THE DEATH OF THE ACTOR

THE DEATH OF THE ACTOR

Shakespeare on page and stage

Martin Buzacott

London and New York

First published 1991
by Routledge
11 New Fetter Lane, London EC4P 4EE

Simultaneously published in the USA and Canada
by Routledge
a division of Routledge, Chapman and Hall, Inc.
29 West 35th Street, New York, NY 10001

© 1991 Martin Buzacott

Typeset in 10/12pt Garamond by Selectmove Ltd, London
Printed in Great Britain by TJ Press (Padstow) Ltd, Padstow, Cornwall

British Library Cataloguing in Publication Data
Buzacott, Martin
The death of the actor: Shakespeare on page and stage
1. Acting
I. Title
792.95

Library of Congress Cataloging in Publication Data
Buzacott, Martin.
The death of the actor: Shakespeare on page and stage
/ Martin Buzacott
p.   cm.
Includes bibliographical references and index.
1. Shakespeare, William, 1564–1616—Dramatic production.
2. Shakespeare, William, 1564–1616—Stage history.   3. Acting.
I. Title.
PR3091.B8 1991
822.3′3—dc20   91–17510

ISBN 0–415–06148–2

CONTENTS

ACKNOWLEDGEMENTS

Thanks are extended to Howard Felperin, Terence Hawkes, Maureen McCusker, Patricia Kramer, Gerard Brophy, Gareth Griffiths, David Ritchie, Tom Burvill, Ian Donaldson, May-Brit Akerholt, Jemal Samir, Jim Sharman, Mark Gaal, Louis Nowra, Jade McCutcheon, Andrew Ford, Margaret Morgan, Leon Cantrell, Laurie Lepherd, Greg McCart, Kate Wilson, Monica Wittenberg, Janice Price, Helena Reckitt and the staff of Routledge, the Association of Commonwealth Universities, the British Council, the Australian Federal Department of Education, the Literature Board of the Australia Council, Pan Books-Macmillan Australia, Belvoir Street Theatre, the Sydney Theatre Company, the Performance Centre and the School of Arts at the University College of Southern Queensland.

INTRODUCTION

What is a Shakespearean actor? It's a simple enough question, and in recent years, it has been provided with an equally simple answer by a scholarly orthodoxy celebrating the rediscovery of performance potential as a crucial element of dramatic text. The simple answer is that the actor is the fundamental figure in Shakespearean drama, the individual who makes the text 'live' and through whose exertions the truly complete form of the Shakespearean play is realised. But why is this so when, historically, actors have rarely enjoyed such authority and respect, often being regarded as no more than slaves? Why is it apparently self-evident that Shakespearean actors are crucial to the enjoyment and understanding of the great playwright's texts?

This book suggests that in sustaining the view of the actor's centrality, modern scholarship has employed as much a rhetorical as a theatrical approach to Shakespearean interpretation, and that its position has been maintained not by the radical critique which it often implies, but by the employment of an extraordinarily conservative theory of origins which is directly opposed to recent developments in modern critical theory.

The performance-critics have employed Charles Lamb and his fellow-Romantic critics and poets as objects of derision for their supposed preference for reading Shakespeare over seeing his plays performed. And so, in questioning the ways in which studies of performance legitimise themselves, one must necessarily re-examine the Romantic position toward Shakespeare in the theatre.

Secondly, because the book seeks to examine the rhetorical foundations of the theoretical position, initially it does not concentrate on the actor himself, but on the discourses which surround his claims to innocence and beneficence. By forcing the rhetoric of Shakespearean acting into a confrontation with various related 'themes' and issues such as terror and terrorism, Carnival, and imperialism, a more accurate assessment of the Shakespearean actor's function can be made, and the relationship with violence and aggression can be established independent of the actor's self-defence.

Once the suppressed languages of Shakespearean acting have been sketched, the attention can then turn inward to the actor himself, with an examination – tied to the various 'themes' – of the traditions of Shakespearean acting from Shakespeare's own company, to Edmund Kean, and then on to Olivier and his colleagues in modern times.

Relieved at last of an *a priori* conception of innocence, the question then can be asked again, 'What is a Shakespearean actor?' And the answer won't be quite so simple, nor so comforting, but rather more tragic.

1

BARDOLATRY

For lovers of Shakespearean theatre, there is nothing more pleasurable than the memories of performances that have been witnessed over the years, the comparisons between individual actors in the same roles, the witnessing of legendary, distinguished and even notorious occasions in modern Shakespearean interpretation. Lined up in the imagination are all the Hamlets – Olivier, Gielgud, Guinness, Burton, Williamson, Jacobi – each with his own distinctive style, each good in some respects and inevitably not so good in others, each a yardstick on which the latest production is measured.

And as each year passes, and the actual performances recede further into the distance, so little by little the nostalgia increases, and the human, ever so subtly and gradually is transformed into the ideal as the good old days imposed their distant grandeur. Olivier's becomes the definitive Hamlet, or Gielgud's does, or Guinness' is remembered more fondly than its hostile contemporary reception would ever have warranted in earlier years.

There is pleasure in such comparisons. In fact the memory of Shakespearean acting, no matter how recent the performances may be, is resonant of an age when life was simpler and there was always time for tea and croquet on the lawns. Quite often, wartime evokes the same pleasant memories of halcyon days in the individual who has been fortunate enough to survive it.[1]

This sentimental reflection on past theatrical events largely independent of the experiences themselves has always been a feature of Shakespearean criticism, but it was never expressed with more beauty nor emotion than by the great Romantic essayists Charles Lamb and William Hazlitt.

By all accounts a delightful, warm and sensitive man whose personal life was sadly restricted by his decision to care for his matricidal sister Mary, Charles Lamb (1775–1834) began his career as a clerk at the India House in 1792 and retired only in 1825. A friend of actors, literati (most notably Coleridge) and intellectuals, Lamb's home became the venue for many famous dinners which live on in various collections of Romantic 'table talk'. His major works include several plays, the famous collaboration with Mary on *Tales from Shakespeare* (1807) and his own *Specimens of the English Dramatic Poets* (1808), which was followed by the notorious *On the Tragedies of Shakespeare* of 1811. He began contributing to the *London Magazine* under the pseudonym of Elia in 1820, often-brilliant essays for which he achieved a certain amount of belated celebrity.[2]

In his mature years, Lamb wrote article after article about his favoured old players, G.F. Cooke, Dicky Suett, Jack Palmer, Bensley, Munden, Jack Bannister, Elliston.[3] According to Lamb in his typical remarks on Suett, they were the sort of actors whom 'Shakespeare foresaw . . . when he framed his fools and jesters',[4] or who, in the case of G.F. Cooke in *Richard III*, seemed

> likely to infuse some *warm blood* into the *frozen declamatory stile*, into which our theatres have for some time past been degenerating.[5]

More than any of his contemporaries, Lamb understood the pleasure which theatre and fine acting could engender, and his often-fanatical support of old actors resounds strangely against his greater fame as the man who supposedly removed Shakespearean drama from the theatre.

William Hazlitt (1778–1830) was a more fiery character than Lamb, with whom he maintained a friendship. A talented painter, Hazlitt dabbled in various arts as well as philosophy (his important *Principles of Human Action* appeared in 1805) before turning eventually to journalism in 1812, a career to which his eclectic artistic autobiography and considerable verbal skills were ideally suited. As a theatre critic on various London newspapers from 1813 to 1818, Hazlitt's criticisms, many collected in *A View of the English Stage* (1817), almost singlehandedly (with the exception of important assistance from his friend, fellow-radical and sometime employer Leigh Hunt) established the standards of modern theatre criticism in Britain.

Another outgrowth of these reviews was the great work of Romantic criticism, *Characters of Shakespear's Plays* (also 1817), in which many of his theatrical reviews and lectures were reworked in more considered form. Despised by conservatives for his passion, courage and political radicalism, Hazlitt continued to write occasional pieces on theatre after 1818 (his *Dramatic Literature of the Age of Elizabeth* appeared in 1820 and there were various literary portraits in *Spirit of the Age* of 1825), but his later life's work was a mammoth four-volume biography of Napoleon.[6]

Generally more severe toward actors than Lamb, Hazlitt too had his favourites over whom he swooned (even if he had damned them mercilessly in previous reviews). On Kean, Hazlitt thundered with characteristic passion:

> Any one who has not seen [Kean] in the third act of *Othello* (and seen him near) cannot have an idea of perfect tragic acting.[7]

Even in the most extreme Shakespearean roles, where the potential for audience sympathy and histrionic failure were great, Hazlitt could never quite adhere in practice to the rigours of his theoretical preference for Shakespearean plays read rather than acted. Years after the event, writing a critical analysis of the play, he could still enthuse on Sarah Siddons' (1755–1831) famous portrayal of Lady Macbeth:

> We can conceive of nothing grander. It was something above nature. It seemed almost as if a being of a superior order had dropped from a higher sphere to awe the world with the majesty of her appearance . . . she was tragedy personified.[8]

The curious thing about such frenzied adoration is that, in transporting the actress from the mortal to the immortal sphere, Hazlitt actually indulged in praise rather in excess of anything he ever offered to Shakespeare, even in relation to the virtuous heroines.

And yet this fanatical support for the theatrical actress is remembered far less than is Hazlitt's highly enthusiastic, but ultimately qualified, admiration for Shakespearean drama. Instead, Hazlitt has become one of the whipping-boys for an indignant gaggle of Shakespearean theatrical polemicists who – without anything but a cursory reference to his voluminous writings on the subject – proclaim him along with Lamb as the enemy of Shakespeare performed.[9]

Lamb and Hazlitt are called Shakespearean 'idolaters', implying that their love of Shakespeare was in excess of their love of actors. Of course Hazlitt himself described his own admiration for Shakespeare as 'idolatry',[10] but the fact that he did so as a preface to a savage attack on the Sonnets tends to reduce its impact as a term of adoration. The word 'idolatry' itself has an immortal but undistinguished place in Shakespearean criticism. Its application to the Romantics is largely attributable to R.W. Babcock's *The Genesis of Shakespeare Idolatry* (1931) whose purpose was 'to point out that the genesis of super-idolatry of Shakespeare lay *in the eighteenth century* – that is, to propose this period as the background of the criticism of Coleridge, Hazlitt and Lamb'.[11]

Babcock then went on to catalogue the relative degrees of idolatry in which each of the critics indulged, concluding that, 'Of course Coleridge was probably the most prominent of the three in Romantic eulogy of Shakespeare. . . . But Hazlitt was not far behind'.[12] In other words, the idolatry was so palpable that it could be quantified, as if perhaps attracting a score out of a hundred.

But since that time, the term has been used to describe virtually every school of Shakespearean critics from Maurice Morgann,[13] through the Romantics (De Quincey as well as those mentioned already),[14] to the biographers and disintegrators of the New Shakespeare Society in the mid-1870s,[15] and even to all modern Shakespearean scholars.[16] In short, rather than a scholarly categorisation, 'idolatry' is actually a term of abuse designed to humiliate predecessors whose love of Shakespeare is deemed to be more intense or less sophisticated than one's own, and can be applied to virtually anyone who has written extensively on Shakespeare. (Indeed one dreads the degree of idolatry which future generations will attribute to the modern jet age of international Shakespearean career-building.)

In vaguely contemptuous vein, not uncommon in his writings on Shakespeare, George Bernard Shaw in the Preface to his *Three Plays for Puritans* (1900) altered Shakespearean 'idolatry' to 'bardolatry', a term which has proved as popular as the original.[17] The synonyms refer, quite simply, to any adoration for and treatment of Shakespeare as 'the source of timeless and universal wisdom',[18] or 'the Godhead'.[19]

Being then a contemptuous term, 'bardolatry' is hurled at most Romantic and post-Romantic critics who publicly dare to remember massacres of Shakespeare in the theatre. For the new breed of scholars who confess their breathlessness at the realisation of the actors' power, the term bardolatry usefully misrepresents the Romantics' theorising on Shakespeare performed. For them, a bardolater is someone who loves Shakespeare but doesn't always and *a priori* extend the same admiration toward his interpreters.

Indeed, in the modern age it seems at times that the Romantics are called bardolaters not because they loved Shakespeare (which, with reservations, they generally did), but because they hated actors (which they certainly didn't, or at least not consistently). As one example of actor-centric allegations of bardolatry, Jonas Barish has suggested that

> though tragedy [in the nineteenth century] continues to elicit a formal respect, if only because of the rising tide of bardolatry, it also becomes increasingly a nontheatrical genre.[20]

This is an attractively simple hypothesis in that bardolatry is to blame for the removal of Shakespeare from the theatre, and scholars feel secure in the knowledge that moderns would never fall into the trap of worshipping Shakespeare and his characters to the detriment of the actors who play the parts. There is a pleasing balance to the argument that the twin evils of bardolatry and non-theatricality enter the scene at the same time and to the same effect.

It would be an even more attractive proposition if it were true.

Barish is just one of many gifted scholars participating in one of the liveliest debates in Shakespearean history. Briefly, the dispute is that between 'close-readers' who champion the written word of Shakespeare as the true site of the drama, and the 'performance-critics' who claim the theatre as the location of the 'real' Shakespearean meaning.[21] Lamb, Hazlitt, Hunt and Coleridge, along with L.C. Knights and the followers of Bradley, are pushed into the former camp while Styan, Beckermann, Goldman, John Russell Brown, Barish and a thousand lesser figures make up the new wave of theatrical champions.

The most strident voices tend to be these of the performance-critics, whose representatives proclaim themselves 'the single most important tradition in contemporary Shakespeare studies'.[22] Each has a variation on the familiar commonsense theme, which, as Worthen says, is that 'performance . . . is naturalised to the drama'.[23] Richard David offers the 'commonplace of criticism' that 'Shakespeare's plays were written for the theatre, and only in the theatre develop their full impact'.[24] John Russell Brown is one of the father-figures of this approach. 'Critics trained in literary disciplines,' he wrote in 1962, 'are apt to think that theatrical experience is coarse and vulgar.'[25] By 1980 Brown had it down to a brief formula: 'Readers and critics have become increasingly aware that the plays were written for performance and reveal their true natures only in performance'.[26] Sidney Holman takes it all even further, noting that the playwright's language 'is complemented, *enhanced*, indeed totally dependent on the visual and non-verbal dimensions of a production'.[27]

In amidst the enthusiasm, the voice of reason has only occasionally penetrated the take-no-prisoners mentality, with Richard Levin and William Worthen reminding their colleagues that the claim that 'these plays can be really understood only in performance, or really that they exist only in performance leads to a subversion of textual authority not desired by even the most extreme performance-critics'.[28] Such claims seem though to have done little to arrest the vigour and extravagance of the performance argument.

Indeed, as the 1980s moved on, so did the extremity of the performance-critics' position. Jean Howard and Marion O'Connor take drama away from textuality altogether: 'Far from distorting the "true" meaning of an unchanging text,' they say in their introduction, '. . . such constructions [i.e. theatrical performances] *are* the text.'[29] Contributions to Marvin and Ruth Thompson's tribute to Bernard Beckermann are scarcely less radical.[30]

The targets of all these golden rules and imperatives are of course those who occasionally doubt the abilities of actors. Such people include not just the titans like Hazlitt and Lamb, but moderns like Harold Goddard who offended sensibilities by arguing that

> Drama must make a wide and immediate appeal to a large number of people of ordinary intelligence. . . . The public does not want the truth. It wants confirmation of its prejudices. . . . What the poet is seeking, on the other hand, is the secret of life, and, even if he would, he cannot share with a crowd in a theater, through the distorting medium of actors who are far from sharing his genius, such gleams of it as may have been revealed to him.[31]

No one would dare say such a thing now, although Harry Berger and René Girard in more recent times have offered more moderate, conciliatory remarks on the same subject.[32]

Using historical evidence Richard Levin makes an interesting contribution to the debate when he proves that the majority of Renaissance authors (with the notable abstention of Shakespeare) actually agreed with the more moderate close-readers in their suspicion of actors and championing of the text.[33] William Worthen on more theoretical grounds continually questions just *which* performance the performance-critics prioritise and notes that 'a variety of ... discourses necessarily intervenes between the text and its stage production', compromising the two positions with the observation that 'To understand the drama, we need to understand all the ways [i.e. through reading *and* performance] that we make it perform'.[34] In this he takes his lead from Terry Eagleton who argues in a different context that 'text and production are distinct formations – different natural modes of production, between which no homologous or "reproductive" relationship can hold'.[35]

Eagleton's remark identifies the irony of the debate, to the extent that there is no clear point of reconciliation between text and performance because both are distinct modes of production. The argument over which is the most appropriate seems to be almost irrelevant in that context.

The fact that the debate is so fundamentally absurd and yet continues with vigour is symptomatic not just of the philosophical discrepancy between close-readers and performance-critics, but also of the the current social and aesthetic supremacy of *actors* in general. Where actors were once slaves, they now become lords, dames, presidents and mayors. Their opinions are sought on anything from their favourite colour to the hole in the ozone layer. And as the most crucial participant within the dramatic culture of the western world, Shakespearean drama and its practitioners have been very much part of the social phenomenon that is acting in modern times. Actors in general and Shakespearean actors in particular have risen to a position of dominance on world stages. But it hasn't stopped at that.

In this historically-bizarre modern theatrical age, the mythology of acting, suppressed for centuries and now liberated with a vengeance, has attacked the authority of textuality with the result that the slave now claims the title of master as a natural birthright. Actors and their supporters, not content with mere liberation and social respect, now attempt to exert their authority over territory which historically has never been, and theoretically never could be, within the bounds of their authority. That area of course is the text, the alternative mode of dramatic production which, in Eagleton's terms, is a 'distinct formation'.[36]

The humour of the impossible dream is accentuated by the apparent willingness of former textual critics to champion actors as the legitimate inheritors of the Shakespearan dramatic heritage. It's the Plautine situation of the master being tricked by the cunning slave into seeing danger, in the form of bardolatry and text-bias, everywhere. In a delightful Carnival inversion, the master willingly submits to the worldview of the slave and is baffled by all around him. And because he sees tricks everywhere, all the master can do is envy the talent of the conjurer and become a member of his party. The first step is to see spooks and bardolaters – one's own kin – and to condemn them roundly.

The temptation for wise men is always there of course. After all, to call someone else a bardolater is to increase one's own self-esteem and to gain the confidence to go on as a Shakespearean critic. And because Romantic criticism of Shakespeare has been so influential in modern times, any new approach has to find an area in which it can rebel against the dominance of Coleridge and his contemporaries.

A presumed weakness in the Romantic position has been created (rather than found) in the area of Shakespeare in the theatre, and with the weapon of the word 'bardolatry' attaching to the Romantics, modern scholarship has set out to establish its original place in the debate by attributing to the great early critics antithetical positions to those which are the current rage. The modern task has been to seize on a few sentences from the hundreds-of-thousands of words which the Romantics devoted to Shakespeare and his acting, and to highlight those which are in any way opposed to the present fad. That way, the myth of originality is sustained and the scholar feels useful and, more alarmingly, objective.

Allegations of 'bardolatry' directed toward the Romantics participate then in a larger trend toward Shakespeare in the theatre which has exerted its influence on twentieth-century Shakespearean scholarship. Indeed it is no coincidence that Babcock's book is contemporary with two of the most influential texts in this trend toward 'actor-centric' criticism, namely Harley Granville-Barker's *Prefaces to Shakespeare* (1930) and Muriel Bradbrook's *Elizabethan Stage Conditions* (1931). Every theoretical position needs an antithetical object of derision, and in misrepresenting Romantic attitudes, these theatrical apologists and their successors created their own particular whipping-boys. It's a sad, and yet largely unacknowledged fact, that they probably seized on the most unlikely and inappropriate opposition of all.

Time, and the mediation of the imagination, can make a friend of an enemy and an enemy of a friend. While Charles Macready, as the greatest Shakespearean actor of the generation succeeding the Romantics, lavished praise on Hazlitt's critical ability[37] (as probably the last Shakespearean actor to do so), conversely the bizarre power of nostalgia ensured that Hazlitt's sometime friend Samuel Taylor Coleridge (1772–1834) became the authoritative source of wisdom on Edmund Kean's greatness, through a truncated version of a decidedly equivocal assessment of the actor's 'flashes of lightning'.[38] Coleridge, of course, expressed as many reservations about Shakespeare in the theatre as any of his colleagues, and despite the frequent misquoting of this comment about Kean, he is usually listed along with Lamb and Hazlitt as one of the misguided zealots responsible for the supposedly unprecedented critical lapse which led them to prefer Shakespeare in the closet to in the theatre.[39]

Theoretical and practical positions alike are idealised by subsequent generations more interested in sorting out the good from the bad in a kind of moral parlour-game, than in acknowledging the complexity of the historical model. The Romantics have been a victim of this process in so far as it affects the interpretation of their position on Shakespeare in the theatre. The treatment which the topic receives in standard Shakespearean texts makes it sound the simplest, clearest phenomenon within a difficult field, usually requiring only a subordinate clause of vaguely contemptuous patronisation.

Nicholas Brooke, as just one of any number of examples, opens his study of early Shakespearean tragedy by referring to the nineteenth century which 'never forgot Lamb's claim that Shakespeare's tragedies ought not to be performed'.[40] Such statements are unjustified and in their tone (impersonating unequivocal truths) make Lamb sound a fool. Even a superficial reading of Lamb's greatest work on Shakespearean theatre would indicate that the situation is quite different from that described by the contemporary scholar:

> I am not arguing that Hamlet should not be acted, but how much Hamlet is made another thing by being acted.[41]

Sometimes reading is a preferable alternative to interpretation, although it can make humiliation of predecessors more difficult.

Edmund Kean (1787–1833), of course, suffers no such modern patronisation, being acknowledged by all who have never seen him as the quintessential Shakespearean actor.[42] The most notorious of the Romantic Shakespearean actors, Kean burst onto the London stage, after a considerable apprenticeship in the provinces, in January 1814 when he appeared as Shylock at Drury Lane. A symbol of wild Romantic passions both on- and off-stage, he was the sometime darling not just of Hazlitt, but of all the Romantic poets and essayists during the height of his career (which was almost exactly contemporary with Hazlitt's time as a theatre critic) between 1814 and the end of the decade. He specialised in roles of villainy and, aside from Shylock, he achieved success as Richard III, Iago and Othello, Macbeth, King Lear, and Sir Giles Overreach in Massinger's *A New Way to Pay Old Debts*. But around the time of his visit to America in 1820, alcoholism, ill-health and unreliability took their toll and after returning to England his powers began to wain and he acted only intermittently.

In modern times, Kean's silence and absence engenders nothing but admiration and to criticise him or his profession is to criticise the very institution of theatre itself. In short, where posterity has trivialised some of the achievements of the Romantic Shakespearean critics, nostalgia has made Shakespearean actors into *a priori* embodiments of aesthetic benevolence and Shakespearean excellence, with the result that genuinely critical discourse is precluded by the theatrical taboo-words of philistinism or Puritanism. The threat of this rhetorical equivalent of having the bone pointed at the violator of the social code ensures that Kean and Siddons remain names to conjure with, not in spite of but *because* no one alive has ever seen them act.

So the term 'bardolatry' in its most contemptuous application to Romantic criticism actively participates in this suppression of critical discretion in the interests of histrionic authority. It is one of the persistent myths which continue to gain in strength as the rhetoric of theatrical Shakespeare exerts its grip on institutions once devoted exclusively to literary studies of the topic.

By distorting arguments and through subtle rhetorical structures establishing implicit hostility and suspicion toward textuality, the myths of Shakespearean acting attempt to prioritise Shakespeare in the theatre as the 'natural' view, over Shakespeare read. Ironically, the argument of the performance-critics is not so much theatrical as it is rhetorical, with some clever literary structures driving home the supremacy of theatricality over literature. A typical example is John Russell Brown's introduction to his book on Shakespeare's plays in performance:

> Shakespeare's verbal art is, in fact, a trap; it can prevent us from inquiring further . . . the very words [of the text] themselves can be fully known only if they are considered in their dramatic context.[43]

This of course is very convincing, and it is convincing for the very reason that everything in the rhetorical structure aims to raise primitive suspicion about the limitations of textuality and to establish the preference for human interaction.

Jonas Barish feels even less need to hide his mistrust of writing:

> only the physical stage, whatever its shortcomings, can be the true site of performance. The theater of the mind is no substitute. What Lamb and his colleagues, with their keen eye for the defects of particular productions and individual players, signally fail to convey is a sense of the *indispensability* of performance, the fact that the script *must* be incarnated by live actors, or it remains forever impalpable and wraithlike, subject to every misunderstanding and distortion of which readers are capable.[44]

It is a sentiment which any number of primitive societies would share, and one which has been at the heart of western metaphysics ever since Plato's *Phaedrus*. There has to be a person speaking, otherwise that which is 'impalpable and wraithlike' takes over, in the form of written communication, that ultimate symbol of mechanised man's descent into inhumanity and technological nightmare.

It is extraordinary to think that such traditions of textual mistrust still endure in the modern world. One would have thought that the simple habit of living with electronic communication would have precluded such sentimental claims to archaic values. But not only have they survived – they have indeed become a dominant force in Shakespearean criticism.

J.L. Styan offers a similar example of textual mistrust in his introduction to Shakespeare's stagecraft. After describing his model Harley Granville-Barker's aim 'to blow away the transcendental fog of the nineteenth century' (which one would think was a rather insensitive generalisation),[45] he goes on to depict the playwright's impotence caused by textual confinement:

11

The playwright may begin with an idea or complex emotion, one seen and felt as people animated in time. He has first to particularise them, through a structure of words which suffer the limitations of words as written.[46]

The argument is convincing in purely emotional terms because these 'limitations' of textuality on which it is predicated are left presupposed. Text is bad, or at least, imperfect. Acting, which supposedly is 'implied' in play scripts, makes them better. It is good.

In the rhetoric of Brown, Barish, Styan and their supporters everything is structured linguistically around absolutes and stresses and imperatives: *only, indispensability, must, has.* Authoritarianism enforcing the principles of textual mistrust are the foundations on which the debate for Shakespearean performance are sustained.

And of course a battle ensues for possession of the illusion of commonsense. Thus, Jonas Barish assures his readers at the beginning of his book that

These pages, again, propose no polemical thesis ... I have sought to avoid, where possible, the dogmatism that the subject [of anti-theatricalism] has often provoked on both sides ...[47]

And by the end of the book he is still claiming his possession of the balanced view, albeit with some quite extraordinary examples:

Borrowing from Jean-Paul Sartre's portrait of the anti-semite, we find that many of its features also fit the anti-theatricalist. A certain mechanism of paranoia, a certain style of fanaticism, seem common to them both, however divergent their specific aims and purposes. In both cases prejudice takes the form not of a mere opinion but of a passion; while indefatigably seeking to fortify itself with argument and observation, it invariably reverts in the end to a stubborn bedrock of irrationality.[48]

How can one argue against such claims, when any observation which questions theatrical legitimacy renders the scholar 'prejudiced', 'passionate', 'paranoid', 'fanatical', 'irrational', and probably 'anti-semitic' as well? If this is the non-polemical view, then one wonders where the extremes of the debate lie. From Barish's perspective there is no rational level on which the debate can proceed, except for that of theatrical legitimacy which has claimed the illusion of rationality for itself.

By such covert rhetorical ploys which suppress and naturalise ideology so that it sounds like commonsense, play-texts emerge as exclusive theatrical property because they are written to be performed. Thus the myths of Shakespearean acting transform the accidents of history into the inscrutable achievements of theatrical nature. There is a self-evident legitimacy in the priority of actors when, in this quintessential demonstration of Barthesian myth-making, occupation is depicted successfully as possession, and historical privileges as natural rights.[49]

Several interrelated 'myths' – reduced as myths must be to a simplistic level so everyone can understand – are employed in this process of naturalisation. For the performance-critic:

(a) Shakespearean texts imply actors;
(b) as a consequence, textual mutilation (in the form of performance in time and space) represents aesthetic maturity;
(c) all of which is predicated on voice enjoying priority over sign;
(d) and a further presupposition of the inherent, *a priori* excellence and 'disinterestedness' of Shakespearean actors and acting.

The myths are easily destroyed simply by questioning them – asking for instance why a bad actor gives a 'truer' account of a text than a good critic – but the whole rhetorical apparatus of the performance-critics is designed to suppress this kind of interrogation, marginalising it beyond the parameters of common-sense. Propaganda always works by these paradoxically extravagant (in the size of the lies) yet subtle (in the forestalling of questioning) means.

The victim of this aggressive appropriation of the imaginative world is the non-histrionic interpreter of Shakespeare, like Lamb or Hazlitt, denied the 'natural' rights and condemned to a secondary position of textual 'limitation'. Their enmity, reluctantly tolerated by actors and their supporters in the interests of clearer definition of histrionic sublimity, is regarded as a sign of imperfection and is caricatured and exaggerated, the better to achieve a peripheral image. They are 'bardolaters', humiliated because the metaphysics of mythical presence condemn them to secondary status, like illegal immigrants devoted to a country which will never make them citizens because they speak the wrong language.

But in diminishing the achievements of the Romantic critics and prioritising the function of the Shakespearean actor, modern scholars have equally drawn attention to the nature of Shakespearean acting itself. As much as their howls of outrage have necessitated a re-examination of early scholarship, so too they have drawn attention to the function of the Shakespearean actor, and demanded that, independent of their obvious amazement and occasional sycophancy at his power and legitimacy, a thorough examination of the nature of Shakespearean acting needs to be conducted.

That appraisal of acting *not* as the theatrical apologists depict it, but as it exists within the wider range of cultural signification, shapes much of the discussion which follows. Shakespeare's plays participate crucially within this cultural life of the western world, and to that extent Shakespearean acting can be regarded as merely an intensified form of acting as it occurs in any text-based western theatre. A study of Shakespearean acting is consequently also a study not just of acting the classic theatre texts, but acting in general. Using Shakespeare as the prime example, the study asks how the rhetoric of the current text versus theatre debate renders the literary critic guilty and the actor and his champions innocent independent of their specific performances.

What emerges from this approach is a kind of 'story' which, with a minimum of alterations to names, places and dates, could reflect the theory and history of almost any field of human endeavour. It's a story about the fundamentals of human existence; quite simply a story of love and hate. It's about the curious love between actors and literary critics, and their attempts to annihilate each other. It's also a story about dramatic texts and the destructive love that they engender. The characters in the narrative are comedians, fools, junkies, poets, preachers, madmen, political activists and intellectuals who, as writers, actors and audiences, span more than four centuries of theatrical and textual productions. But mainly it's a curiously Romantic story, filled with the paradoxes of agony and ecstasy, *sturm und drang*, and accordingly, the crucial historical episodes occur in that period. Centred on aesthetics, it's a story about passion and possession and the rage of men and women to become one with the sublime.

The paradoxes are immediately obvious. Selective memory and active promulgation of myths has imposed on both Romantic and modern Shakespearean acting a rhetoric of innocence (which pleases the mind) and authority (which impresses the desire for servility), with Sarah Siddons and Edmund Kean being typically rewarded with the reverence reserved for virgin deities. Contradictory enough

14

as simultaneous qualities, innocence and authority are not characteristics usually associated with the diabolical artistic temperament of
the Romantic era,[50] nor with godless modern times. And specifically
they played no part in the Romantic or post-Romantic exegesis of
Shakespearean drama, which was more fascinated by the earthly
terrors of lust, greed, obsession and the other sins which litter the
plays. Fevered response to the plays themselves was typical.

As one example of this, where Sarah Siddons' famous performance
of Lady Macbeth encouraged Hazlitt to align her acting with
heavenly supernature, Siddons' own testimony of her first encounter
with the part invoked thoughts of *infernal* supernature, much more
in keeping with the Romantic ethos. Reading the part at night, as
was her custom, Siddons

> went on with tolerable composure, in the silence of the night (a
> night I can never forget), till I came to the assassination scene,
> when the horrors of the scene rose to a degree that made it
> impossible for me to get farther. I snatched up my candle, and
> hurried out of the room, in a paroxysm of terror.
>
> My dress was of silk, and the rustling of it, as I ascended
> the stairs to go to bed, seemed to my panic-struck fancy like
> the movement of a spectre pursuing me. At last I reached my
> chamber, where I found my husband fast asleep. I clapt my
> candlestick down upon the table, without the power of putting
> the candle out, and threw myself on my bed, without daring to
> stay even to take off my clothes.[51]

Shakespeare was responsible for the Gothic horror, and Christian
values – no less than narrative convention – demanded that the
terrified but virtuous heroine-actress who was to confront the horrid
part implicitly emphasised her fear at the prospect.

The successful portrayal of the role, which had already been
completed when Siddons wrote her thriller,[52] became a demonstration of the inherent morality of the actress subduing the
diabolism of the Shakespearean text, a triumph of courageous
benevolence over cowardly malevolence and a transference of moral
repugnance into theatrical approval. Hazlitt's hyperbolic publicity
for Siddons in the role was the response of all good men to a semantic
environment controlled by the alternatives of dramatic evil and
histrionic good. Before even entering a theatre, the extra-theatrical
hostility aroused by the play itself ensures that the audience is already
of the actor's party, a sly tradition of sympathy-manipulation which

continues with the modern reputation of *Macbeth* as an 'unlucky' play for actors.[53]

In other words, a gulf exists between the often-implicit but furious rhetoric relating to (and sometimes emanating from) Shakespearean analysis, which can sound like that of the Marquis de Sade, and the language applied to Shakespearean acting, which sounds more like that of his virtuous creation Justine. This schism is nowhere better evident than in *Macbeth*, where the purity of description evoked by the actors contrasts drastically with the macabre details of the play itself, and the even more ghoulish scholarly responses to it.

And so this rhetoric of evil which attends on all but the histrionic aspects of Shakespearean drama and performance, creates a theatrical cult of heroism and virtuosity in which actors, as the physical representatives of worldly good struggle, always successfully, against the abstract and imaginative threat of diabolical terror embraced by the text. Symptomatic of a struggle between voice and sign in a newly print-bound society, the debate has continued into the modern day, with the issue still centring on the voice's claim to reduce the infinity of play in the textual sign.[54] Intellectual conservatism has always favoured this victory of the finite (voice) over the infinite (sign) and in its theatrical incarnation, acting has benefited from the apparent theoretical victory of the human over the mechanical.

Perhaps though there is another language of acting which is cast aside by this rhetoric of innocence. Walter Benjamin has noted that

> without exception the cultural treasures he [i.e. the historical materialist] surveys have an origin which he cannot contemplate without horror. . . . There is no document of civilisation which is not at the same time a document of barbarism. And just as such a document is not free of barbarism, barbarism taints also the manner in which it was transmitted from one owner to another.[55]

But there is no indication of this barbarism or, to use a more relevant modern term, terrorism, in the rhetoric of Shakespearean acting. On the contrary, everything in the art is depicted as wondrously-controlled and geared toward the furtherance of aesthetic and social progress. We are told that Shakespearean actors demonstrate the perfectability of the text. They are never depicted as wreckers.

No, the rhetoric refuses to identify Shakespearean actors with barbarians, and certainly not in the literal sense of uncouth, uncivilised, violent and ignorant people. Is this because acting disproves Benjamin's thesis, or is it because the language with which acting depicts itself has effectively suppressed the discourses of barbarism and violence on which it is constituted? The contention of the chapters which follow is that the latter applies. And the suggestion is that to understand the nature of Shakespearean acting, as art rather than propaganda, one must attempt a reconstruction of this barbarism whose articulation has been suppressed in the interests of refined debate.

Of course we're never invited to contemplate that barbarism. Set against Shakespeare's terror which goes on and on, the actor preserves integrity because, unlike the text, at least he gives the audience a smile at the end of the performance and eventually leaves them alone altogether. The critical and dramatic text, on the other hand, survives to torment every successive generation with its potential for meaning. Shakespearean criticism, as a discipline committed to teasing continually-new meanings out of Shakespeare, has played a major part in creating these conditions through which an actor's humanity is deemed to represent a victory over textual tyranny.[56] And in regard to *Macbeth*, Thomas De Quincey (1785–1859) has done more than most to confirm by implication and through an extraordinary description of textual horror, the division between the evil of characterisation and the (contrasting) good of its acting.[57]

As the most notorious Romantic opium addict, a man with a morbid lifelong fascination with murder, and perhaps as a consequence of both habits, an acutely-developed sense of paranoia, Thomas De Quincey was well-qualified as a judge of horror. His daughter, Mrs Baird-Smith, remembered that:

> It was an accepted fact among us that he was able when saturated with opium to persuade himself and delighted to persuade himself (the excitement of terror was a real delight to him) that he was dogged by dark and mysterious foes.[58]

Few papers on Shakespeare have been more celebrated than De Quincey's extraordinary 'The Knocking at the Gate in Macbeth', written in 1823 and published originally in the *London Magazine*.[59]

Meditating on the impression of 'awfulness' and deep 'solemnity'[60] which the said event had produced on him since boyhood, De Quincey devoted his paper to the elucidation of the psychological and structural phenomena in the Porter scene which establish the conditions through which the drama of the knocking produces its dreadful effect. Conveyed dramatically, the assassination of Duncan is different from ordinary murder in that the interest must be transferred from the simple instinct of self-preservation in the victim to the quintessentially Romantic 'great storm of passion'[61] creating a hell within the murderer, and while not necessarily approving Macbeth's actions, the drama ensures that the audience nevertheless achieves some degree of sympathy for the man of violence.

De Quincey argues that the most affecting moment during a loved one's fainting-fit is not the actual collapse or coma, but the point when a sigh announces the return of suspended life. This proto-structuralist argument for semantic creation through contrast and transitory delineation of rhetorical boundaries – in De Quincey's words, with action being measured by reaction – identifies the knocking at the gate as that audible moment when the pulses of life begin to beat again, thereby, through the return of normality, heightening the awareness of the abnormality which has just transpired. The murderers are isolated from ordinary human affairs at this sublime moment when the knocking announces that 'the human has made its reflux upon the fiendish'.[62]

Extending De Quincey's argument from dramatic narrative to the present context of Shakespearean acting, precisely the same effect can be observed when, at the completion of *Macbeth* or any other play, the audience breaks into applause announcing that sublime transition from the fictional evil of characterisation to the normal beneficence of the everyday human status of professionalism, thus emphasising both the horror of the preceding story and the joy of the actor's safe return from that terrible world. Both effects directly contribute to the establishment of solidarity between the actors and their audience, founded on the isolation of the text and the drama.

With smiling actors and clapping spectators closing the dramatic action, the performance effectively represents the triumph of the human world over the fictional, and the dominance of the pulses of life over the flights of the imagination. This conservative and 'actor-centric' return to reality is the gist of Feste's concluding song in *Twelfth Night*, and it is most shamelessly indulged in those extraordinary Elizabethan pleas for audiences to give actors some applause.[63] At those moments of transition, the urgency of corporeality and normality render the author and the text as unnatural as Duncan's murder, and the actor as of the audience's own party.

And so De Quincey's paper – among many other achievements – offers an insight into the nature of horror and violence, and the thrilling appeal thereof, and it suggests a mode of analysis in which an emotional or aesthetic phenomenon is determined not internally, but by its interaction with the antagonistic discourses which surround it. To come to terms with the impact made by these events, exegesis necessarily must focus on the points of intersection between the existent and the series of external articulations out of which it is constituted. In the case of Shakespearean actors, this understanding must occur not simply through a passive acceptance of the performers' difference from the rhetoric of terror which surrounds them, but from an active examination of the boundary which divides and unites them.

In tracing this common border between the innocent and the terrible, similarities cannot be suppressed in the interests of idealised rhetoric, and the actor, whose career is founded on his isolation from the terror which he enacts, is once more made answerable to the allegations of complicity in acts of horror. Just as the knocking at the gate reaffirms Macbeth's ultimate accountability to the very code of human justice which he has suppressed, so too the very clamour of the innocent rhetoric surrounding Shakespearean actors makes them liable to the allegations of horror which they continually displace in rhetorical self-defence.

And so the new knocking at the gate is that of the text and its defenders, who will survive the temporary domination of the mortal actors and ultimately render justice if justice need be done. So the following pages are not a theoretical nor historical study so much as they are an examination of the modes of cultural signification in general, and in particular the cultural discourses on whose promotion and suppression the current legitimacy of Shakespearean acting would appear to be predicated.

Such an approach will inevitably run the risk of being depicted by performance-critics as a facile exercise in actor-loathing. This would only be partially correct. No one denies the pleasure which actors can afford, but additionally, it is incorrect to ignore the offence which they may also give. Indeed, a major contention of the chapters which follow is that the pleasure and offence of Shakespearean acting are both integral to the fascination which we experience in the performance of Shakespeare's plays. Loathing has never been, and can never be, an impediment to loving. In fact it can only add to the passion.

So hatred or otherwise toward actors is not the issue here. It is more complex than that. Indeed any study of Shakespearean acting runs the gamut of emotions, embracing all those feelings which rise to the surface when watching a slave prancing about extravagantly in top hat and tails. For the spectator there is an abundance of amusement, pity, sadness, love and, above all, pleasure. The awareness governing all these sentiments is that we know the spectacle of wrongly-assumed power can only last a little while and that one day we'll feel nostalgic for these delicious moments of absurdity. We'll be just like Lamb and Hazlitt, reminiscing about the good old days when, just for a tragicomic moment, actors could actually enjoy a blaze of glory to which they were never entitled.

2

TERRORISM

I accept being maimed, but I refuse to remain powerless.
(Sarah Bernhardt after her amputation in 1914)

Terrorism is fundamentally anti-democratic because through violence it allows imperfect, inexperienced and irresponsible minorities the opportunity to wield enormous power and influence. Often this ill-gotten position solidifies into permanent authority. Sixty per cent of the world's governments are in fact under one-person, one-party, or military rule[1] and current or former terrorists often figure prominently among these dictators and despots.

This fundamentally-absurd capacity of terrorism to invest the mortal individual with the responsibility of a national culture results in a bizarre form of masquerade, wherein the impostor, who cannot reasonably serve the civilisation which he has acquired, employs every method at his disposal to sustain the illusion of authority and control. Generally, these deceptions are unsuccessful unless there is at least tacit support on the part of the community suffering the autocracy, and the best way to engender that is through an unequivocal display of force. Marcos in the Philippines and Amin in Uganda are just two examples of tyrants whose patent inability and lack of desire to address the needs of the societies which they ruled resulted in a curious displacement of the political focus from the concerns of the people to the theatrical display of force.

The success of these brutal dictators in part lay in their ability to convey their tyranny as an heroic response to the imperfections of a corruptible and immature political community peopled by wimpish democrats and liberals who feared the responsibility of power.[2] In other words, the concern about the validity of their own position was deflected into an implicit, paternal questioning of the ability of

21

their societies to exist peacefully and happily without them.

According to the terrorist position, it wasn't the leader who was weak and corruptible, but the community itself, and as the society wondered if it really was incapable of self-regulation, the dictator seized the advantage and established himself as the national hero. Power was substituted for truth and through rigorous military support and extreme political corruption, the strength to rule was exerted on a broken and suffering community, effectively being created in the very image of imperfection which the terrorist had ascribed to it.

And so, knowing that her project can never be justifiable or complete because of her own mortality and sympathetic limitations, the terrorist abuses her constituents to keep them in submissive awe through the drama and the violence of her actions. Being nothing in herself and knowing that it is better to be feared than loved, the usurper can only manipulate the seductive power of machismo to make her audience stand and applaud in amazement at her brilliant triumph over its limitations and her extraordinary enthusiasm for committing violence on beloved institutions and icons. While in theory nothing can be justified in the usurper's seizure of power, in practice the illusion and apparent brutality combine to make the imposture irresistible.

It's not so different in the theatre, where demonstrations of terror and energy often overcome any shortcomings in interpretive legitimacy. For Michael Goldman, one of the most prominent of the modern theatrical apologists, theatre presents a confrontation between an actor and her audience, the actor functioning as, in Goldman's words, a 'terrifying' and 'terrific' primary being onto whom is built character, plot and the other formal elements of drama.[3]

According to Goldman, audiences feel an energy present in any good actor's performance, that goes beyond the demonstration of what some 'real person' is like:

> When we watch a play the actor establishes before us a particularly interesting and energetic human being, who is not simply the actor and not properly the character, but the actor as character, to whom we relate in a special way.[4]

The individual becomes multiple, at least in terms of the rhetoric and fable in which she is clothed. Quite simply, from this perspective the actor becomes impossible, superhuman. When the actor is not properly the actor, nor properly the character, but the actor as character, audiences have succumbed to her spell and necessarily stand in awe of the supposedly not-quite-physical creature on stage. This primitive and endearing attitude is crucial to a theatre relying on ritual and the complete trust (or gullibility) of its audiences and it has no shortage of champions anxious to spread the power of the myth.[5]

More alarmingly, the myth of the superwoman embraced in such depictions of the actor leaves its possessor susceptible to the very same problems which necessarily confront political despots – namely, the potential embarrassment of mortality being revealed in immortality, and the susceptibility to charges of terrorism masquerading as administration. The same technique of creating an imaginary dependence on the violence of the dictator is employed in both cases, in the hope that brute force and destruction will be applauded by an awestruck public.

If the report of Michael Billington in *The Guardian* is accurate,[6] then a typically imperfect terrorist attack leading to wider cultural acceptance and even historical grandeur, occurred at the Round House in London in March 1969, when Nicol Williamson played the title role in *Hamlet*. Having already achieved a reputation as one of the finest actors in the younger generation at the Royal Shakespeare Company, Williamson's initial triumph had come in the role of Bill Maitland, the tormented hero in *Inadmissible Evidence* of 1964. But five years later he was to offer a Hamlet which was to achieve for him even greater fame and notoriety. Billington wrote of the performance:

> No doubt about it: Nicol Williamson's Hamlet undoubtedly leaves a lot out. The observer's eye is mercilessly there but scarcely the scholar's tongue or soldier's sword ... and yet, for its excess coarseness and over-reliance on a note of unmasked contempt, this is the most exciting Hamlet since Redgrave's 1958 Stratford performance.... This is not a complete Hamlet.... It lacks irony, delicacy, gentleness. Its virtues, however, plead trumpet-tongued on its behalf. It matches the play's questing feverishness with a bottled hysteria of its own. It informs the lines with a bristling, bruising intelligence and is constantly showing Hamlet to be testing those around him.... And it provides the rarest of all sensations: the feeling that the actor rejoices wholeheartedly in his presence on the stage ... it is refreshing to find a man-sized,

ravenously hungry attack on the part. Some actors take the stage by default: Mr Williamson takes it by storm.[7]

The two separate lines of argument developed in this review – that Williamson destroys Hamlet in delivering only a portion of the character, and that his performance is one of the greatest of modern times – can only be rescued from absurd contradiction by an awareness of the attraction of terroristic violence, and the fascination of a man who, incapable of doing justice to the role, survives through the emphatic illusion of his confidence in wielding the weapon of destruction.

Billington's diction ('mercilessly', 'excess coarseness', 'unmasked contempt', 'bruising', 'man-sized', 'ravenously hungry attack', 'takes it by storm') is enough to confirm his delight in the aggression directed against Hamlet by the actor who would (and avowedly did) mutilate the character in an effort to reduce him to human dimensions – in other words, through reduction making the character dependent for his existence on the actor.

Williamson was like the terrorist, and in adjudicating between the destruction of Hamlet and the aggressive actor's display of force, Billington's preference for force aligns him – metaphorically of course – with the supporters of Marcos and Amin in applauding strength over and above justice and the maintenance of human rights. The critic bows before the actor who cannot offer anything but a mutilated Shakespeare, but who does so with power and conviction, as if the violence were voluntary rather than inevitable.

Thus is sustained the terrorist project, when the ferocious compulsion of that which is plausible takes over from the modest claims of that which is right, and on this basis of praise for strength over justice, both terrorism and Shakespearean acting have reached unprecedented heights both of authority and delight in the years following World War II.

Just as Williamson was perfectly imperfect as Hamlet, Donald Wolfit's greatness as a Shakespearean actor lay in his similar ability to play characters badly and confidently. One of the most ubiquitous performers on the English stages between his debut in 1920 and his death in 1968, Wolfit achieved a reputation not just for his preference for inferior casts (which allowed his own undoubted talents to shine), but also for his extraordinary performances of virtually all the great Shakespearean roles. Described by Kenneth Tynan as:

an actor with a comedian's face and a tragedian's soul and for this reason nearly always looks mysteriously miscast . . .[8]

Wolfit survived as a creative artist through the emphatic demonstration of conviction and heroism in his travesties. According to Frank Granville-Barker:

> So many other actors play down Lear, Hamlet, Macbeth, Othello and Antony whereas Wolfit lets us see them in their full heroic stature.[9]

So great was Wolfit's unsuccessful presence in *Tamburlaine* that he could make Marlowe seem like a second-rate playwright:

> Only the death scene where, like a great bear in shaggy fur, he stumbles to and fro across the outspread map of the world, doesn't quite come off. But this is surely Marlowe's fault.[10]

But it was always in Shakespeare that Wolfit's imperfections were seen to greatest advantage, and never more so than as Brutus in the highly successful *Julius Caesar* of 1949. Writing of this performance, T.C. Worsley offered a truncated version of Billington on Williamson, with only the names having been changed:

> Brutus is not a part [Wolfit] does well: indeed it reveals more of his weaknesses than his gifts. Yet he stands there and he speaks, and his mere presence and the pitch of his voice swell and expand the entire emotional atmosphere, broaden it, deepen it, lengthen it – carry us, in short, into a larger and intenser mood . . .[11]

From Leigh Hunt and William Hazlitt through to Kenneth Tynan and Michael Billington, this abuse of Shakespearean actors leading to praise is a constant motif, always beginning with a grievance about the deplorable mutilation of the character, followed by admiration for the actor's total performance, and it renders the legendary conflict between the two parties as more apparent than real. Ultimately, the critic abandons his function of safeguarding the icons, and instead achieves popularity by relinquishing his right to Shakespearean authority in favour of the actor. The confrontation between actor and critic becomes the kind of puppet opposition much-favoured by political dictators who like to create the illusion of democracy by installing family or business partners as political rivals.

So the extent to which an actor's style and temperament suit the character is not as important in the final analysis as is her self-conscious display of conviction in the histrionic enterprise. Like Barthes' wrestler, the actor's object is not primarily to achieve a conclusion or a closure within the ritualised narrative, but to imitate those motions which are expected of her as a performer.[12] The rise and fall of the fortunes of her character are only an incidental aspect of her presence; what really matters are the transient images of passion which the actor brings to the performance, images which ultimately bear no causal relationship with the character being represented.

In non-Shakespearean drama, where the characterisation does not participate in a wider cultural signification, such intrusions of the real into the mythical are not nearly so great a problem nor delight, except for the playwright whose inventions are hijacked by the attention-seeker. Fortunately, the author's death precludes her from witnessing the desecration. But in Shakespearean drama, much more than a dead author is at stake, because the centrality of the characterisation within the western imagination ensures that the inheritors of the Shakespearean cultural heritage – the audience – are present in the theatre to monitor the performance of those who would animate that which is already known.

There is then a fundamental hostility established between the mortal who would assume the immortal roles, and the audience whose project is to safeguard the integrity of the cultural icons. But as with terrorists and their hostages, this enmity, which is a cause for war, is continually deferred because of the prevailing conventions of theatre which depict both the actor *and* Shakespeare as providers of pleasure in excess of pain, and the oppression is viewed as beneficent in the greater interests of sheer survival.

Just as through disinformation and extreme psychological pressure a dejected hostage believes that her survival is dependent on her captor, so too theatre audiences have difficulty conceiving a Shakespearean drama which can exist outside of the actors' responsibility for it. Both of course are myths designed to sustain the authority of the aggressor, and both offer considerable appeal to the dedicated algolagnist.

The objective of sado-masochism is to rail against the pain as explicitly and graphically as possible, but ultimately to conclude with an apparently-spontaneous outburst of pleasure which is both the result of, and a complement to, the previous discomfort and disaffection. This offence leading to delight, this aggression between unsuitable and jealous lovers, is the essence of the relationship not just between terrorists and their hostages, but also between Shakespearean actors and their critics. So too it is the characteristic of the frenzied Romantic descriptions of the encounter between the whore and her client:

> You tell me that [the whore] Kuchuk's bedbugs degrade her
> in your eyes; for me they were the most enchanting touch
> of all. Their nauseating odor mingled with the scent of her
> skin, which was dripping with sandalwood oil. I want a touch
> of bitterness in everything – always a jeer in the midst of our
> triumphs, desolation even in the midst of enthusiasm.[13]

Every offence, every travesty, every imperfection, is noted and derided, and yet the conclusion – that the parodic libertine nevertheless has served an admirable purpose – is always already in existence, and indeed has even been the presupposition on which the exercise has been founded.

In Shakespearean drama too then, the individual appearances and actions of performers are a cause for continual critical lament, but the broader function of the actor is never in question because of the satisfaction which her offence affords. The popularity of actors, terrorists and whores rests on this identity and legitimacy developing largely independent or even because of their specific atrocities.

Actors are bodies corporeal; Shakespearean characters are bodies politic. The one belongs to private physical beings, the other to the public imagination. The one is transient and powerless to withstand the simple progression of time, the other moves with the times, sustaining its influence over generations and drawing strength from its status as a venerated institution. Where dependence confronts authority in this way, it is unreasonable to expect that an individual (corporeal) could make any significant contribution to the development of the universal (politic), because their areas of signification are fundamentally opposed and because the latter is largely self-sustaining, possessing an hieratic constitution whose identity acquired through history has the capacity to intimidate and oppress even the most gifted practitioner. In short, on the imaginative level, the body politic always wins.

As a director, John Gielgud was thus silenced by the monolithic cultural grandeur of Hamlet:

> When I attempted to direct Burton [in Hamlet] I found it impossible to do anything new or interesting. I was surrounded by ghosts, not just that of Hamlet's father, but of all the other productions I had seen, acted in and directed.[14]

So established is the icon by its historical significance, and so imbued with implied authority, that it permits no further mortal interpretation beyond that which has been achieved already. Its plenitude of meanings are pre-existing and independent of individual theatrical realisation. And so as a body politic, Hamlet cannot be answerable any longer to rhetorical agitation alone, just as established political regimes eventually silence and render irrelevant the voices of those who would reform their constitution through democratic means.

This termination of debate leads to only one brutally-effective alternative. Forced into an awareness of her physical strength compensating for imaginative weakness, the mortal abandons creative conciliation in favour of violence, removing the debate from the realm of language to that of force. With all avenues of reform closed, revolution and its instrument, terrorism, eventuate, as fallen archangels resolve with Milton's Satan,

> To wage by force or guile eternal war,
> Irreconcilable to our grand foe,
> Who now triumphs, and in the excess of joy
> Sole reigning holds the tyranny of heaven.[15]

Terrorist actions begin at this moment when the debate surrounding authority is exhausted, with emphatic victory to the imagination, and with the alienated flesh in consequence demanding eternal vengeance. Terrorism then becomes not merely the violent expression of wicked men, but the inevitable outcome of cultural maturity's contempt for fallen mortal heroes who will not be silenced or humiliated.

In terms of Shakespearean acting, this dialectic of establishment-created anarchy is manifested in the predestined terrorism of the actor directed against the character for whom conciliation is irrelevant and aggression the only coherent means of address. It's that sublime ironic moment when the former defender, now dispossessed of her creation, monomaniacally sets out on a course of destruction which tragically seeks to re-establish her claim to respect through annihilation of its cause.

28

That is the terrorism of Shakespearean acting, that Satanic violence committed upon the very icon which the jealous actor may have once possessed but which, partially through her own exertions, has now been denied her. The result of this removal of the actor from her traditional function as custodian of the theatrical individuals is that there is no longer any 'interpretation' of Shakespearean roles – there are now only 'attacks' on the parts.[16]

And so in its most obvious form, the articulation of Shakespearean dialogism actually proceeds monologically, with the primary discourse of character orthodoxy already in silent existence while the actor makes the noise. Because the character is largely undefined in physical terms, the secondary but physically-immediate presence of the actor affords the terrorist the opportunity to distract audience attention from the presupposed by strenuous exertion and compelling assault. The stability of characterisation condemns the actor to this undignified demonstration of desperate violence. Unable to possess her love, she turns instead to a flamboyant practical demonstration of her faith through murdering the object of devotion. Thus the terrorist succeeds by dramatically shifting the terms of debate from the rhetorical to the physical, and through the sheer violence and audacity of her action winning the admiration of the audience which sustains her beyond the revolution.

At this point, where the terrorist restakes her claim to the lost territory, euphemism enters immediately, with a profound difference appearing between the language employed and the action performed. Generally in Shakespearean productions, actors avowedly set out to make the texts 'live', and the first task is to slash into them, cutting out as much as half of the text in the case of *Hamlet*. Supposedly liberated from its cancers in this way, but with many of its vital organs impaired as a result, the text is dependent on the actors for its survival.

In prolonged terrorist actions, this is always the objective, to take hostages and through mental and physical deprivation to make them dependent on the aggressor, and eventually to turn them into loyal mouthpieces for that opposition. This procedure is familiar from the many statement-reading American hostages appearing with guns at their heads on propagandistic videos from Beirut. The violent objective then in both hostage-filming and Shakespearean stage-editing is to reduce complexity to such an extent that it can be delivered effectively by a performer whose very presence is theatrically-arresting over and above the content of her message. In other words, through brutal coercion, the text is rendered subservient to the human appearance and voice which seeks to embody it.

In Shakespearean theatre, the difficulty for the actor (or the director) arises when these surviving limbs of the text are identified as something less than an 'improvement' on the previous whole form. In addressing this potential embarrassment, the conjuring trick of actors is facilitated by appeals to a cultural code which suggests that the text is only fully-realised when so disfigured for the purposes of ritualised public display. For the (editorially as well as physically) knife-wielding actor, the plays have to be reduced and paraded before the public to overcome their textual imperfection and immaturity. A few slashes that won't hurt very much and the ability to show off the scars in public afford the text a newfound respect in a community which values above all else the ability to withstand pain.

It's a familiar argument, this depiction of physical mutilations as aesthetically-beautiful signs of cultural maturity, and so uncompromising is its support that it is not easy – indeed not always polite – to argue against it. To question the morality of circumcision, tattooing, cicatrisation or Shakespearean textual mutilation in societies which support them as ritual is to risk ostracism, humiliation and contempt.

Euphemism, such as that of 'improvement' (which justifies all) restores to terror the rhetorical power which had been denied it before violence transformed the debate from the mental to the physical level. At this point, where the violence of the function is disguised by the innocence of description, the myths of Shakespearean acting come into play, and none with more seduction than this eminently-plausible and sensual depiction of mutilation as a prerequisite for maturity.

Appealing both to the logical and communal sympathies, the myth is founded both on the ambition of actors and the trust of the audience, as the work of the text is appropriated by, and converted into, the work of people. Taking advantage of a (literally) absent author, and through a naturalised liberal–humanist perspective refusing to acknowledge the (metaphorical) death of the same, the actor slithers into the text as the one confident source of authority and closure, offering to a bewildered audience a guiding hand through the vague, the threatening and the inhospitable textual wilderness, just as the terrorist sinisterly offers to become the eyes and ears of the hostage in the frightening and unstructured world of the abduction crisis.

Should these myths which sustain violence be challenged – and they rarely are because to do so is ultimately to reject community standards and label oneself a philistine or savage – terrorism nevertheless has a surefire final line of defence in the sheer beauty of its project. Nothing thrills the emotions nor invigorates the senses like the threat or the onslaught of violence directed toward self and others. Shelley called it 'the tempestuous loveliness of terror' and its literary echoes reverberate throughout the Romantic age.[17] It's the cruel and erotic beauty of the Medusa, inspired by severed heads, snakes and vile animals and contorted images of death, which sent the Romantic poets into ecstasy even as it identified them as explicitly of Milton's Satanic persuasion.

By these furious standards, the blinding of Gloucester, the tortures of *Titus Andronicus*, and the euphoric lovemaking between Cleopatra and her asp are among the paradigm illustrations of a Shakespearean beauty which exhilarated the Romantic critics even as it made their moralistic contemporaries rush for their editorial scalpels in a bid to respond to the exquisite offence.

This rage to do ill and to do it beautifully is the active inversion of Rousseau's dictum 'All is beautiful, all is the work of God', reworked into the Marquis de Sade's more thrilling 'All is ugly, all is the work of Satan',[18] a revised code which embraces its own undeniable fascination and which is eminently-amenable to mythical representation in euphemism and justification in aesthetic excitement. 'What do the victims matter if the gesture is beautiful?' asks Laurent Tailhade.[19] Destruction, if it leads to some kind of transformation which is emotionally appealing and socially advantageous, can be justified as the work of the artist on the icon, a reinterpretation and improvement which finds support on the grounds of novelty alone.

So potent is this desire for the shock of the new (to employ Robert Hughes' memorable phrase) to defile the relics, that the euphemisms of 'radicalism' and 'avant-garde' become synonymous with the propaganda surrounding any artistic enterprise. Eschewing the trappings of conservatism, every work of art attempts to attract these novel epithets. They express an attitude of hostility which exists independent of the fate of the victim, a statement of intent rather than concern. They do so because art and terrorism are means predicated on the beautiful; victimology, on the other hand, is an end which is the domain of science alone.

Thus, actors, masquerading as humanists of the Rousseau school, set about their joyous destruction with all the evil fury of Praz's 'divine Marquis',[20] secure in the knowledge that the erotic appeal of their project will forestall any opposition to its depravity. In consequence, Shakespearean texts become the virtuous Justines upon whom every degradation and every climactic shiver is perpetrated by an ecstatic butcher performing his atrocities for an audience deriding the abnormality of purity. Impressed by the conviction of the oppressor, spectators either through their silence or active support, condemn the Shakespearean Justine to the humiliation which in a world of satanic heroism is the just reward for unmutilated virtue. Nature being hostile toward virtue in this way, Justine's demise in the novel occurs appropriately as a consequence of a thunderbolt which strikes just as her life seems to be improving.[21]

And Shakespeare, as morally inviolable as Justine, gets exactly the same meteorological retribution from actors performing as instruments of inscrutable justice:

> To see [Kean] act, is like reading Shakespeare by flashes of lightning.[22]

> I think of the lightning which a true actor flashes from *all* corners of his mind and face, and of the thunder that follows such flashes and such only . . .[23]

Founded on the myth of the natural being unnatural, these quasi-biblical thunderbolts and lightning-strikes roar up from Hell to annihilate all that would retain chastity – heroine and play-text alike. And the debate for debauchery is thus established on the bottom lines of beauty and divine compulsion.

From the actor's perspective, to oppose the mutilation and rape of Shakespeare in performance (in other words, to oppose nature) is to risk the wrath of supernatural vengeance and to become the victim of, rather than the audience for, the terror and the beauty of the meteorological metaphor. Through her 'attack' (which is a demonstration of the primacy of nature over culture) the actor becomes the representative of elemental fury which the text alone is not.

And so there is a struggle at the centre of Shakespearean acting, between the characterisation which is imaginative, huge and chaste, and the actor who is physical, small and violently lascivious. The rhetorical project of the actor is to render the physically-passive characterisation imperfect and ultimately dependent on the active party by reference both to a brutal code of cultural initiation and the imaginary hostility of a corruptible divinity. In depicting Shakespeare as needing to be 'prepared' for maturity, and in arguing for the heinous artificiality of autonomous textual existence, the actor ultimately adopts a moral position which is both primitive and aggressive, necessitating the institution of savage and arcane public ritual, which is the fundamental characteristic of both theatre and terrorism.

Mutually-founded on these same primitive foundations, Shakespearean acting and terrorism share many of the same images and properties. Aside from the storms which blow up whenever the violation of the natural order occurs, the two arts also share masks and weapons as their essential properties, the latter being the symbol (which in either case may or may not be real) of force and conviction, the former the suicidal denial of the self in the interests of the greater cause. From the tubercular heroines of nineteenth-century melodrama, to the feverishly-anticipated martyrdom of the hijacker, both theatre and terrorism know the incredible seductiveness of death and these attendant images of destruction.

Unable to contain his excitement at the beauty of mortality and its cadaverous visage, Clement Scott swooned over Sarah Bernhardt as Sardou's Tosca in 1887:

> She looked superb, pale as death with distended eyes and the fierce glare of a Judith. Sarah Bernhardt, knife in hand, is the nearest thing to great tragedy that has ever been seen in modern times.[24]

This adoration of both the violent image and the corpse sustains the public interest in theatre and terror, and an awareness of its capacity to engender audience sympathy has occasionally driven criminals to demand their own public execution as an extravagant final bid for public acknowledgement.[25]

There is an ideal quality attached to these horrible actions and images of terror and theatre which removes both from the realm of the personal to that of the universal. In both cases, the dramatic action – which of course is real in itself – avowedly refers to another reality beyond the actual scene on the stage. In the case of Shakespeare, audiences are encouraged to

Suppose within the girdle of these walls
Are now confin'd two mighty monarchies,
Whose high upreared and abutting fronts
The perilous narrow ocean parts asunder:
Piece out our imperfections with your thoughts:
Into a thousand parts divide one man,
And make imaginary puissance[26]

while in terrorist situations, the actual drama of the hostage crisis is meant explicitly to draw attention to the plight of oppressed peoples, often far away from the scene of performance. Palestinian actions in Europe are just one example of one reality serving the purpose of another.

The result of this alienation is that the immediate violent actions of actors and terrorists are intended not so much as personal attacks against the audience or hostages as they are symbolic actions whose direction is always outward. In other words, the relationship between the aggressor and her victim is not causal and is not so important as the significance of the actions which transpire between them. Usually a hostage is killed because of what she represents, not because of what she has done. This provides an excellent alibi for the aggressor, because it allows responsibility to be deflected from her onto some ideological cause, with the result that, in the case of acting, the performer is usually blameless and enjoys the advantage of being applauded for her good deeds and being excused for her bad. There is usually some powerful faceless person behind the scenes – a director, a playwright, or the terrorist leader who bears the guilt of the atrocities.

The visible action then becomes a symptom rather than a cause, and with the support of that illusion, the present violence is removed from the real to the ideal by the actor proclaiming herself a hero as she stands to take the applause, and a pawn in the game when asked to defend herself. Through the power of physical idealisation, her visibility deprives her of guilt as it deprives the audience of imagination.

The result is that Sarah Bernhardt can indulge her deadly intent toward the text, and wield her knife without compunction, assured that the initial reaction toward her is always-already one of for-giveness. The greater cause of the histrionic project means that her individual actions performed under its auspices will be pardoned by appeals to the legitimacy of acting as a whole, and the sheer passion of the performer. A similar argument has been ventured in support of wartime atrocities, when murders can be justified on the basis that they are committed under duress and prevent further murders.

In such situations, the project of the aggressor relies for its success on extravagant displays of emotion which engender sympathy through the demonstration of human frailty, and fascination through their visual representation of commitment. Hamlet is not the only audience member who has been moved to pity and wonder by the tears of a passionate player. The better to accentuate this human identification with roles, actors are eager to emphasise the extremism of their passions, often bordering on the fanatical or the perverted.

Sarah Bernhardt's menagerie was one of these extra-theatrical indulgences which have passed into legend as an illustration of the exotic fetishes into which she channelled her empathies and creativity. Biographers of the great French tragedienne (1845–1923) are fond of cataloguing the three dogs, a parrot, a monkey, a cheetah, a wolfhound and seven chameleons which she acquired during her visit to London in 1879.[27] Being evidence of a kind of weakness, but weakness which is both dedicated and realised, the menagerie anecdote is just one of hundreds of factual and fictional references to Bernhardt's behaviour which contributed (and still contribute) to an intense appreciation of her extreme corporeal vigour and inverse mortality.

Surrounded by such a reputation for all manner of lively appetites, Bernhardt was well-qualified to become the most famous actress of death scenes in modern theatre. The emotional extremity of her life made her portrayal of the termination of those energies all the more poignant, as the extravagant emotion of her life was triggered imaginatively by the physical imitation of death on stage. A few coughs and chest-clasps would be enough to make this point effectively, given the extra-theatrical factors determining the significance of the action. Being a more talented actress than this, however, Bernhardt realised the potential of underlying emotion with such physical and imaginative impact that greatness was created.

Theatrical and extra-theatrical codes operate in this way to ensure that no matter what happens to the text in performance, the action of the performer is still more than significant enough to generate meaning which can be regarded as the point of the play. Actors take the place of authors as the mouthpieces for the play's argument. But a curious thing happens when this assumption of intellectual supremacy by the physical body achieves anything more than symbolic or conventional form. When the actor 'dries' and has to improvise or surreptitiously lean toward the prompter, suddenly the actual possession of the desired power becomes an intolerable and humiliating burden. At that point when the actor finally does take charge, rather than pretending, her helplessness makes the audience laugh at her.

A similar embarrassment can be observed when the terrorist finally gets her chance to make her broadcast about the injustice which she suffers. Usually speaking in a language which she does not understand, she falters, making laughable, amateurish errors, which are hilariously at odds with her stated ambition to supplant the established voices of power. The terrorist feels much happier shooting a gun than interpreting a text, and for the sake of her pride (not to mention her project), the ultimate ambition of the overthrow of dominant linguistic and cultural control acquires more rhetorical power when it has not been achieved.

In this sense, both the actor and terrorist are sisters in arms, trapped inside the rhetoric of their own failure – magnificent and frightening figures when they demand their own (denied) rights to control, but pathetic and forlorn when ultimately achieving this goal. Failure being a form of success and the pressing necessity to disguise weakness either as strength, affectation or injustice, means that the actor is ultimately in the saddest position of all in the theatrical enterprise. She is the emperor trying to pass off her nakedness as the richly-embroidered robes of authority.

To sustain this bizarre illusion of metaphorical dress, the actor supplements her aggressive posturing by an attractive packaging of meaning which renders even the most complex details of dramatic signification as capable of physical interpretation and ultimately reducible *only* to that form. Bearing similarities both to Ronald Reagan's favourite dictum prefacing speeches on the budget and trade deficits, 'Now let's keep this simple so everyone can understand', as well as Coleridge's remark following Pythagoras that 'The definition of beauty . . . is the reduction of many to one',[28] the passionate and histrionic delivery of the awesome semantic complexities of many longer Shakespearean speeches is one example of this theatrical function, resulting in the reduction of poetic meaning to elementary audience responses such as 'Leontes is angry' or 'Hamlet's putting it off again'.

By attempting to *act* that which is already over-determined in the text, the actor ultimately reduces the poetic and philosophical to the physical, and trivialises the argument to the point where it is quite capable of representation in dumb show alone (as 'experimental' productions have proved).

This is not to say that acting is ineffective in Shakespearean drama. On the contrary, any psychological project which demands mind change in its subjects as a prerequisite for its success *must* remain highly selective in the information which it distributes if it is to achieve its ambition of winning support for its cause. Certainty presented with appropriate conviction is the only way to win over a reluctant audience and, as Feyerabend suggests, 'where arguments *do* seem to have an effect, this is more often due to their *physical repetition* than their *semantic content*'.[29] This is why both acting and terrorism are eager to articulate their cause through sloganeering ('Actors make the texts live', 'Death to America') and why their own methods of performance are to reduce everything to a simple, repeatable and recognisable emotional formula or method.

It may well be the case then, that Shakespearean acting would lose audience support if it concentrated more on Shakespeare's meaning and less on actors' frantic arm-waving and regal posturing. A charismatic fanatic shouting and sweating with the passion and apparent self-evidence of her argument is always going to present a more popular theatrical spectacle than an intellectual speaking in archaic blank verse and depicting the world as intricate, perplexing and ultimately unknowable.

The trick is to align this oversimplification with an element of surprise, so that uncertainty is created everywhere but in the gestures of the actor. The sudden appearance of apparently unequivocal truth in a world of confusion achieves a dramatic impact known both to actor and terrorist alike. As the perpetrators of this illusion, the aggressors are always eager to justify their actions on the grounds that they represent the will of the people. That disingenuous assurance of a public mandate both increases the conviction of the actor, and encourages the sycophancy of the audience. And as audiences applaud these travesties, they effectively support their own oppression in the interests of a disaffected and politically ambitious minority. Thus do actors survive in a society which has never recovered from its Romantic infatuation with the heroic villain.

3

THE STOCKHOLM
SYNDROME

One of theatre's most extraordinary powers is its ability to immortalise and deify even the most pathetic of society's losers. Through its scene-mounting and mythologising, it provides the opportunity for any coward or incompetent to achieve (in Andy Warhol's phrase) his fifteen minutes of fame, before forcing him back into the anonymity and humiliation that he usually deserves.

Sometimes this repeated promotion of charlatans to temporary but very public positions of power makes it seem that the theatre is interested more in novelty than in artistic responsibility. The brief stage careers of countless child prodigies and rock stars attests to the fact that sometimes bad things in theatre can be passed off as good long enough to collect the cheques. Sometimes indeed they're *so* bad that they *are* good. When either of these conditions become permanent, however, an aesthetic shift eventuates and the one-time buffoon becomes an establishment figure, against whom subsequent buffoons can rebel.

Consequently, in politics and in theatre, concepts of good and bad are frighteningly fluid and the fool is always a chance for the monarchy. To describe a performer as 'good' is to make a comparison with some pre-existing, but usually temporary and arbitrary, standard. But to borrow a well-known histrionic quote, goodness has nothing to do with it, because theatre turns talent into a useful quality rather than an essential one, a fact which often galls traditional actors as one novelty act after another forces them into the background.

So anything and anyone can succeed in the theatre if there is an appropriate context of heroism. This is not to say that theatre is an easy profession. On the contrary, creating that context of heroism is difficult and most who try to do so end in failure. Try as actors might to take a permanent grasp on talent, it does not exist in any one natural and permanent, nor instantly-realisable form. It's on loan while certain aesthetic and social conditions prevail, and may change as soon as they do.

The best actors in the long term are those who can adapt to the changes as if they are part of them. Through brilliant illusion, they appear to be permanently located in the avant-garde. The insecurities caused by this philosophically-absurd position, have driven many actors into eccentricity and even insanity. There are few things more damaging to one's mental health than the self-destruction of the illusion of power.

Theatre's judgements and developments are enigmatic and inscrutable, and the individual can never know when, or even if, his fifteen minutes will eventuate; nor will he know if his deeds may endure in legend, or disappear without trace. This is the sorry fate of the dispossessed, those who can borrow but never own. The sixteenth minute is crucial, because at that point theatrical history delivers its judgement and the actor may find himself permanently relegated below the fool, consigned to the scrap-heap of old newspaper clippings.

Such a fate has befallen the Swedish would-be bank robber Jan-Erik Olsson. Few people now know this man's name, but his quasi-theatrical feats have altered the languages both of modern psychology and terrorism. Olsson's character, and what he did, can illustrate much about the nature of theatre and theatrical appreciation.

Jan-Erik Olsson had no credentials for a matinée idol. A convicted felon, painfully-thin, unattractive, and with a history of psychopathic disorders, his life had been wasted away in various Swedish prisons, until his escape allowed him to undertake one more highly public display of vicious incompetence.

It began in August 1973 when Olsson, then aged 32, wandered into the Kreditbanken in Stockholm's busy Norrmalmstorg Square and began firing shots into the ceiling.[1] He moved to the teller's cage and demanded money. The inherent theatricality of this spectacular, but traditional, entry was jeopardised momentarily by the intrusion of a genuine hero – an anonymous plain-clothes policeman who stepped in to challenge Olsson. In vaudeville fashion, the bad guy was so frightened by the intervention of the good guy that his evil plans were thrown into chaos and he reacted in desperation. For Olsson, this panic resulted in the taking of four hostages and their incarceration with him among the safety-deposit boxes in the bank's massive vault (the 'center stage for the drama', according to the report in *Newsweek*).[2] The straightmen in the ensuing six-day 'psychological drama' (again, quoting from the *Newsweek* report), were the four hostages, comprising:

> Kristin Enmark, black hair, 21
> Elizabeth Oldgren, blonde, 23
> Brigitta Lundblad, mother-of-two, 31
> Sven Saefstrom, bachelor, 25

All were bank employees. Other crucial small parts were played by the Swedish Prime Minister Olof Palme, the Chief of the Stockholm Criminal Police Gunnar Aastrom, and various policemen, psychiatrists and media representatives.

One of Olsson's first requests after holing up with his hostages in the vault was that his friend Clark Olofsson, 26 and like Olsson an inmate at Stockholm prison, be allowed to join him. This request was granted immediately, and the bewildered Olofsson took his place as the sixth performer in the vault. Once the negotiations began, with Olsson shouting instructions over a telephone, Swedish television and radio began live broadcasting of the event. Contemporary newspaper accounts suggest that millions of Scandinavians tuned in to listen and watch, as the regular programmes were either rescheduled or interrupted for updates on the hour.[3]

Olsson's demands were for $750,000 in cash, a getaway car, an aeroplane, and guaranteed safe passage out of the country. During the first days of the siege he delivered these demands directly by telephone to Olof Palme. At one point during the conversation, Olsson threatened to shoot the youngest hostage, Enmark, unless his demands were met within sixty seconds. As Olsson counted back from sixty, Palme heroically refused to be bluffed and would not relent. At zero, Olsson did not pull the trigger. However, Palme's extreme control under pressure was only an incidental detail in the media reports of the proceedings. Olsson as the deranged man-of-violence was the centre of attention. The audience found him a more appealing character.

Conditions for the hostages were appalling. Aside from the obvious threats to their lives posed by Olsson and his firearms, they were used as human shields whenever their captor met with police negotiators. With nooses around their necks, they were connected to the top of the security shelving to dissuade the police from pumping gas into the vault – if the hostages lapsed into unconsciousness they would die. And during one dramatic telephone call, Olsson actually used his hands to choke one of the hostages – whose terrified gasps were clearly audible on the broadcasts of the event – to demonstrate that he was serious in his demands. Outside of negotiations, Olsson began to approach the women sexually and after the siege, traces of semen were detected on the floor.[4]

The next telephone call to Olof Palme came not from Olsson, but from hostage Enmark. The 21-year-old chided the Nobel Peace Prizewinner for his inaction, and affirmed her complete trust in Olsson. Not only had he not hurt the hostages, but in fact he had 'been very nice'. She made it clear that she trusted the robber more than the police and later reaffirmed that 'I'm not in the slightest afraid of him'. So great was her trust that she *wanted* to go with him when the siege was over. Palme and she began arguing, and with a sarcastic 'Thanks for the help', the hostage hung up on the Prime Minister.[5] Stockholm psychologists at the time described this bizarre phenomenon as a 'defence mechanism'.[6]

At one point, the Police Commissioner was allowed to inspect the hostages, and was dismayed to find them cheerful and relaxed, with one of the convicts even affectionately putting his arms around two of the women. Swedish paper currency amounting to $350,000 was dropped through the ceiling after this inspection, to complement the stylish blue Mustang parked nearby as the getaway car.

Finally, after six days, the police decided to use gas. After a camera lowered through the ceiling confirmed that none of the hostages was strung up, a jackhammer was employed as a diversion on one part of the ceiling while gas was sprayed in from silent aerosol cans at another point. Simultaneously the police forced down the door with a hydraulic jack and with everyone gasping and choking, Olsson finally surrendered.

But while he had given up on the siege, the hostages had not given up on him. Their fear was that the police would gun him down as soon as he emerged from the vault, and so they stage-managed their own exits, forming a human shield around him, to ensure the safety of their failed captor. In short, at the end of the performance they volunteered their own oppression, through emulating and thereby implicitly approving the techniques of their captor. They were the theatre audience at the end of a gruelling and unenjoyable performance, nevertheless offering their applause and affirming their care for those who had put them through the ·

ordeal. It seemed only appropriate that they should exchange roles as a gesture of solidarity at the end.

At the affectionate parting of the two groups, the one to jail, the other to the psychiatric ward, Enmark promised Olsson that they would see each other again, a promise which she honoured before and during Olsson's resultant ten-year sentence.[7] On the way to the psychiatric hospital immediately after the siege, Enmark and Oldgren pleaded with the Chief of the Stockholm Criminal Police not to be too hard on the robbers.

Months after the event, still none of the hostages would condemn their captor.[8] For his part, Olsson lamented his softness, saying he should have shot one of the hostages but that he couldn't because of the personal bonds that had developed between them.[9]

And thus, with the notorious failure of this forlorn and bumbling Swedish felon, was born the celebrated psychological phenomenon of the 'Stockholm Syndrome'. In psychoanalytic terms, the Syndrome is a curious version of the Freudian 'identification with the aggressor' – although strictly speaking it cuts both ways, with the aggressor also identifying with the victim – which has been documented in countless subsequent studies of terrorism and psychology.[10]

There is no shortage of spectacular examples of the phenomenon, but none better than the case of the TWA airline hostages of a Croatian hijacking in 1976 who contributed funds toward some of their jailed captors' legal defence,[11] and none more notorious than the American heiress Patty Hearst who, following her abduction, became 'Tania' of the Symbionese Liberation Army and the lover of one of the terrorist group's leaders.[12]

The Stockholm bank siege was quite an extraordinary event, and yet typical of the close interpersonal relations which can develop between aggressor and victim in a closed environment. The many reports of the 1973 siege described the violence of the convict Olsson and his acts of aggression toward the police and hostages, but they did not mention the many quieter hours during the siege when Olsson told his middle-class captives of his own childhood and his wasted life in prison, his fears of being returned to his cell and his sufferings at the hands of an arbitrary and unjust criminal system.[13]

The hostages further exchanged roles with their captor to the extent that they exercised the power of pity toward him, thereby concentrating on his acts of kindness instead of his more obvious aggressions, and in so doing, probably saved their lives. Hans Joachim Schneider has described the textbook example of this phenomenon:

> The more the terrorists come to look on the *victim as a human being and as an individual* the harder they will find it to exert violence. If the victim is not injured or killed in the first three days, there is a growing probability that he/she will not be injured or killed at all.[14]

The fact is that a terrorist project is jeopardised if the aggressor begins to see his hostages as individual human beings. Pity begets pity.

For the terrorist, victims should be mere trade objects or at least only faceless symbols of an antagonistic regime, and when their value as trade objects diminishes – such as when illness makes them require too much care or attention or when they possess an irrelevant nationality – they are usually released unharmed.[15] So from the criminal's perspective, the necessarily desensitised attitude toward his captives relies on as little personal contact between terrorist and victim as possible, to avoid the amateur Olsson's mistake.

Hardened professionals know that gags and blindfolds are helpful in preventing identification with the victims, but even these extreme measures may not prevent the development of bonds between the groups. The temptation to love one's enemy is ever-present, both in the victim and in the victimiser. And if the terrorist or survival action is to succeed, every effort must be made *not* to see oneself in terms of the other.[16]

South Moluccan terrorists failed to achieve this with Gerard Vaders, a 50-year-old Belgian newspaper editor and one of their train siege hostages in 1975.[17] They heard Vaders' confession to his wife before his impending execution and were unable to perform the deed. They shot someone else, a 33-year-old father of two named Bierling, instead.

And while the Moluccans took pity on Vaders, the reverse was also true. Vaders described how his captors' minor acts of kindness – the proffering of cigarettes and blankets – took on immense dimensions in the minds of the hostages:

> ... we ... realised that they were killers. Yet you suppress that in your consciousness. And I knew I was suppressing it. I also knew that they were victims, too. In the long run they

would be as much victims as we were. Even more. You saw their morale crumbling. You experienced the disintegration of their personalities. The growing of despair. Things dripping through their fingers. You couldn't help but feel a certain pity. For people at the beginning with egos like gods – impregnable, invincible – they end up small, desperate, feeling it was all in vain.[18]

Such a description in style and tone is not unlike that which William Hazlitt churned out in a rush of belated sentiment whenever he bade farewell to some fading star of the Romantic stage.[19] But more to the immediate point, such generosity toward his captors seems extraordinary from an intelligent man like Vaders who for almost a fortnight had been incarcerated, physically abused, and subjected to extreme psychological torture by a band of homicidal foreign thugs.

Vaders too is another extreme example of the theatrical audience that feels obliged to applaud even the most appalling of performances. He too has fallen for the same trick as his captors did with him. In the words of the criminologist Hans Joachim Schneider, he has recognised his

> targets as men or women, as fathers or mothers, as loving husbands or wives, as human beings who laugh and cry, who cherish hopes and harbour fears.[20]

That way madness lies, because from the hostage perspective, after that point captors become lovers, sadists are seen as benevolent, and pain masquerades as pleasure.

In this vicious Carnival world of inversion, self-respect and human dignity lapse into a tragic infatuation by passivity for unattainable action. The spectator develops enthusiasm for the actor. And from the perspective of the captor, the potential frustration of political ambitions is complemented by a rare sense of being hailed as a hero or saviour. For fifteen minutes, the barbarian becomes a star of the stage, watched and discussed by everybody, without ever having to demonstrate any particular talent except the fanatical ambition toward destruction.

Because the social and psychological pressures to identify with an aggressor are so great, theatre practitioners need never be reluctant to align their profession with acts of violence. Indeed, there is an enthusiasm to employ metaphors deriving from aggression.

These clichés include the ubiquitous 'danger' of the stage, the 'precariousness' of a theatrical career, the stage as a 'scaffold', the descriptions of actors 'dying' during a poor audience response, or 'killing them' during a success. In fact there must be as many violent descriptions of theatre as there are theatrical descriptions of violence (bank robberies, for instance, are always 'dramatic'). Actors are urged by Grotowski to 'confront' a text[21] and Richard Schechner explicitly equates drama with violence, especially political and sexual violence.[22]

By equating aggression (a somewhat different term to 'violence')[23] and theatre, a certain mystique, a kind of heroism, is attached to the art form. The theatrical event is aligned with the fundamental experiences of life and death, or on the grand scale, survival and apocalypse, and the theatre is situated in the forefront of human endeavour and ambition. This of course suits the theatrical propagandist very well. It is so much easier to endure claims of violence than those of irrelevance. Violence makes good promotional copy, especially when it has been liberated from the reality of the victimisation on which, by definition, the violent act has been predicated.

Once it is established that violence exists in theatre, the types of this violence that prevail need to be distinguished. The obvious violence is that which makes the audience want to commit murder or hurt others – or from a pro-theatrical standpoint, which prevents them from doing so. Gloucester's eyes being put out in *King Lear* is just one example out of literally millions. Few plays, comedy and tragedy alike, do not physically represent some violent act, or at least have an off-stage act of aggression or threat as an integral part of their development.

But a second, and more intrinsic form of violence in theatre relates to the curious effect of actors upon an audience in the confined space of a traditional theatrical building. The suggestion is that simply by performing their impersonations in front of an audience, actors afflict their spectators with a range of devices deriving from the aggressive arsenal of professional terror and oppression.

In respectable theatrical terms, this histrionic capability is acknowledged implicitly in catchy titles like Artaud's 'Theatre of Cruelty' (and even to some extent in Grotowski's 'poor theatre'), and explicitly in the descriptions that attend on them. Artaud for instance makes it clear that there can be no spectacle without an element of cruelty as the basis of every show,[24] although he remarks elsewhere that it is not cruelty in the sense of slit noses and so on but cruelty 'in its broadest sense.'[25]

That broad sense of cruelty is something other than the first form of theatrical violence. It is more the sort of cruelty which oppresses the audience (through 'massaging' or 'lacerating' them – two favoured Artaudian terms) through the presentational mode itself, rather than from the subject of the various dramas in which it occurs. In his fevered way, Artaud explicates that the way to a mind is through a body (the famous statement of this thesis, not by Artaud, is 'grab them by the balls and their hearts will follow'). Artaud didn't invent cruelty in theatre. He found it there already and in his uninhibited and unsystematic way attempted to realise its potential.

The Artaudian statement of theatrical cruelty is an extravagant acknowledgement of the simple fact that every actor wants to affect his audience emotionally, and that when this occurs most successfully, the audience members feel it physically. Exhaustion, hollow legs, tears, active libido, shouting and applauding, are all manifestations of the physical changes that audiences undergo at a good theatrical spectacle. Whether it's called cruelty or violence or aggression or acting, it remains as one individual's physical imposition on another, a fact that could justify any of those labels.

Naturally when there is an element of complicity between the parties, it is harder to apply the labels, but there remains the problem that violence of any kind is difficult to control, and it is never entirely clear where voluntary pleasure ends and imposed pain begins. The potential for the actor's abuse of his audience in 'physical' theatre is a constant reality, and an actor knows that he can always achieve some response – although it may be disgust – if he is desperate for it. It's the old story – better to be violent than irrelevant.

Strangely, this theatrical violence is a positive force according to Richard Schechner:

> It has been my experience that the more violent the actions dealt with in performance – the more physical the work, the more risky the taboos revealed or violated – the stronger the bonds formed among the group making the performance.[26]

Schechner of course writes from the perspective of the actors (through himself as the director), a fact which explains his emphasis on the bonding between the violators. But he might equally have described the bonding which violence engenders between actors and audiences – in other words, he could have elaborated his theory to embrace the theatrical equivalent of the Stockholm Syndrome, wherein audiences not only endure but enjoy that which is unpleasant to them, and even targeted directly at them. Artaud could batter an audience with his oppressive images and fury and still be assured of many who would defend his work against the perceived threat of some 'out-group'.

Violence, however, is an extreme act of communication and cannot exist in and for itself. It has to have a target, and those who describe acting as violence without citing the object of this violence are only giving half the picture, usually in the interests of publicity for their cause. In Schechner's case, there is a violator, but no violated:

> The high incidence of sex and violence can partially be explained as redirected activities; performers frequently seek to work in the theatre as a way of 'getting out' their feelings.[27]

Theatre then, from this perspective, is a form of therapy for the psychopathic personality. The subject of this kind of theatre is the actor, working out his neuroses and aggressive instincts in a manner which is supposedly less destructive than blowing up a jumbo jet. But there is aggression nevertheless, and there has to be a victim somewhere amid the theatrical rubble created by these disturbed egos.

Theatrical apologists would have their readers believe that there is no victim, but this is only a curious feature of acting and terrorism's publicity campaign which glamorises and mythologises violence in such a way that it can be admired privately, even if not espoused publicly (except by fanatics). The hero rides into battle, overcoming dangers through his physical prowess and unbounded courage, and ultimately the audience celebrates his victory with him. The victims on whose suffering and extinction his victory is predicated, are suppressed in the epic narrative. Audiences glory only in the violence and ignore its necessary cruelty.

So too Schechner is excited by the violence of drama, while avoiding any comments about the victimisation on which it must be founded. This leads to a strange tension in his writing between the explicit statements that theatre is 'problematical, taboo, difficult, liminal and dangerous',[28] dealing with themes of 'sexuality, violence, conflict, obscenity',[29] and his implicit claim that theatre is nevertheless simple, beneficial and, more alarmingly, innocent as well.

He resolves the tension by opting for the 'safety valve' theory of theatrical performance and Carnival espoused by liberal authorities since the Renaissance. 'Drama', he says, 'is about the I-want-but-can't/shouldn't-have; or about the I-have-but-will-pay-for, which amounts to the same thing',[30] which is also a description of most terrorist motivations.

He goes on to argue that 'instead of causing further anxiety the performance of forbidden actions relaxes tensions'.[31] He sees laughter as aggressive but reassuring, serving the double purpose of threat and bond.[32] And to this end, he approvingly quotes the well-known ethologist Konrad Lorenz who once argued that 'There is no nonaggressive animal able to form personal bonds'.[33]

So Schechner argues from ethology (and Aristotelian catharsis) in his celebration of morally-beneficent violence in theatre. Theatre for him 'is transformation, not conflict' and it deflects man's natural violent instincts which otherwise would result in a 'difficult confrontation'.[34] It is theatre designed to produce a 'safe', non-violent society by diverting the impulses of nature into the confines of culture. It stresses the fun of it all and aligns the release of pent-up emotions with farce.

Unfortunately, however, the reality is that in a non-utopian world this 'safety valve' theory of theatrical aggression often malfunctions, and while theatre clearly can have beneficial effects in terms of social control (therapy) through catharsis, nevertheless, under the guise of neutrality and aggression displacement, theatre can equally embrace *actual* aggression and partiality. The supposed moral beneficence of theatre is not inevitable, and alternative perspectives on ethology and Carnival (the cornerstones of Schechner's theory of theatrical aggression) provide overwhelming evidence against the naïve populist views of socio-historical reality. Carnival inversions have a nasty habit of staking a violent claim to legitimacy, and the 'fun' of the festival has so often throughout history given way to ugly scenes of genuine social unrest.[35]

But in spite of these problems with his conclusions, Schechner's work is valuable in that it attempts a systematic (even if defensive) evaluation of the integral function of aggression in acting. From Schechner, scholars know that the connection between the two is more than a clever literary conceit designed to condemn actors, and in comparing aggression and acting seriously one does far more than to depict plays like Peter Handke's *Offending the Audience* as a paradigm of the theatrical experience.

What a re-evaluation of Schechner's work suggests, rather, is that in assessing the functions of the actor, scholarship has to take into account not just the individual (who in isolation will inevitably be depicted as a hero), but also those 'others' on whose oppression the actor's success is dependent. Specifically, it necessitates an examination of the actor's aggression, which may or may not be manifested in physical violence of the Handke kind. And just how this aggression is received by the oppressed (who can be cited as texts and audiences) needs to be understood.

It is easy for a terrorist to abuse his hostage (indeed that is the basis of their relationship). It is far less easy for a hostage, who by definition is powerless, to abuse his captor. The best he can do is appear in a court after the event, using words rather than weapons to attempt retribution.

The same kind of relationship pertains between actors and audiences in the theatre, where simply by paying money at the door, the audience is implicitly submitting to the power of the performance. The actor then has not only the audience's consent, but he has the full technical capability of the theatre, a number of colleagues in the ensemble action, as well as the respect of society, with which he can then proceed to alter the captive audience either physically (Artaud), emotionally (Shakespeare), intellectually (Beckett), politically (Howard Barker), or morally (Brecht).

In comparison with such potential antagonism, the audience's power to boo, demand their money back, or write rude letters, is minimal and ineffective. Collective action may damn a particular instance of acting, but the activity itself will not be destroyed. Indeed, there is a chance that the activity will be promulgated by such events, because controversy is a part of publicity and publicity is the lifeblood of acting. So the actor and terrorist are disproportionately powerful in relation to their audiences and this kind of indiscriminate (quasi-absolute) power breeds its own fascination. It can in part explain the much-vaunted mystique and charisma of the best terrorists.

The audience is in an invidious position when this mutable and duplicitous 'actor' achieves a position of power, because with the continual alternation of the real and the fictive, the effect of disorientation on any spectator is extreme, and in true 'Stockholm' fashion, the confused immediate response is often one of complete trust and identification. The pressures on a spectator to adopt this absurd position are easy enough to see, because with the established modes of perception rendered irrelevant (what's the point of distinguishing between the real and the feigned when each is manipulated into a part of the other?), the safest and most comforting alternative is to adopt another easily-assimilated standpoint which *does* offer relevance – namely, the viewpoint of the actor.

And once confusion gives way to this adaptation to the actor's world, sense and coherence emerge, just as in a hostage crisis where the apparent reluctance and impotence of the previously-trusted authorities turns the hostage first to disillusionment and ultimately to an enthusiastic acceptance of the world of his captor. A successfully-disoriented hostage will opt for an authoritative semantic structure when it is offered as a means of salvation, in preference to the established modes of perception. This in part explains the reversal of loyalties that occurs in the Stockholm Syndrome. The mutability which it represents in the hostages is determined by the criminals to be a form of victory.

Not only do the hostages come to identify with the terrorists in ideology, but their mutability means that they also employ the same techniques and methods, 'fitting the face to the situation'. To accentuate this transformation, and to ensure its effectiveness, terrorists – especially kidnappers – employ an array of devices beyond mere ideology to disorientate their hostages and to make them more effective victims of brainwashing. Richard Clutterbuck, in his book on responses to kidnapping, remarks that:

> Interrogators are likely to use Pavlovian techniques of contrasting brutality and kindness, light and dark, noise and silence; and to attempt mental disorientation by sensory deprivation, probably keeping the victim permanently blindfolded, with ears plugged, without any means of telling the time of day, with deliberately irregular and unpleasant food (perhaps none at all for a time) and repeated interruption of sleep (if any).[36]

Under such extreme physical and psychological pressure, with the hostage relying totally on his captor for food, information and human contact, the temptation for rapport and even trust to develop between hostage and kidnapper is immense and mutually beneficial. The hostage feels comfort and trust in the (re-)ordered world of his captor, and the captor gains the admiration and vindication that the illegitimacy of his project demands.

It requires very little alteration to transfer these techniques of terrorist interrogation and disorientation onto the grid of the theatrical experience. The traditional western theatre is, in design, an efficient but overcrowded space like a bank vault or an aircraft cabin, where individuals are confined for the purposes of mass transformation at the hands of the few. The space is constructed (or in the case of airline hijackings, chosen) in such a way as to discourage escape and to make the claustrophobic effect serve the purposes of the powerful few.

As much from peer pressure as from physical confinement and social etiquette, theatre audiences are denied the right to speak or stand up, so that their sole attention is focused on the new 'world' transpiring before them. No sooner has the confinement begun than the auditorium is plunged into darkness as the houselights dim, or in cases where this effect of disorientation is deemed to be too familiar, the lights stay up.

Darkness and light are employed for surprise and for fore-grounding of the spectacle transpiring on the stage. They can depict rapidly-succeeding days and nights, moods and even themes within the drama, but most important of all, they manipulate feelings of comfort and fear within the audience, and establish the victim's essential powerlessness. An audience knows that somewhere, an invisible person is sitting behind switches which can plunge them and the spectacle into darkness, but they never know when or why that decision will be made.

The kinder lighting directors usually employ a fade to black, the less kind simply flick the switch. In either case, the audience is at their mercy and it would be an easy task for a lighting director to throw an audience into panic. All he need do is refuse to turn up the lights, or put a screwdriver into the fusebox. When he does not do this, the audience trusts him, or even forgets him altogether.

Theatrical scenes are constructed and juxtaposed so as to accentuate these transitions, not just from darkness to light and back, but also from noise to silence, action to inaction, lyricism to discord, and brutality to kindness. There is just enough of the contrasts found in life to make the transitions comprehensible, but never enough to induce the torpor of familiarity. Thus there is a theatrical version of 'estrangement' inherent in the most successful theatrical productions, but in terms of the techniques employed to achieve this, a greater degree of physical and mental violence is required than in Jakobson's poetic theory.[37]

51

Theatre proudly boasts that it involves all the senses simultaneously and in attempting to disorientate on this broad base and with a captive audience, it necessarily must operate with far greater intensity than is required in successful literature. That is why the most innovative theatrical practitioners attract compliments that in any other field would be terms of abuse – 'disturbing', 'shocking', 'terrifying', 'radical', 'daring'.

In the theatre, there is usually no way for an audience to tell the real time, although on the stage the fictional hour is always hammered home ('The west yet glimmers with some streaks of day'), nor can an audience obtain food until the demands of the unknown performance blueprint have been satisfied. It would not only be highly improper, but also ludicrous, for a hungry audience member to seize the bread and wine furnishing the table on the stage (like the yokel in the audience shooting the villain of a melodrama).

There is no capacity within the confines of performance for normal human needs to be accommodated, and natural urges have to be suppressed in the interests of the supposedly greater aesthetic pleasure. Falling asleep, for instance, is treated with contempt by peers as evidence of philistinism – a failure of the initiation rite and demonstration of incomprehension at the 'danger' of the event. An audience exerts pressure on its own members in a gesture of solidarity with the actors.

On the stage itself, characters alternate brutality and kindness, with the result that the audience identifies with some individuals and warms to them, while rejecting others. Police officers, terrorists and playwrights all know the power of this device, interrogating a victim – to the victim's disadvantage – through a duo (one sympathetic, one unsympathetic) of bully-boys. One interrogator swears at and threatens to assault the victim unless he divulges the information. Then he leaves the room, at which point the other apologises for his colleague, explains that they don't really mean to hurt the victim, and that this second interrogator will protect him from the 'animal' now out of the room (usually, permanent teams of interrogators take turns at playing the tough guy). When the victim necessarily warms more to one than the other, his demonstration of this fact usually results in a weakening into trust, and the divulging of information to the supposedly less harmful of the two.

The interrogators have imitated the world known to the victim, and deceived him into believing that the lesser of two evils is the good. Thus the victim is condemned because his fundamental need for trust to be set against distrust led him to identify with his aggressor. Politicians, terrorists (as the prototypes of politicians) and theatrical performers all rely on the success of their acting to engender this Stockholm Syndrome response of trust in their victims, and they all tend to employ the same methods, simulating white in a world which is all black.

An analogous display of teamwork in the alternation of brutality and kindness occurs not just in characterisation, but in acting itself. Through its implementation, audiences develop a sense of favoured and less-favoured performers. The criteria for this division into good and bad (or bad and worse) include familiarity (Hazlitt's and Lamb's 'old favourites'), the liberties taken with the 'known' (as opposed to 'realised') texts, general appearance (attractive or unattractive), and acting style (Kean versus Kemble). Acting, like Saussurean language, is a system of gestural differences with no positive terms, and the result is that, in context and comparison, the morally heinous can be interpreted (by comparison with that which is worse), as histrionically superb.

The performance provides its own modes of interpretation and once 'inside' its world, the spectator need not refer to any extra-theatrical prejudice. The confining capabilities of theatrical archi-tecture and powers of disorientation embodied in theatrical effects accentuate this phenomenon. That which is deplored 'outside' of the theatre can be admired from the inside, because theatre is as much a world in itself as the world is a theatre. If an audience has submitted to the 'spell' of the theatrical experience, it will not only endure the physical and psychological assault on it, but will applaud the perfection of the oppression.

With their senses altered by technology and trust, audiences are deluded into the belief that their borrowed judgements are their own, and that their critical and moral faculties are being exercised to the point of exhaustion. This is usually a good feeling and hopefully provides for satisfaction at the conclusion of a performance.

If, however, the audience feels dissatisfied at the end, they can usually find a scapegoat in the playwright (if the play is new) or the director (if the play is old). Actors are rarely held responsible individually, and virtually never *in toto*, because after having spent the hours of the ordeal together, audiences feel at one with these visible performers – they tend to be regarded as friends and fellow strugglers, while those who are removed from the scene of the ordeal in positions of authority are much easier targets for condemnation. Familiarity with the personalities and bodies within a closed environment has been denied and they remain faceless symbols of antagonism, custodians of the coldly-printed text and the distant and shadowy manipulators of present action.

Once in this position of identification, an audience will not interpret violence as threat, but as art. They will not only tolerate but enjoy the shocks of sudden gunfire which makes their hearts pump faster, the simulated murders and lacerations which make them tremble, the foul and aggressive language directly targeted at their conservative sensibilities. They won't question the deprivation or alteration of their normal intellectual, emotional, physical and psychological responses, and the cramped and uncomfortable conditions will be accepted as necessary rather than imposed. The common experience, in fact, will be one of enjoyment.

All this happens from the audience perspective, but when the obverse form of the Stockholm Syndrome applies and the actor begins to identify with the audience, the success of his project is jeopardised, because his concern for the victim as an individual outweighs the victim's value as a trade object or a faceless symbol of an antagonist. Actors often describe their misgivings about performing for friends and relatives and are reluctant to act except under optimum conditions.[38] Objectivity – and not direct human contact – are essential to the project. Terrorists find that to achieve as little identification as possible with their victims, blindfolds, hoods, gags and silence are the best dehumanising devices to employ.[39] Similar techniques are often employed in the traditional proscenium-arch theatre, where the audience is 'blacked out' and quiet, allowing the actor to indulge himself without the awareness of human eyes upon him, and with a consequent lack of temptation to see his spectators as individuals with everyday concerns like his own.

Under such optimum conditions, spotlit, solitary and hidden behind costume, the actor is safe from the 're-sensitised' temptations which proved the downfall of Jan-Erik Olsson and the South Moluccans. The Stockholm Syndrome is reduced to a one-way expression of trust and with the anonymous and unseen-but-present audience in awe of him, the advantage lies entirely with the actor. A combination of personality and technology establishes him literally and figuratively in the theatre as the one source of light.

Ensemble acting thus exists as the audience realigns its sense and sensibilities, deciding on the individuals with whom it will sympathise and offer trust, and those whom it will dislike and distrust. A successful ensemble is one whose collective talents are diverse and contrasting enough (even though they are all directed toward the same end) to satisfy an audience's desire for feelings of love and hate that it has come to exercise in real life, prior to theatrical realignment. In these cases, the audience's submission to the performance is deemed by them to be voluntary.

An experienced ensemble knows that if one member is hated, the rest benefit from the resulting displacement of affection, which is why Sir Laurence Olivier was never harmed by his appearance among woeful casts in worse productions,[40] and why Yasser Arafat is now regarded as a moderate Palestinian in comparison with the extremist campaigns of Abu Nidal. It is desirable for theatre as a whole to permit the audience enough latitude to despise parts of it, because if that happens, the illusory world of theatre makes sense to its auditors, and the Stockholm Syndrome is allowed to exert a persistent and nefarious grip on its victims. Queues form and money is paid in the rush to become passive recipients of the action. For the audience, this point of entry into the theatre comes as a liberation from embarrassment and mistrust, like the thrilling and illicit moment of rolling into a lover's arms and pleading to be abused.

So the impression that guilt and responsibility for the victimisation lies solely with the actor should not go unchallenged. Modern scholarship in psychoanalysis, criminology and victimology has argued persuasively that the visual symptom of obvious aggression does not in itself always convey the reality of motive. The arts have always known this fact, that the pleasure of being victimised sometimes exceeds the thrill of victimising.

Toward the end of Act One in Mozart's opera *Don Giovanni*,[41] for instance, the amorous Don on his tomcat prowl to Hell arrives at a peasant wedding, where his eyes fall on the pretty Zerlina. Only the intervention of Donna Elvira prevents the peasant from becoming yet another of the Don's sexual conquests. Safely returned to the bosom of her forgiving lover Masetto, Zerlina is reluctant to plead her innocence and begs him to beat her, because she knows how close she came to submitting to the randy devil. The distinct impression conveyed by her excited pleading for punishment (*Batti, batti, o bel Masetto*) is that she sees her victimisation at the hands of Masetto as an adequate substitute for her intended tryst with the Don. Poor Masetto makes an unlikely thug, but as her lover he must play that role. He can't disappoint her.

This brief incident in the opera has parallels outside of the theatre, not just in the obvious cases of sexual perversion, but in a range of social activities where violence works to the advantage of the victim. Especially where the victim pays the victimiser, total guilt cannot always rest solely on the shoulders of the aggressor. It's rarely as simple as the good guy getting beaten up and hating it and the bad guy doing the beating and enjoying it. Studies have shown that, on the contrary, there are various psychological types who either through personality or action are predisposed to be victims and who actually invite victimisation on themselves, in extreme cases like Zerlina's even reversing the tables and rendering the victimiser as the more passive party.[42]

In the theatre as in life, guilt and suffering possess undoubted if apparently perverse appeal, which makes them ideal targets for religious and political ideology. To watch the violence, to perpetrate the violence, and to be the victim of the violence all at once characterise the phenomenon that is known as the feeling of passion. In its theatrical incarnation, the emphasis on one of these ambitions over another usually determines whether the individual is known as performer of the theatre or the audience, but in greater or lesser degree they are characteristics shared by artist and non-artist alike. Zerlina's implicit equation of a beating with the finer physical and emotional pleasures is as much an aesthetic manifesto as it is a confession of guilt.

So every pain contains within itself the possibility of a feeling of pleasure[43] and the difference between the two conditions is fundamentally that between the activity and passivity of the sexual perversions known as sadism and masochism. The *activity* of the Marquis de Sade and *passivity* of individuals like Mozart's Zerlina are extremes of the phenomenon. More frequently, it occurs as a combination of the two, sado-masochism, in which the oscillation between activity and passivity works to the advantage of both the subjugator and the subjugated. The pleasure and pain derive from the antagonists' resistance succumbing through means other than conciliation. Each takes a turn at being the victim and through violent means each ultimately operates in the interests of the other.

In many cases of voluntary victimisation, the fundamental physical, moral, sexual or spiritual need to endure hurt is aligned rhetorically with prevailing social ideology. Thus the fanatic dancing with spears and spikes piercing his body attributes his survival to his religious faith, while the Filipino Christian enjoying his annual

Easter crucifixion in the name of biblical piety also pretends to serve a higher cause than his own. And so too the sumo wrestler gorges his way to an early death in the interests of art, sport and victory.

All of these zealots, freaks and self-mutilators confront an audience whose initial (uneducated) response is based on pity, fear and revulsion at the act, and the complete fascination with it. The reaction is both a heightening of sensual awareness and an affront to established modes of perception.

As familiarity with the violent act develops, however, the naïve shock is replaced by established modes of perception, which render the spectacle meaningful. Sadism and masochism are superseded by ritual, and that which *was* bad and irresistible (the screaming of the initiates, the mutilation of the body) is rendered good and routine. Sadism and masochism become unrecognised parts of the process, rather than ends in themselves. Founded on cruelty and oppression, the ritual assumes the status of nature and its violence is only an issue to the outsider. Reason and objectivity are luxuries that the *aficionado* abandons as soon as he agrees to abide by the tenets of a society.

In its artistic version, this very abdication of the rational faculties demanded by commitment to a social ideology led Plato to his celebrated censorship of the creative arts from his Republic. The Platonic mind, made up of higher and lower elements, is eminently corruptible and by the subtle manipulation of aesthetic seductions, the poet's appeal to the weakest parts of moral resistance could lure even a philosopher-king to sell himself into slavery:

> this recalcitrant element in us gives plenty of material for dramatic representation; but the reasonable element and its unvarying calm are difficult to represent, and difficult to understand if represented, particularly by the motley audience gathered in a theatre, to whose experience it is quite foreign.[44]

Throughout Plato's theory of art, there runs a constant awareness of man's corruptibility and tendency to victimise himself given the encouragement of an attractive Iago or Hilarion. It is a theory based not just on the power of art but more crucially on the weakness of individuals, specifically, individuals who are all too willing to submit their control in response to emotion and seduction.[45] Plato knew that in every individual there exists a victim waiting for his turn in the chamber of horrors, and removing the catalyst of art is one method of forestalling that particular ritual humiliation.

Plato's work, being theoretical, is not challenged physically like that of the Romantics (who essentially in their attitude to Shakespeare on the stage were arguing a similar theoretical point), but there seems little doubt that if put into practice, the sheer illicitness of the artistic spectacle would have corrupted even Plato himself. He, like the Romantics, would have fallen in love with Kean even as he condemned his kind.

Already in The Republic is the embryonic veneration of the antagonist that characterised the Romantics' writing on Shakespeare in the theatre. As Hazlitt called Kean the greatest commentator on Shakespeare,[46] so Plato treats his poets 'with all the reverence due to a priest and giver of rare pleasure'. He anoints them with myrrh and crowns them with fillets of wool, before collecting himself and finally sending them packing.[47] Defenders of the arts despise Plato, but his tendency toward victimisation in the presence of the charismatic artist is not so very different from their own, and he is saved from embarrassment and ecstasy only by the chastity of pure theory. Put him in a darkened room with his antagonist and they may emerge as lovers, unwilling but passionate victims of the Stockholm Syndrome.

4

VIOLENT COMEDY

The annual Carnival in Rio de Janeiro is one of those local celebrations that has become an international event. Along with the running of the bulls at Pamplona, the Pope's Easter Mass at St Peter's, and the Academy Awards in Hollywood, the images of the Rio Carnival convey to the western world the message and myth that all is well – crazy but well – and that the tradition, no matter how debased or transformed, endures. With the benefit of distance and alienation, television and newspaper audiences can bask in the extravagant Romantic sentiment and the comforting ritual of these celebrations, reassured that they as individuals are not affected nor affronted by the reality faced by the participants.

This is the modern incarnation of Renaissance Carnival, where the major transition has occurred to a strict division between actors and audience. The modern Carnival, unlike its Renaissance predecessor, now means different things for the participants than it does for the spectators, because the perspectives on it are opposed and divided between the active and the passive.

Inevitably then, with the perspective of millions of non-participating outside (international) observers dominating the trans-mission and reception of the event, the impression is the sentimental one engendered by alienation and affection. The emphasis is on personal liberation and social stability reflecting the essential satisfaction of the populace with their lifestyle and position in the (reaffirmed) homogenous society.

In relation to the Rio Carnival, this external sense of assurance is conveyed by the image of sweaty, bare-breasted mulattos gyrating to the samba down the streets, resplendent with tropical fruit on their heads and a virgin-whore look in their eyes. Noise and smiles and endless rubber hips flash across television screens, and the western world feels grateful that in spite of the contemporary political, economic and social catastrophes of the time, the party continues indefatigably from year to year.[1] Absence makes the myth grow stronger.

Then, some time after the Rio Carnival concludes, a small paragraph will appear in the international pages of western newspapers, conveying the official statistics for murders which occurred in the city during the celebrations. Usually this figure is around 130 dead, with an unspecified number raped, robbed, assaulted and infected, far in excess of the average for the rest of the year.[2] No reasons are usually offered for the violence but the implication is that drunkenness, heatstroke and intense sexual jealousy could be to blame. It's a tragic consequence of an event whose distanced depiction and defence is always conducted in the rhetoric of comedy.

To question this ritual of partying and then counting the dead is to deny the priorities of myth over fact and the sentimental over the rational, and renders the critic a Puritan. Consequently, the celebrations and the murders continue annually with the full support of fevered libertarians for whom the violence of Carnival is accidental and incidental, a product of their too-much-of-a-good-thing perception of the festival.

From a less secure, less alienated perspective, however, one determined by history and tradition, the tragedy and violence of Carnival appear to be as intrinsic to the event as the much-vaunted comedy.[3] As the work of Natalie Zemon Davis, Peter Burke and others demonstrates, since Renaissance times, Carnival throughout Europe has been characterised by its ritualisation of aggression, with mock battles, brutal football matches and its savage attacks on Jews (pelted in the street on their annual race through Rome), cocks (pelted to death) and dogs (tossed in blankets). Records show that the number of street killings in Moscow always increased during Carnival time, and an English visitor to Venice at the end of the sixteenth century reported that:

> There were on Shrove-Sunday at night seventeen slain, and very many wounded; besides that they reported, there was almost every night one slain, all that Carnival time.[4]

The violence could manifest itself in countless less-homicidal ways than this, from ladies on balconies throwing eggs, stones and fruit at festival participants, to men rushing about striking at bystanders with pigs' bladders and sticks.[5] But whatever the form, Carnival took its cue from ritualised acts of aggression and a popular expression of the time was that ' 'tis no festival unless there be some fightings'.[6] The danger occurred when the licence to fight liberated more than the desire for ritual combat, and symbolic violence turned into mass bloodshed.

In 1376 in Basel, a Shrove Tuesday celebration turned into a massacre. At Bern in 1513, the Carnival became a peasant revolt. Four years later, May Day in London resulted in a riot against foreigners.[7] At Romans in Dauphiné in 1580, one of the licensed Abbeys of Misrule carried a placard reading:

> The rich men of the town have enriched themselves at the expense of the poor

– the result of which was a shocking outbreak of violence which spread from the town to the surrounding countryside.[8] In the country, the local gentry 'went hunting through the villages, killing the peasants like pigs'.[9] In Switzerland, the Netherlands and France, there are records of similar atrocities resulting from Carnival violence.[10] The revellers of Lyon in the 1580s flouted their Carnival licence to protest the folly of religious war, the high cost of bread and the poor state of the economy, just as they had in 1540 at the Mardi Gras in Rouen. Winegrowers revolted at the Carnival in Dijon in 1630 and there were disturbances at Palermo in 1647 and in the following year.[11] In other words, the annual carnage in Rio has any number of historical precedents in a supposedly 'green' world of Carnival which has an embarrassing habit of turning a bloody shade of red.

Through centuries of carnival brutality, fighting has been the mode, aggression the stimulus, and humiliation the objective. The *charivari*[12] (which survives in media show trials and persecutions) was one of the more repressive and malicious forms of this Carnival humiliation, taking the form of a noisy demonstration of popular justice in which the wrongdoer was paraded through the streets and his crime re-enacted:

> If anything singular occurred in town, like thefts, murders, bizarre marriages, seductions, then the Chariot and the Infantry got on foot; people in the troupe were dressed the same as those to whom the thing had happened and represented them realistically.[13]

The re-enactment of husbands beaten by wives in Lyon in 1566 saw the victims assaulted with sticks, knives, forks, frying pans, trenchers, water pots and even tripe. Some had stones thrown at them, some had their beards pulled, and others were kicked in the genitals.[14] An enquiry into injuries caused by *charivari*s in a region of south-west France found five cases of the victim firing at his tormentors, two people blinded, two killed and one suicide. In Scotland there is a record of a suicide 'from remorse' and in the Basque Country, one *charivari* resulted in one killed, two wounded and one suicide.[15]

For their participation in these punitive morality plays, the revellers were rewarded with the Renaissance version of Horatian *dulce et utile*, comprising an instructive awareness of the dangers of sin and social transgression, together with the pleasure of assaulting and humiliating a lesser mortal. The supreme example of this artistic indulgence was public execution, wherein Tower Hill in London (and similar venues throughout Europe) became the major entertainment venue in England, drawing crowds of up to 40,000 for the best attractions such as Anne Boleyn and Sir Walter Ralegh.[16]

To ensure this kind of attendance, public holidays were often proclaimed when important individuals, in Ralegh's words, marched playing to their latest rest, in the procession up the hill from the Tower, allowing the spectators to taunt and pelt them for one last time. The scaffold was mounted, the crowd addressed, the gods invoked and the moral pointed. Then the head was chopped off and held aloft for the delight and instruction of the assembled, cheering throng. Drawing and quartering the corpse, perhaps a public display of the head at another venue, and then a slow procession back to the Tower closed the performances, but as great art always generates lesser art, it would not be long before ballads recounting the last moments of the deceased were hawked about London streets.[17] This mass attendance and literary perpetuation ensured that the pleasure and instruction was spread further afield than Tower Hill, defying the constraints of time and distance.

Carnival has played an influential role in literary and theatrical criticism, particularly that devoted to the study of Renaissance authors for whom the distance in time and space between author and critic is quite extreme.[18] Inevitably, the result of this alienation from the historical and social reality of the author's time is that Carnival is interpreted affectionately as a community 'safety valve' in a theory which bears a striking resemblance to Aristotle's 'catharsis' defence of the arts.

By censoring the historical precedents of Carnival as an outlet for aggression and disaffection, the 'safety valve' theory argues that by allowing for a temporary reversal of the social order, Carnival as comedy effectively renews the mandate for established authority. As long as innocent laughter is the appropriate response to a fool becoming a king, then the status quo prevails and Carnival remains the most insidious, desirable and effective means of social control. It will also remain a delightfully censorable phenomenon about which nothing but goodness can be conveyed to other times and places.

So from this alienated perspective on Carnival-as-comedy, literary and theatrical critics such as Barber and, to a lesser extent, Bakhtin and Bristol,[19] are necessarily limited in the texts which they can identify as 'Carnivalesque' and in which they can trace elements of Carnival 'doubling'. Like reporters searching out the literary equivalent of the sweaty Rio mulatto, they mythologise the innocent and attractive part of the popular event to the detriment of the greater reality. But because of the cruelty, violence, humiliation and tragi-comedy of Carnival itself, its influence on literature must necessarily extend beyond the simple comic inversions from reality to illusion, from the sacred to the profane, and from the top to the bottom half of the body which Barber and Bakhtin find in their chosen texts.[20]

That extension of the historical Carnival spirit emerges in Shakespeare's tragedies, typified by *King Lear* where the fools and kings and noblemen-disguised-as-bedlam-beggars prance about the storm-swept heath like Queens of the May debating whether a madman be a yeoman, gentleman or king.[21] Here too is the rapid Carnival juxtaposition of the celebratory and repressive, and the comic and the violent, with the mad trial scene on the heath suddenly giving way to the all-too-real blinding of Gloucester, and then the gentle reconciliation of Lear and Cordelia rapidly descending into the brutal triumph of their oppressors.

These Carnivalesque transitions, comic inversions and identity changes are accentuated further if, as suspected, the Fool and Cordelia are doubled, because with such casting, the festive image of the fool appears as the effigy of the wronged daughter, in *charivari* fashion, perpetually tormenting Lear with the physical embodiment and imitation of his offence.[22] The tragic error, transferred into a brutally comic re-enactment by the demands of popular justice and folk ritual, drives the victimised offender to the limits of his physical and mental endurance, as a means of private punishment and public entertainment. Lear's insanity emerges from the same remorseful impulse, exacerbated by torture, which drove the historical victims of *charivari* to suicide.

Outside of the drama, the Abbeys of Misrule appointed as the agents of *charivari* retribution, consisted initially of young bachelors within the community and only later included married men as well. Typically, by the sixteenth century, Lyon with its 60,000 inhabitants had about twenty such Abbeys, each with its presiding Abbot and titular office-bearers.[23] Because of their power and potential for corruption, these and other Carnival institutions were particularly susceptible to infiltration by authoritarian spies. The French lawyer Claude de Rubys, as part of his 'safety valve' theory of Carnival repression, was one of many conservative doctrinarians who advocated such espionage in the late sixteenth century, in his case for the purpose of disseminating Catholic propaganda.[24]

So the youth groups 'monitored' their victims, and the authorities 'monitored' the youth groups' 'monitoring', in a paranoid environment of meta-surveillance which Shakespeare would appear to have emulated in *Hamlet*, a play in which everybody, from the tormented amateur Hamlet observing the King at the play to the professional sleuth Reynaldo dispatched to follow Laertes, takes their turn at skulking along the suspicion-ridden corridors of Elsinore.

Shakespeare's plot in *Hamlet* bears the character of a staged *charivari*, wherein a bachelor sets out to avenge both the murder of his father and the social transgression of his 'adulterous' mother.[25] (Statistically, wrongful or bizarre marriage was one of the most frequent causes for *charivari* retribution.) Under the deceptive guise of holiday humour, deemed by most observers to be madness, Hamlet enlists the aid of his fellow-bachelor Horatio, in concert to form a kind of Abbey of Misrule devoted to the punishment of the offences. Through the agency of Rosencrantz and Guildenstern, the authorities make an unsuccessful bid to infiltrate the Abbey, and the quick exposure of the impostors makes them too the objects of humiliation and ridicule. They do not distract Hamlet from his Carnival purpose which is to confront the King with a comic theatrical image of his transgression, thereby eliciting the murderer's confession and his torment.

He enlists the aid of the players, selects a comedy, and makes his own additions to the traditional text of it, the better to weaken the King's defences through submission to the opponent's humour:

KING: Have you heard the argument? Is there no offense
            in't?
HAMLET: No, no, they do but jest, poison in jest; no offense
            i'th' world.[26]

It's the familiar routine of terror adopting the seductive euphemism
of humour to distract attention from the viciousness of the motive
and the means, and ruthless political ambition (in this case Hamlet's
desire for revenge on his father's death) masquerading theatrically as
comic madness. At this point in the play, the King doesn't yet realise
that Hamlet is always at his most dangerous when he's smiling. And
that is his fatal mistake which soon results not in the grin of laughter
but the grin of death.

So the humorous inversion of established social order which seems
to have influenced Shakespeare's comedies was not the only form
of Saturnalian behaviour on which literature, theatre and political
activism could be fashioned. In fact it coexisted with various rigorous
and oppressive devices for social control and purgation, including
humiliation, violent re-enactments, rioting and ritual aggression.
Carnival was much more than an amusing expression of the second
selves of a naïvep people, and the Bergsonian comedy which it
precipitated was characterised by the cruelty which could kill or
drive its victims to suicide.[27] Once the restrictions of passivity and
removal from the action are overcome, the observer of Carnival
notices that the obvious capacity of the fool for acts of wisdom is
aligned with an equal talent for malevolence.

In its stage manifestation, this potentially duplicitous function
inevitably raises doubts as to the theatrical motives and interpretive
ambitions of Shakespeare's so-called 'wise fools'.[28] The safety of
distance and the survival of contemporary publicity have ensured
that the greatest comic actors such as Richard Tarlton and Robert
Armin are remembered affectionately as valued influences on and
collaborators with Shakespeare in the creation of the great fool roles
in *Twelfth Night*, *As You Like It* and *King Lear*.[29] But the social
and theatrical tradition of folly which they inherited and developed
was much less innocent than this sentimental expression of goodwill
would suggest.

The fool appeared in both comic and tragic modes in Shakespeare,
and Armin acted both the wise Feste and the mongrel Thersites. The
indications are that the latter's brand of bitter railing and violent
contempt possessed a more distinguished theatrical heritage than

the former's middle-class wimpishness, and that the actor Armin, far from being the humble colleague or servant of Shakespeare, acted as a kind of terrorist, not just offending Hamlet by speaking more than was set down for him, but through violence, viciousness and vanity effectively subverting the artistic ambitions of the greater theatrical spectacle itself.

Through a century of theatrical development, the Elizabethan stage fool descended from the Devil and, through various transformations and hybridisations remained of the diabolical persuasion. His inheritance of Carnival cruelty founded on Satanic temperament was ideally suited to the medium of comedy, and the success of his terrorism-through-laughter endured both on- and off-stage in every country where the comic actor was mistaken for a friend, and where the sweaty body of the rampant mulatto obscured the view of the city morgue.

But folly needn't be as sinister as this of course. Under the illusion of liberation, the Carnival licence restricts its participants to the adoption of one fictitious persona, whose appeal rests both on the traditional characterisation within the ritualised social drama, and on the tension created between the known actor and his assumed role. When Carnival operates in its conservative mode, the entertainment resides in the simultaneous presence of the image and the reality within the characterisation, resulting in an irresistible potential for comedy. Robert Weimann employs the comic example of Ampleforth to demonstrate this simultaneous presentation and representation which constitutes the duality of stage acting:

KING: I'm a King and a Conqueror too,
        And here I do advance!
CLOWN: I'm the clown of this noble town,
        And I've come to see thee dance.
KING: The clown come to see a King dance!
CLOWN: A King dance! Ask thee good fellow?
        didn't I see thee tending swine 'tother
        day – stealing swine I meant to say?
KING: Now you've given offence to your Majesty,
        thee must either sing a song, or off goes your head.[30]

The Clown's sabotage of the illusory seam between the ritual and the mimetic action exposes the artificiality of the stage event and mocks the pretentiousness of the swineherd who through acting would be

King. Essentially it's an anarchic ambition on the part of the actor, rendered acceptable by the humour, but if ever the comedy lapses or oversteps its authority, the fool's appropriate punishment is the whip.

In a passage from Thomas More's *History of Richard III* where *theatrum mundi* is invoked to liken the perception of political ambition and ceremony to that of playing, the dangers of the serious calling of the bluff are manifest. According to More, at a play everyone may know that the man playing the sultan is in fact a cobbler, but if anyone is foolish enough to 'call him by his own name while he standeth in his majesty, one of his tormentors might hap to break his head'.[31] Humour allows the comedian to get away with murder, but once deprived of that Erasmian cloak of folly, the observer no longer perceives distance between himself and the drama, thereby abandoning the sentimental view and identifying the comedian as an antagonist devoted to the destruction of the dramatic conventions.

These traditions of Carnival which shape the ritualised cruelty in the actions of the fool are supplemented on the Elizabethan stage by a degree of alienation between the actor and his character which is equally as amenable to manipulation by terrorist agitation.[32]

To state the nature of this potential alienation in its most succinct form, it can be said that actors as anonymous or, alternatively, famous figures, have the ability to make their acting facilitate or disrupt the theatrical illusion. The extent to which the purely textual meaning of a play is transferred onto the theatrical stage depends on the way in which actors convey, or are permitted to convey, their parts to the audience. Actors are simultaneously presenters and representers, a situation which has wide-ranging ramifications in theatrical productions and literary criticism. Richard Burbage, Edmund Kean and Laurence Olivier all presented and represented a different Hamlet, which may or, more likely, may not have approximated the Hamlet as conveyed, devoid of an actor, in the printed text.

Just as hostages sometimes fall in love with their captors, there are times in modern theatrical performances when an audience necessarily wants to believe that it sees reality, and on those bizarre-but-conventional occasions, the sentimental view of Carnival duplicity necessarily fades as theatrical *dulce* is superseded by *utile* and the victim's delight in deception overcomes the compulsion of reality. From the Romantic perspective of Hazlitt, this is the point at which great acting begins, wherein the thespian achieves 'acting degree zero' or a total disintegration into the role which he is playing.[33]

This rare illusion of successful syncretism perpetrated on the audience is an extreme and usually hyperbolised version of a theatrical relationship between actor and role which exists more commonly in a continual struggle between the two antagonists for supremacy in the theatrical action. The opposite extreme is the situation wherein an actor appears explicitly as himself within a fictionalised dramatic performance, such as that in Webster's Induction to Marston's *Malcontent*.[34] It occurs as rarely as 'acting degree zero', and is equally as susceptible to critical misrepresentation and hyperbole.[35]

The more common duplicity of stage characterisation created by the problematic relationship between the actor and his role(s) has been a crucial issue in twentieth-century theories of acting. The theatrical potential of the tension between acting-as-presentation and characterisation-as-representation has particularly excited the more radical theorists seeking alternatives to the dominant illusionist modes of theatrical production. Indeed the theoretical and practical distinction between the actor and character has been something of a rallying point for anti-Stanislavskian theatrical theorists approaching their topic from such diverse perspectives as popular culture and folk theatre, political agitation, semiotics and even speculative Shakespearean casting.

Bertolt Brecht's *Verfremdungseffekt*, deriving from Shklovsky's 'estrangement', realises this potential for division between actor and character by advocating that the actor should not aim to be an illusionist but must invest what he has to show with a definite gesture of showing,[36] thus not allowing himself to become completely transformed on the stage into the character he is portraying.[37] He speaks his part like a quotation[38] and adopts a particular attitude toward his character.[39] The anticipated result is the familiar 'alienation effect' (*Verfremdungseffekt*) designed to make the spectator adopt an attitude of enquiry and criticism in his approach to the incident being depicted.[40]

The problem with this approach, however, is that it theorises and desensitises a spontaneous characteristic of the passionate theatrical experience, with the result that, in the words of Jerzy Grotowski:

We watch performances inspired by the 'Brecht theory', and are obliged to fight against utter boredom because the lack of conviction of both actors and producers takes the place of the so-called 'Verfremdungseffekt'.[41]

Because non-Brechtian theatre possesses the capacity to subvert its own ideological impulses, at their worst, Brechtian productions only realise the ever-present potential to create a distinction between the message and the means at the expense of the underlying emotion of the event. The dramatic theory serves to emulate the function of the Shakespearean fool by providing an ironic commentary on the events within the plays, but in Brecht's case, risking a reduction of the drama to the level of political rhetoric while making this ideological point. Shakespeare proved that in fact the same political functions of alienation and critical awareness could be achieved through exclusively theatrical means, in drama of less-overtly homiletic function and infinitely greater histrionic conviction.

A more flexible attempt to theorise the relationship between actor and character is that of Petr Bogatyrev in two articles on the European folk theatre which have been influential in recent semiotic theory.[42] Bogatyrev's studies of the naïve drama established the fundamental opposition between actor and character which Brecht sought to formalise, and the crucial example of the division occurs when a spectator observes a friend on stage or an actor with whose work he is familiar appearing in a new role.[43]

In Bogatyrev's theory, there is a constant interaction between the real and illusory modes of dramatic representation, with the spectator sometimes forgetting that a fictional performance is occurring, but never enough to constitute a complete performance. The actor's function is curiously ambivalent; on the one hand he takes great care with costumes and make-up to look different in each role, and yet in spite of these precautions throughout the performance he deliberately adopts gestures which make his identity known to the audience.[44] The result is that the folk theatre has the capacity to embrace both the realistic and fictitious modes simultaneously in a performance which, at varying times, could satisfy the demands of Brechtian alienation *and* Stanislavskian method acting. To isolate one mode from the other would be alien to a theatre built on an awareness of the simultaneous existence of ritual and mimetic action.

In the writings of J.L. Styan, S.L. Bethell, Robert Weimann, Michael Goldman, Stanley Wells and others,[45] the differing emphases brought to the theory of acting appear as the local colour in messages which are essentially the same. In the words of Glynne Wickham, there is a 'person representing' and a 'person represented', and both modern and ancient audiences 'possessed the capacity to accept mimetic action on two levels simultaneously'.[46] The advocacy of the 'double view' in the work of these Shakespearean scholars suggests the potential for highly self-conscious acting implicit in the Elizabethan texts, typified in the illusion-breaking devices of *As You Like It* where boys play girls playing boys, and where references are made to the improbability of the stage action.[47]

As a reaction against dominant theatrical naturalism, this theory influenced by Shakespearean drama sometimes finds it difficult to gain practical application in criticism. A theatre and a criticism still largely enclosed by three walls and dominated by 'scratch-and-mumble' acting occasionally needs to be reminded of the self-evident fact that theatrical acting is not the same as dramatic characterisation. And Shakespeare, in his texts and on his stage, is one of the better teachers of that salutary lesson.

And so modern theatrical theory acts in concert with socio-historical studies of Carnival, to provide a theoretical foundation illustrating that the nature of comic acting which emerged with such force on the Shakespearean stage was the result both of the cruelty and violence associated with ritualised social celebration, and the tendency of actors to present two often contradictory personae to a sympathetic public. For the comic actor, both approaches could be guaranteed to keep the loyal audience laughing, and from that position of power, the real work of the comedian began.

The cruelty of stage comedy during the English Renaissance was doubly effective because the audience, even if they could escape the hypnosis of affection, could never be sure precisely who their target must be. Actors hiding behind characters and characters behind actors ensured the development of an Elizabethan version of Artaud's theatre of cruelty, wherein the oppression on the spectator was palpable, yet the direction from which it was coming could never be determined and the confusion only added to the bitter-sweetness of the theatrical pleasure-in-pain.

But putting the theory into practice in theatrical criticism is not as easy as might appear. One of the problems in the Shakespearean context is that the original actors who complemented or contradicted the great Shakespearean characters are known only by name and repute. Except in a few cases, their physical appearance is vague, and so the best the practical critic can do is to allude, for instance, to Burbage's singular portrayal of Lear, without actually describing the performance itself. In the case of the comedians, the practical application of the theory is still difficult, but the singularity of their appearance together with the conventionality of their roles, makes them a less impossible object for study.

From the pictorial representations of Tarlton, for instance, it is possible to infer the relationship between the actor as a famous individual and the dramatic roles which he is known to have assumed in extant plays.[48] As comedians, Tarlton and his successor Armin were the products of a vicious theatrical and social history dedicated to the oppression and humiliation of revellers and moral miscreants. As actors they existed as multiple beings able to distance themselves from the emotions and characters whom they overtly represented. And as inheritors of both these comic and histrionic heritages, they were slippery identities, possessed of the urge toward mayhem and able to wriggle and charm their way out of the blame for its creation.

The Devil, in his capacity as a complex moral being, had faded from the stage by about 1500, because his many sides became impossible to represent in allegorical stage action.[49] His place was taken by the various Vices who, individually, embodied a single moral idea and dramatic function in congruence with their names. Coming into the plays first as an attendant on the Devil and an opponent of mankind, the Vice gradually assumed centre stage and became both a figure of amusement and an interpreter of the events within the plays.

Under the guise of Carnival madness, the Vice scurried back and forth between the fiction of the drama and the theatrical reality of the stage event, at one moment fully integrated with the other characters in the play, at the next offering to make love to a woman among the spectators. Relying on Carnival's capacity to render evil and violence enjoyable, the Vice in his most developed incarnations came close to the status of satanic hero, thrust into the centre of stage action and precipitating calamities, while all the while acting as the eccentric confidante of a confused but admiring audience.

But with the arrival of scepticism and the related demise of monothematic stage impersonations from around the late 1560s, the Vice too went the way of his diabolical commissioner. Secularisation of the Vice's identity and function meant that allegorical certainty no longer reflected the social, scientific, theatrical and literary preoccupations of the age of Montaigne, nor could it keep pace with the increasing sophistication of Elizabethan stage practice as permanent theatres began to be built in London.

And so in the final third of the sixteenth century, the sophisticated fools of Shakespeare's stage emerged as the role of the Devil's advocate became morally ambiguous and histrionically versatile, demanding impersonation by comic actors with extra-theatrical identities and sometimes anti-theatrical motives. Where the transition from the Devil to Vice had begun with the Carnival enjoyment of entertainment-within-evil, the Vice in turn became a fool as his actor began to appear as a stage figure in opposition to the traditional characterisation.

This transition from Vice to stage fool was facilitated by the rise of the London theatres from the 1570s, because actors and audiences gained the opportunity to spend much more time together, further enhancing the familiarity so necessary to the psychological phenomenon of identification with the aggressor. Within a known and dedicated theatrical space with regular performances, regular audiences, and especially, regular casts, the appeal of the play centred not just on the plot and characters, but the performers as well. The concept of 'old favourites' among actors, later to become so crucial to the Romantics' enjoyment of the theatre, was made possible by this Elizabethan stabilisation and industrialisation of theatrical performances.

In this age of theatre-building and resident company-forming, the comic actors preserved the traditional separation of the Vice from the mythos of the drama not merely by their equal familiarity with those on stage (in the play) and those in the audience, but by their theatrical and extra-theatrical status as known figures. Actors themselves began to approach the mythical, being the objects of collective imagination, wonder and instruction.

Once the physical conditions for comic acting – a committed audience, close proximity between stage and orchestra, playwrights devoted to the comic cause – were established at the permanent London theatres, ugliness became a crucial attribute in raising the comedian to star status. From the surviving records, it would seem that few were uglier than Richard Tarlton, nor more influential in transforming the Vice into a modern stage figure, *presented* as well as *re*presented by a known actor.

The most famous clown of the Elizabethan stage, and probably the model for Shakespeare's Yorick,[50] Tarlton (d. 1588) was an author as well as an actor, and completed a lost play of *The Seven Deadly Sins*. Quite possibly, he was the author of the surviving play *The Famous Victories of Henry the Fifth* (described on page 74) in which he certainly appeared. Just possibly also, he was 'one of the first actors in Shakespeare's plays',[51] but whether this is true or not, he was undoubtedly known to Shakespeare, as he was to the whole of Elizabethan England, through his reputation and through his stage performances with Queen Elizabeth's Men. At one stage he had been a personal favourite of Queen Elizabeth herself, until a scurrilous joke at the expense of the Earl of Leicester resulted in his banishment from Court.[52]

With Tarlton, physical deformities like squints, squashed-tomato faces, button-noses, dwarfishness and hunchbacks became theatrical virtues which made their actors instantly identifiable on a crowded stage. As the apparently blessed possessor of all these disfigurements, Tarlton was well-endowed not just to achieve fame, but to gain the sympathy of his audience because of his apparent powerlessness.

Modern Pakistani beggars know that if they continually break the legs of their children, by adulthood the children's bodies will be so crippled that their ghastly appearance will elicit more generosity from the horrified alms-givers. The same tendency to pity the afflicted as if under divine compulsion underlies the project of the Tarltonian Elizabethan comedians. And yet while the sensibilities of theatrical audiences and tourists are affronted by the Elizabethan fools and Pakistani spidermen, the presumed miserable spastics employ the hypnosis of their grotesque appearances to achieve their own, often-ruthless ambitions.

An audience feeling pity is as susceptible to deception as one laughing. Tarlton possessed the enviable ability to create both responses in the theatre. He was so ugly, so pitiable, so laughable, and so talented, that his transgressions of the Carnival licence to mayhem were rarely likely to result in the whip or pillory.[53] The dominance of Christian ideology manifested in charity and forgiveness, together with innocent conceptions of Carnival and laughter, to this day results in feelings of identification and compassion toward the Tarlton-inspired fools who emerged on the Elizabethan stage. They're always ugly and sometimes funny, and because of that they often get away with murder.

The medieval idiot who had achieved popularity in Europe was not on the whole a rebellious figure. His presence at court was approved by the society which he often subverted and by the religion of which he was irreverent. Under the special protection of God, the fools were able to display what Kempis called their 'holy simplicity' and what Cusanus described as their 'learned ignorance'.[54] But under the pressures of Renaissance scepticism and personal ambition, the fools of Tarlton's day no longer implicitly affirmed the order of the world through simple contradiction, and their jests were less a 'safety valve' for the tyrannies of social inequality than they were immoral, blasphemous and rebellious attacks on social custom and courtly privilege.

Gradually, this absurd and radical figure began to assert a grip on the imagination of the English Renaissance, supplanting the sober and benevolent monk, pilgrim, knight and scholar, who for centuries had acted as the protagonists in a more ordered Utopian universe, with a prodigal reformer whose sympathies were decidedly picaresque. According to Harry Levin, this trend toward comic infamy began on the continent and moved north and west:

> Across Europe, along the drift from Renaissance to Reformation, from Italy to Germany, stride two gigantic protagonists, the rogue and fool.[55]

Through the secular diversification of the Vice in the drama, the rise of the permanent theatres and the talent of Tarlton and his successors, these rogues and fools – sometimes as separate individuals (Autolycus), sometimes as the one character (Thersites) – entered Britain and there, through actors like Tarlton and Armin, established a commanding stage presence which was to last until the closure of the theatres in 1642.

The actions of Tarlton's one known stage character illustrate the vicious heritage from which the Elizabethan and Shakespearean stage fools derive. In *The Famous Victories of Henry the Fifth*,[56] Tarlton's character of Dericke creates comedy through vindictiveness, maliciously savouring the impending punishment and even death of his enemies:

THEEFE: I prethee be good to me honest fellow.
DERICKE: I marry will I, Ile be very charitable to thee,
For I will never leave thee, till I see thee on the gallows.[57]

The audience's laughter at the aggression is predicated on the belief that the character lacks the power to achieve his ambitions, so the idea of violence is divorced from its reality.

This apparent impotence to fulfil evil intent, combined with an undeniable charm, results in an audience sympathy which turns hundreds of spectators into would-be assassins of the thief because they have mistaken a postponement of the reality for its impossibility. But power is transient and the motive remains, so the fool's violence has been deferred instead of contradicted, and he remains of the vicious persuasion regardless of the amused and admiring response of those who mistake his humour for honesty.

The similarity between Tarlton's clown, the Vice, Carnival agitators and political dictators exists not only in this simultaneous presentation of cruelty and comedy, but also in his love of strutting and attracting attention from the moment he enters the drama. In *Famous Victories*, Tarlton announces his presence by charging on and off and on again while making as loud a racket as possible:

Enter Dericke roving

DERICKE: Who, who there, who there?

Exit Dericke

ROBIN: O neighbours, what meane you to sleepe,
and such adoe in the streetes?

AMBO: How now neighbour, what's the matter?

Enter Dericke

DERICKE: Who there, who there, who there?

COBLER: Why, what aylest thou? here is no horses.

DERICKE: O alas man, I am robd, who there, who there.[58]

In line with Castiglione's precept for courtly self-promotion, the entry of the star performer is flamboyantly staged to achieve maximum dramatic impact, a skill for which, to judge by contemporary references, Tarlton was famous:

> Tarlton, when his head was only seene,
> The tire-house doore and tapestrie betweene,
> Set all the multitude in such a laughter,
> They could not hold for scarce an houre after.[59]

> . . . the people began exceedingly to laugh when Tarlton first peeped out his head.[60]

One of the reasons that Tarlton's other stage roles are unknown is that writers beside Peacham and Nashe always described Tarlton as himself rather than as his character. As if to emphasise the greater attraction of the actor, Greene wrote of Tarlton coming in 'apparelled like a clowne, and singing'[61] in another variation on the attention-grabbing entry which seems to have its counterpart in *Famous Victories* where, in an echo of the Tudor Vice's 'Who am I?' *lazzi*, much is made of Tarlton's clothing on his first appearance.[62] With his performance partly traditional stage routine and partly freak-show, it was inevitable that the impact of the characterisation was offset by the dominant histrionic personality, and that 'Much of his merriment lay in his very looks and actions'.[63]

The sympathy for human misery which is usually associated with the fools of Tarlton's successors is never apparent in Tarlton's role of Dericke. His preferred method is rather one of vehement denunciation. Thus, in one of the better Elizabethan examples of passionate misogyny, Dericke denounces John's wife as 'a stinking whore, and a whorson stinking whore' for daring to serve him 'a dish of rootes, and a peece of barell butter', and he leaves the stage with the intention of breaking all of John's windows as retribution.[64]

It's the violent Carnival spirit personified, and so too it's the tradition of the Vice. Indeed, on Dericke's next appearance he is dressed for battle like the old Vices, bound for the wars with a potlid for a shield and an enthusiasm for battle matched only by his desire to insult John's wife further. In typical morality style, John's wife gives Dericke a thorough beating with the potlid in an assault which, unfortunately, does not prove fatal.

Tarlton's character displays little sympathy with the issues of the play and a moment of poignant dramatic appeal only fills him with disgust, as when the tearful John bids farewell to his wife:

JOHN: Come, wife, lets part lovingly.
WIFE: Farewell good husband.
DERICKE: Fye what a kissing and crying is here?
           Sownes, do ye thinke he will never come againe?[65]

The comedian's Carnival licence for cynicism and contempt means that he has no time for scenes whose sentiment reverberates in the moral or thematic patterns of the play. A rare moment of genuine warmth such as this is anathema to the Vice whose historical character, from the anonymous Thersytes onwards, is scurrilous and whose development, even in the 1580s, is already heading toward the grotesquery of Shakespeare's Thersites.

In subsequent years, the great tragic themes of heroism, love and honour all begin to suffer from the development of this scorn for ritualisation of emotion. The object for the comedian is usually, through humour and *charivari*-like humiliation, to distance the audience from the events occurring on the stage and to prevent them from identifying too closely with the situation or characters. Through this, they facilitate a 'double perspective', that of the play world and the real world. And the sympathy thus displaced inevitably falls onto the comedian himself.

The presence of a famous actor and his freakish form means that the issues conveyed and the emotions aroused can never achieve independence from the physical environment of the performance itself. The fool's presence positively encourages the kind of reduction and trivialisation which turns King Lear into an old hoon with a stick. High emotion and heroism may be possible in opera when familiarity allows for the illusion that the obese soprano is in fact consumptive, but in Shakespearean theatre the fool's very function is to ensure that the hero's imperfections are never naturalised in that way. Tarlton's speeches attacking the very emotions of the drama only confirm the alienation from and antipathy toward the events which his body has already asserted. And thus when the fool succeeds, theatrical tragedy becomes a tale told by an idiot, full of sound and fury, signifying nothing.

Since the Classical age, one of the functions of the stage fool had been to subvert the emotion of the stage in this way. In a fragment of an Iphegenia play, the tragic invocation of the gods for a safe return is parodied by a farting fool, for whom the only deity is the goddess of flatulence, Porde.[66]

In adopting these positions which overtly oppose the mythos of the main action, the fool subverts the theatrical and structural foundations of the play while establishing a specific actor–audience relationship. He offers an alternative perspective from which the heroic theme is set contrapuntally against the contemptuous critique of anti-heroism, as the audience is offered both a 'mythical idealism'[67] and a caricatured realism. The fool oscillates between both worlds, just as the artful Feste negotiates between the upstairs world of Orsino's and Olivia's courts and the downstairs, drunken world of Toby and Andrew. He is welcome in both worlds because he is an integral part of neither, and because of that distance between himself and the world, his hostility and contempt is interpreted as entertaining.

This distancing occurs in most of the roles which Robert Armin (1568?–1615) is suspected of playing.[68] The First Gravedigger in *Hamlet*, for instance, is a less scurrilous relative of the Iphegenian *stupidus*, singing his happy ballad about death in the presence of the morbid Hamlet.[69] The character places himself outside the narrative and thematic concerns of the play at a climactic moment (his jokes make it clear that he is digging Ophelia's grave). He is 'inside' the play only to the extent that he appears on the stage and speaks to Hamlet, but 'outside' in that *his* world makes the world of the play seem inconsequential. He is an unconscious antagonist toward the unity of the drama, whereas Thersites, the violent, foul-mouthed and quintessential Arminian fool, is very much a conscious critic of the dramatic mimesis in *Troilus and Cressida*.

Doubling as a figure of the real and mythical worlds in the finest Shakespearean illustration of Carnival cynicism and disaffection, Thersites' dismissal of the seven-year siege of Troy – out of which the intensity of the play has derived – as nothing more than an argument over a cuckold and a whore, is both a violent critique of the artifice of courtly love and a continuation of the vicious stage folly shared by his namesake Thersytes.[70]

Armin's fame today rests on his courtly characters Feste, Touchstone and Lear's Fool, but these comparatively gentle souls are only the Arminian version of the sweaty mulatto, being a seductive diversion from the main thrust of the actor's literary and theatrical preoccupations.

Enjoying the soubriquet of Tarlton's successor,[71] Robert Armin was not only an actor, but also an author of plays, pamphlets and translations of Italian poetry.[72] He probably joined the Shakespearean company around 1598 after travels with Lord Chandos' Men, and his appearance as a presumed successor to Will Kemp as leading comic specialist in the company is usually aligned with Shakespeare's transition from the writing of rustic clown roles to those of the (supposedly) more sophisticated fools. But like all the members of the Shakespearean company (with the possible exceptions of Burbage and Lowin), his creative relationship with Shakespeare is largely unknown and the increasing number of biographical writings on him are based largely on speculation.

In 1600, Armin made his contribution to the contemporary revival of the jest-book genre with the Quarto publication of *Foole Upon Foole*, comprising a series of jests about six real and imagined fools.[73] It's a grotesque pamphlet, filled with gratuitous acts of violence and callous descriptions of amusing suffering. Even at a distance of four centuries, scholars have to work hard to adopt the sentimental view of its anecdotes. Armin's fools are victims and idiots. They choke on live falcons, break bagpipes over rivals' heads, climb into hot ovens, and are laughed at when 'blistered grievously' by nettles – before dying the next morning. The humanity which had once characterised the books of folly, such as in Brandt's *Narrenschiff* where affection attends on man's imperfections, gives way in Armin to a weary cynicism and an intolerance toward society's follies, a contempt which was reinforced by the additions in the subsequent version of the text, published as *Nest of Ninnies* in 1608.[74]

So the Carnival fools which Armin created were not just the famous three, but also Thersites and Lavache, those scurrilous cynics who perpetuated the saturnalian techniques of inversion while turning a licence for celebration into an excuse for vehemence. Autolycus, a roguish social outcast, was the ideal toward which Armin's fools moved as, under the guise of traditional stage entertainment, they withdrew more and more from social affirmation and reliable interpretation. Using the potent device of corruption of words, they exposed chaos, challenging established beliefs and social practice while refusing to articulate a coherent alternative worldview in a frequently frightening invocation of a Carnival devoid of renewal. Their ambition was always to reach a point where they could turn on their audiences and demand, 'Who's the fool now?'[75]

In theatre and in politics, that supreme moment of triumph comes as the audience, entertained into trust, acknowledges the innocence of the fool's two identities. Familiarity with, and pity on, the comic body eventually extends to faith in the motives and delight in the character. At that point, with overt acting diverting the attention, covert action begins, and laughter is forced to pay.

5

THE ROMANTICS

Thus, on our narrow boards, shall you bestride
The whole Creation's prospect, far and wide,
And travel cunning, swift as thought can tell,
From Heaven through the world and down to Hell.

Goethe, 'Prelude in the Theatre' to *Faust*

Violence, victimisation and suffering need have nothing to do with
unadulterated hatred. Of course there are frequent cases where the
emotions causing and generated by acts of aggression are in extreme
and unequivocal forms, and these require no interpretation. But in
many other examples, the negative sentiments are also accompanied
by positive feelings of pleasure and its various sensual or intellectual
manifestations. On these equally regular occasions, two languages
speak simultaneously within the one utterance, as, for instance,
hate can imply love, fear imply thrill, and aggression imply lust.
In these infinitely more interesting cases, interpretation *is* required
and the generalisation and discrete categorisation of attitudes is
inappropriate.

Such a situation where opposites and contrasts cohere in the
interests of a greater, often sensually-oriented unity is of course a
definitive characteristic of Romantic writing, and it is a courageous
critic who would depict men like Charles Lamb, Samuel Taylor
Coleridge, Leigh Hunt and William Hazlitt as entirely committed
to only one extreme of a potentially paradoxical whole. In the
Romantic period, the tendency to love the unlovable was intensified
and supplemented by aesthetic ideals in which, for instance, beauty
was typified by the horrible form of the Medusa, and agony was
one of the greater sensual pleasures. This context of pleasure in pain
undoubtedly informs the Romantic attitude toward Shakespearean

acting and is a timely reminder that occasionally, no matter how fleetingly, antagonists fall in love and lovers feel the urge to destroy their object of adoration. One would expect no less from an age of passion.

The Romantic era in Britain began around 1792, when Prime Minister William Pitt announced that 'unquestionably there never was a time when a durable peace might more reasonably be expected than at the present moment'.[1] Pitt was not a gifted forecaster. The next 23 years were to be among the most turbulent in British history, with not only the intermittent and bloody war against Revolutionary France placing extreme demands on the resources of the nation, but also a series of internal crises related to the demands for extension of the franchise.[2]

As industrialisation and its consequence, urbanisation, altered the social fabric, a growing band of disaffected working- and middle-class activists began a series of social protests against the rule of the few and the result – achieved after decades of hatred and violence – was the limited Reform Bill of 1832, extending the franchise to a larger, but still far from significant, proportion of the population.

The first decades of the nineteenth century were consequently an ineluctably political age, with passion and prejudice characterising not just the political debate, but also the works of literature that emanated from it. Indeed the border between literature and politics was virtually non-existent, with the great (and opposed) political treatises – Burke's *Reflections on the French Revolution* (1790) and Paine's *Rights of Man* (1791) – being outstanding works of literature, and the great essayists who succeeded them – men like Godwin, Cobbett and Hazlitt – being similarly diverse in their interests and influence.

This was the age in which men-of-letters were original social reformers speaking the language of life, rather than specialists with a dialect that needed to be taught. Writers moved back and forth between the disciplines, and it was common for creative artists of all kinds to be political activists as well. Political terror and aesthetic pleasure were the synonymous activities which led Byron and Shelley to Europe, and which fuelled the love and then hate at home between the prickly colleagues Coleridge and Hazlitt. A knowledge of, an opinion about, and even participation in revolution and political agitation, were almost prerequisites of literary activity in this intense and admirable era.

It was a symptom of the age that the author of the great works on Shakespeare and the contemporary stage, William Hazlitt, later became Napoleon's most sympathetic English biographer, because the latter 'terrorist' had a significant, if indirect, impact on English theatre. The author Thomas Colley Grattan maintained that Byron had modelled himself on Napoleon and that what Byron was to Napoleon, the great actor Edmund Kean was to Byron. Grattan used the comparison to invoke the nineteenth-century version of *theatrum mundi*, concluding that 'They were each acting the self-same part – straining for the world's applause, not labouring for their own delight'.[3] Such statements are symptomatic of an age when the equation between political terror and theatrical innovation was literal rather than figurative.

Theatre had traditionally been associated with the monarchy and court, but now, with revolution and regicide the fashions of European political life, the metaphor transferred to the new Continental dictator who had come to power through bloodshed and deeds of military heroism. Napoleon's cast for the tragedy included monarchs, heads of state, and other entrenched hoodlums and bureaucrats, all doomed for a terrifying and symbolic meeting with a masked figure of medieval justice. The scaffold was the public stage on which Napoleon first drew crowds to these performances of theatrical politics, and his resonant message of good and liberty overcoming evil and decadence was represented by the striking theatrical images of heads dropping into baskets and bad blood washing down the gutters. The purity and intensity of this theatrical spectacle of execution resulted from the actors' necessarily complete submission to the ultimate ritual of public humiliation. Lives were given in the creation of roles, and audiences could expect nothing less than total commitment from their performers.

It seems, however, that the commercial theatre in Britain, because it was authoritarian rather than revolutionary, chose to create far less impressive attractions, and by all accounts the English stage of the Romantic period was by comparison with Napoleon's French street theatre a dreary and unpleasant affair.[4] If anyone was going to lose their head, it was more likely to be the audience than the actors. Certainly, admission prices meant that they lost their money, and with the dubious privilege of entering the pit or gallery they were under threat from fire, riots, poor texts, vain actors, hostile managements, general discomfort, and worst of all, boredom. Supporters of Napoleon like Hazlitt, and those who grew increasingly hostile toward the French like Coleridge, were of the one mind when they wrote about the experience of the English Romantic theatre.

For the lover of Shakespeare, there were only two theatres to choose from, Drury Lane and Covent Garden, which under terms of a Patent granted by Charles II in 1662, held a monopoly on 'serious' drama in the City of London.[5] After Covent Garden had been burned down and rebuilt, Kemble abolished the shilling gallery and reopened the theatre with a performance of *Macbeth* in which the Italian Madame Catalani played the Lady. The combination of these abominations resulted in the famous O.P. (Old Prices) Riots, which were to become a form of class war in London theatres for the two months following the reopening, rendering performance virtually impossible and ultimately forcing Kemble to back down on his price hike.[6] The less hardy (and more wealthy) among the elite promptly abandoned the theatre in the face of these riots, and the textbook view is that

> for the next fifty years, polite society quitted the theatre for the opera house and the play for the novel.[7]

But the riots may have attracted as many punters as it drove away, just as English soccer today repels the gentry and attracts hoodlums.

Once the immediate battle over price rises had been won, many of the rowdies actually became patrons of the theatres, refocusing their protests onto the stage and heckling plays, performers and fellow audience members. All of the great Romantics refer disparagingly to these vociferous interrupters and the detrimental effect which they had on the quality of the theatre. Coleridge's experience was that he heard:

> a wit's ... slang voice call out 'the gallows', and a peal of laughter would damn the play. Hence it is that so many dull pieces have had a decent run, only because nothing unusual above or absurd below mediocrity furnished an occasion, a spark for the explosive materials collected behind the orchestra.[8]

And Charles Lamb, like Coleridge an aspiring and aspired playwright, also had the misfortune with his play to encounter:

> a theatre like that, filled with all sorts of disgusting sounds, – shrieks, groans, hisses, but chiefly the last ...[9]

The enthusiasm of these 'explosive materials' must have been quickened by the fact that they were not, at this point in theatrical history, blacked out. They could perform their atrocities within full view of the other patrons, thereby providing an alternative (and often better) spectacle to that offered on the stage.

Amid such a rabble, it was difficult for the Romantics to indulge their love of Shakespeare by attending in minute detail to every syllable uttered on the stage. The less committed among them perhaps acknowledged defeat and adjourned to a recently-advanced dinner hour,[10] or availed themselves of the whores who could usually be found soliciting at the back of the boxes.[11] Those of more sturdy disposition and poisoned pen reacted by conducting a savage campaign in print against the ignorance of popular audiences. Their rhetoric bore an uncanny (but secularised) resemblance to that of the Puritan moralists who sustained the anti-theatrical prejudice in earlier years.[12]

For those who could tolerate the audiences, however, there were numerous other obstacles to overcome, not the least of which was the smelly and garish gas lighting which, used initially only for the front of the house, in 1817 came to be employed as a standard method of lighting the stage as well. Contemporary accounts testify to the pungent odour which permeated the Patent Theatres while this technique of lighting (as well as the other innovation, limelighting) was being perfected.[13]

On the stage itself, audiences could expect to see some minor French play, bought cheap and hastily translated in a Romantic but familiar illustration of war being unable to prevent trade between antagonistic nations. The expense of commissioning native English drama, combined with a popular demand for melodrama and light Continental entertainment, meant that in this one area of English life at least, the ideological and military war against revolutionary France was replaced by voluntary submission to Gallic cultural imperialism.

This triumph of commerce over art and politics does not reflect positively on the courage of contemporary theatrical managements, although in fairness to them, it has to be said that the economic pressures under which they laboured were extreme (even if self-created). With the rebuilding of the theatres, they now had huge halls to fill – Drury Lane seated 2,283 and Covent Garden 2,800.[14]

From a modern aesthetic perspective, the impact of these massive caverns on acting and theatrical productions was disastrous and even laughable. The broadening of style required to project into the back galleries meant that all thought of subtlety and nuance – those crucial elements of great Stanislavskian acting – had to be abandoned in favour of the sweeping gesture and the grand rhetorical delivery.

Comic acting in particular suffered, as the intimate audience involvement and split-second timing that it relied on became swamped in the huge spaces of the theatres. Comedians had to revert to stock types in a move that sabotaged the huge advances made in sophisticated comic acting in England during the sixteenth century and culminated in the great comic roles of Shakespeare.[15] Performances of Shakespeare during the Romantic period either cut the fools entirely (Lear's Fool is the classic example, murdered first by Tate and not reappearing until Macready's version of 1838), or at best removed them from the centre of the drama.[16]

Even the strongest theatrical voices could not always be heard in the more distant seats of these new buildings. To compound the problem for actors, vast sets and excessive spectacle – designed originally to 'project' the drama into these larger halls – began to take over the productions, dwarfing the actors and in the worst instances reducing their function to that of inaudible supernumeraries.[17] A curious and (for the actors) insulting outcome of this phenomenon was the rise to popularity of animal and novelty acts. Under the dubious and stormy management of Sheridan, Drury Lane had witnessed the departure of Kemble and his sister Mrs Siddons for Covent Garden, and their replacement by a variety of performing elephant and dog acts, an artistic policy thankfully terminated by the fire of 1809. The career of William Henry West Betty, billed as a child prodigy and freak, was also annihilated around this time, after his performance of Richard III had been hissed off the stage in 1808.[18]

Men of passion like Hazlitt and Hunt, so impressed by the deeds of heroism and terror emanating from the French political stage and eager to raise their new profession of theatrical criticism to a position of genuine social relevance, must have torn out their hair at the imbecility and triviality of so much contemporary English theatre. Every age despises its contemporary art, but in this particular case the rejection was directed not at the usual 'crimes' of modernism, but at the *refusal* to embrace the modernist impulse which was being so clearly demonstrated in the spirit of Napoleonic France.[19]

It must have seemed to the early critics that while the Jacobins remembered the awesome spectacle of the storming of the Bastille, the English could only offer a few performing dogs and spectacular aquatic displays as their contribution to the theatre of the terrible and exhilarating new age. In the nearly two centuries of professional theatrical criticism in Britain, this was surely the only time when the critics were more disposed toward radicalism than the performers.

The Romantics stood at the threshhold between Classicism and modernity when, in terms adopted by Foucault, words ceased to intersect with representations and to provide a spontaneous grid for the knowledge of things.[20] With meaning now irreducible to voice as it had been through the metaphysics of presence, the critical attitude to acting was determined by the frustration which resulted from the inability of words to be represented accurately on stage, and the actors' apparent unwillingness to effect a genuine reconciliation between text and performance. The liberation of meaning through textual encoding meant that for those interested in interpretation, performances were always likely to result in dissatisfaction.

This critical exasperation could be triggered by any number of offences committed on the English stage, particularly in the performance of Shakespeare's plays. One of the most irritating and consequently famous of these was the continued employment of aborted Shakespearean texts, the victims of eighteenth-century 'improvers' like Cibber and Tate, whose castrations of *Richard III* and *King Lear* were still regarded as the definitive texts.

With the rise of printing and the development of the concept of textuality, the sanctity of authorial property found articulate and savage champions in the great Romantic critics, and the 'improvers' received a barrage of belated abuse. With his customary honesty, Hazlitt stated that:

> The manner in which Shakespeare's plays have been generally altered or rather mangled by modern mechanists, is a disgrace to the English stage[21]

– a comment which preceded an attack on the 'foppery and ignorance of the promptbook critics'.[22] Hunt too attacked the adaptors,[23] and even Lamb's characteristic generosity was stretched when he was confronted with:

> such ribald trash as Tate and Cibber, and the rest of them . . . have foisted into the acting plays of Shakespeare.[24]

The revolutionary spirit was one which could no longer tolerate the abuses of corrupt authority and tradition. Decorum and gentle wit had died with Classicism, and been replaced by an angry and impatient language that sought to instigate action rather than engender polite admiration.

Thus fired by revolutionary zeal, the Romantics were intolerant of a debased theatre sustained only by, in Leigh Hunt's memorable words, 'puffing and plenty of tickets'.[25] But for the committed Romantic, the issue was not simply the hyperbole of stage publicity legitimising the emasculation of the great playwright, nor was it just that the 'inherent fault' of stage representation turned the magnificence of *King Lear* into 'an old man tottering about the stage with a walking-stick' (in Charles Lamb's equally memorable words).[26]

The crude adaptations of Shakespeare were symptomatic too of a hostility which the contemporary theatre had developed toward English playwrights past and present. The hypocritical importing of French comedies was another manifestation of it; the cruel receptions given to plays by Coleridge and Lamb was another still. Lamb recalled that

> In that memorable season of dramatic failures, 1806–7, in which no fewer, I think, than two tragedies, four comedies, one opera, and three farces, suffered at Drury-lane theatre, I was found guilty of constructing an afterpiece, and was *damned* . . .[27]

Lamb was referring to his unsuccessful farce *Mr H–*, performed at Drury Lane in that season with Elliston playing the lead. Coleridge could have told a similar tale about his own excursions into drama, although when nearly two decades after its completion *Remorse* (originally named *Osorio*) was produced at Drury Lane it failed less miserably than *Mr H–*.[28]

To judge by contemporary accounts, managements were so unsupportive, actors so contemptuous and audiences so vindictive that few English plays – new or old – had any chance of success. The conditions for playwrights were so bad that the *Morning Herald* advised authors,

> never write for Drury-Lane Theatre, so long as the present system continues; you but waste your noble energies; and subject yourselves not only to disappoint, but to insult.[29]

The implication here is that management was to blame, but in fact the notice came in response to another of Kean's celebrated run-ins with authors.[30] The talented little man with the ferocious ego made a habit of commissioning authors and then forgetting his commitment to them. Other important actors and actor-managers never even got that far, as the difficulties encountered by Coleridge with *Remorse* and Lamb with the tragedy of *Sir John Woodvil* (turned down by Kemble among others) indicate.

For the actors who triumphed in spite of the spectacular theatre – thus creating the so-called 'actor's theatre' of the age of Kean – playwrights were insufferable members of a theatrical underclass. And the feeling was mutual. Sir Walter Scott, whose novels were so adaptable for stage realisation, was asked by Robert Southey if he had the intention of writing a play specifically for the stage. For all Scott's political differences with the Romantic poets and essayists (Southey, Wordsworth and perhaps Coleridge excepted), his reply must have struck a chord with them:

> To write for low, ill-informed, and conceited actors, whom you must please, for your success is necessarily at their mercy, I cannot away with.[31]

All of the great critics and failed playwrights took up the theme and, seemingly, John Philip Kemble, the fine but pedantic Classical actor in the 'teapot' tradition of one-hand-on-hip, the-other-extended-in-gesture style, was the man in everybody's sights. Hunt humiliated him with a satirical condemnation of his method of eliciting audience applause, finishing a big speech with a thrust of his clenched fist and then running off stage 'as if . . . in haste to get to his pint of wine'.[32] Hazlitt too regularly despised his self-conscious and outmoded style which labelled its perpetrator 'an icicle on the bust of Tragedy'.[33] Most succinctly of all, Coleridge (in a fragment which is rarely mentioned by scholars), referred to his 'insufferable coxcombry'.[34]

With such egos as Kean and Kemble calling the shots and being hailed as the saviours of the theatre from economic ruin, and with all the aesthetic eccentricities which afflicted the Romantic stage, the chances of any brilliant and radical author being attracted to the theatre in anything but a critical capacity were remote. And so they proved to be. The wonder is that Lamb, Coleridge, Shelley and Byron wrote for the stage at all, given the limitations that a conservative and actor-dominated artistic policy foisted upon those possessed by Shakespearean influence and revolutionary zeal.

For those whose aesthetic credo was based on the disinterestedness of the imagination (or in its Keatsian form derived from Hazlitt, 'negative capability'),[35] an ego-ridden theatre was incapable of sustaining either their own writing or that of their beloved Shakespeare. And as activists as well as aesthetes it was inevitable that they would respond. That kneejerk response, shared by Hazlitt, Coleridge, Hunt, and its most famous (or rather, notorious) advocate, Lamb alike, has become one of the most resounding and reviled theories of theatrical history.

Reduced to its facile form, as it usually is, the Romantic argument was that because of the stage's inherent unsuitability for representing complex characters of the imagination, Shakespeare read was preferable to Shakespeare performed. In Lamb's celebrated sentence, the practice of stage representation reduced everything to a controversy of elocution[36] and Shakespeare's magnificent creations when performed seemed not much different to any other journeyman playwright's jottings.[37] Further, in performance the trivialities ('non-essentials') which in stage presentation *are* essential – costumes, scenery, props – 'are raised into an importance, injurious to the main interest of the play'.[38] Lear becomes as notable for his walking stick as for his poetry.

As an enthusiastic patron of the theatre, Lamb must have known the experience of attending a Shakespearean performance where the interval conversations have centred on the actors' hairstyles and clothing, or on the lead's skinny legs and lisp. And so in order to avoid these distractions and trivialisations, Lamb made a point of realising the potential inherent in the post-industrial growth of literacy and mass publishing. He and his distinguished contemporaries – like the university professors who succeeded them – argued for the joys of reading Shakespeare and reconstructing his dramas in the theatre of the mind.

Such a view is naturally anathema to any theoretician obsessed by the self-evident historical fact that most plays are written to be performed. One of the more recent of these persistent gasps of outrage has come from J.S. Brattan in discussing Lamb's treatment of *King Lear*.[39] Attributing Lamb's preference for the play to be read rather than performed to 'the anti-theatrical pressures of nineteenth century evangelicalism and middle-class snobbery', Brattan, herself with a touch of evangelical zeal for the self-evident, goes on:

His lavish praise of *King Lear* amounted, in fact, to a wholesale condemnation – for if a dramatic poem is not a play able to be staged, then it has already failed, and any attempt to produce it will only demonstrate the inadequacy of author and actor alike.[40]

This view, which is typical of nearly two centuries of abuse for Lamb, is predicated on the primacy both of orality (over textuality) and authorial intention (over audience interpretation). From this curious, pre-literate perspective, a work of literature has to succeed in the (implied) terms set down by its (implied) author, otherwise it is 'already a failure'. In the specific case of that which is supposedly drama, this means that it has no option but to work in a building called a theatre and in a physical spectacle called a play.

But of course, given five hundred years of printing, sixty of New Criticism and thirty of structuralism in the English-speaking world, such a primitive passion for categorisation is of historical interest only. Shakespeare's plays are now texts as well as performances.

Theatrical apologists, confronted by the perennial conservative dilemma of a world which changes, may be distressed by this textual reality, but they cannot refute it. In a modern literate and text-based society, reading a Shakespearean playtext and seeing its performance are two viable alternatives. That other modern innovation, democracy, demands that individuals retain the right to choose.

Lamb chose the modern option in his capacities as a visionary and experienced artist in both literature and the theatre, but he in no way abandoned the Shakespearean theatre in practice. In his offending essay 'On the Tragedies of Shakespeare', Lamb provides all of the provisos and rejoinders that would satisfy his most severe critics had they cared to read them, but in theatrical theory as in war, propaganda allows for no depiction of subtlety or probity in an opponent. Crucially, Lamb makes the point that he is *not*

> arguing that Hamlet should not be acted, but how much Hamlet is made another thing by being acted.[41]

This of course is a very, very different thing to advocating so-called 'closet criticism' as a general rule in theatrical practice. It may not sit comfortably with conservative literary scholars who strain their talents to appease the whims and vanities of theatrical practitioners, but there is no doubt that in the context in which it was argued, Lamb's statement is fundamentally correct.

Lamb was at pains to stress that he made the statement *only* in relation to Shakespeare (significantly, the title of the essay describes it as about Shakespeare in particular, not about theatrical theory in general)[42] and made no such claims for the work of other playwrights:

> I mean no disrespect to any actor, but the sort of pleasure which Shakespeare's plays give in the acting seems to me not at all to differ from that which the audience receive from those of other writers; and, *they being in themselves essentially so different from all others.*[43]

In other words, independent of origins, Shakespearean texts were ideally-suited to the new modes of textual dissemination.

As a man of the theatre and of the revolutionary world, Lamb realised that no amount of fine modern stage productions could alter the fact that the characters of Shakespeare, because of their predominantly extra-theatrical dissemination in the modern world, exist with more force in the mind than they do on the stage. They may (or may not) enter the mind through specific stage performances, but they lodge and reverberate there in a distinctly mythical way. The characters of Shakespeare are huge monoliths in the English cultural heritage. Implicitly, Lamb was acknowledging that because Hamlet now exists outside the theatre,[44] to witness a performance of the play is only to observe a (disappointing) physical imitation of that *a priori* reality.

In this extreme case, one could now even go *beyond* Lamb to express a preference for neither reading *nor* seeing the play of *Hamlet*, because both activities tend to reduce the magnificence of the character conveyed by socially-derived knowledge and expectations of him. Hamlet superstar is so famous and loved that he is used by advertising agencies to sell products.[45] To read the text or to see the play is only to recognise – and be disappointed by – the mortality and indecision of this (imaginatively) heroic figure.

So even though theatrical champions find this and Lamb's extra-theatricalisation of major Shakespearean characters heretical, it is in fact an acknowledgement of the universality of the metaphor, like the myth of Atlantis being removed from Plato's *Timaeus*. It is pro-theatrical in the sense that it argues for the greater significance of theatrical characterisation.

This persistent misrepresentation of Lamb on the issue of Shakespeare in the theatre has not been helped – although it should have been – by the support of Hazlitt, Coleridge and Hunt. Sadly, the fondness of these provocative authors for spontaneous rhetorical outbursts has sometimes meant that modern scholars, raised on precise, dispassionate and systematically-developed argument, have confused the colour of their prose with its fabric. An unfortunate example of this comes in response to Hazlitt's declaration that 'We do not like to see our author's plays acted, and least of all, *Hamlet*',[46] or the similar condemnation of the 'delightful fiction' of *Midsummer Night's Dream* being turned into a 'dull pantomime' when acted, 'because poetry and the stage do not agree well together'.[47]

The standard scholarly patronisation of these forthright opinions is that expressed most recently by Stanley Wells:

> Perhaps he did not see quite deeply enough to realise that this [perceived failure of the stage] was not the fault of the plays, or of theatre as a medium, but rather of the theatrical conditions of his age.[48]

This is of course an altogether glib assessment of the man who was the greatest theatrical critic of his age. No one possessed a deeper perception of the strengths and weaknesses of the Romantic English stage than Hazlitt. His voluminous writings on theatre consistently contain the extraordinary passions and perceptions of a man who devoted the most productive years of his professional life to the medium. And if Hazlitt made the assertion that he preferred to read rather than see the plays, scholars must respond with less smugness and more sensitivity than simply arguing that he didn't know what he was talking about, especially when he had the support of the other great writers of his day.[49] The issue is far less clear-cut than the contemptuous hatchet critics would like to believe, and infinitely more interesting, in that while the justifiable Romantic advocacy of Shakespeare read was a striking rhetorical and theoretical ploy (conceived in the spirit of revolution), in practice it contributed to an undisguised delight in the theatrical experience shared by all of the Romantics.

Nearly two decades have passed since Joseph Donohue observed that apologies for Lamb's (and by extension the other Romantics') judgement, explaining it as a reaction to the deplorable tendencies of the theatre of his day, were misleading.[50] And it is nearly as long since Joan Coldwell demonstrated that while apparently rejecting contemporary theatre, the Romantics actually based their arguments on it.[51] New questions are now needed to further the debate.

It is no longer relevant to argue whether or not the Romantics were reacting against the contemporary theatre, but why they were both attracted to *and* repelled by it simultaneously. The conflicting arguments for them either loving or hating, and understanding or misunderstanding, the theatre have to be superseded by the much more intriguing examination of the way in which their love necessitated their hate and vice versa. The response of the Romantics to the theatrical experience is symptomatic of the curious duplicity of reaction engendered in most western theatrical audiences, and in anyone who has ever felt the need to be oppressed as they are loved.

These extraordinary men went to the theatre to enjoy the intensity of the experience. For Lamb:

> We carry our fire-side concerns to the theatre with us. We do not go thither, like our ancestors, to escape from the pressure of reality, so much as to confirm our experience of it; to make assurance double, and take a bond of fate. We must live our toilsome lives twice over . . .[52]

In rejecting theatre as escapism, Lamb's strange emphasis on the amplitude of the medium in a tone of weariness and resignation is typical of his ambivalence toward the topic. In a selective reading, such quotes could establish the preconditions for a withdrawal from the theatre into the closet, but they have to be set against an inverse and generally more frequent theme in his writing:

> Comparison and retrospection soon yielded to the present attraction of the scene; and the theatre became to me, upon a new stock, the most delightful of recreations.[53]

But it remains a 'delightful recreation' which nevertheless is frequently the source of anger, frustration and regret:

> Take the play-house altogether, there is a less sum of enjoyment than used to be.[54]

Yet he remained throughout his life a staunch patron and champion of the theatre, numbered many actors among his friends, wrote the most generous tributes to individual performers (among them Munden, Bannister and Elliston) and like Hazlitt expressed extraordinary sentimentality at the decline of their powers.[55]

It was a widely-shared mixture of indifference and affection. Even Coleridge, who also preferred his Shakespeare removed from the theatre, could qualify a discussion of dramatic illusion by noting that:

> The most important and dignified of this genus is, doubtless, the Stage.[56]

Underestimation of the power and appeal of theatre was not one of Coleridge's faults and nor was an inherent distrust of the medium, especially considering that he expended more effort on *Remorse* than on so many of his more successful creative works. One of Coleridge's most sensitive interpreters has argued that in fact:

> Coleridge's complaints about the performance of Shakespeare's plays and his advocacy of the closet as a more appropriate place for them are not intended to be anti-theatrical in any general sense.[57]

But as a brilliantly-gifted individual liberated from the tyranny of theatre's overdeveloped concept of exclusive property, Coleridge too felt the urge to make an exception of Shakespeare. And like Lamb and the others, it was expressed as a preference, rather than as a rule.

The fact is that while the Romantics undoubtedly felt nostalgia for a 'golden age' of theatre which they knew in their youth,[58] this did not necessarily imply a rejection of contemporary staging techniques. Hazlitt made it clear that the modern stage was 'not unfruitful in theatrical genius'[59] and Hunt like Lamb was a spirited defender of modern actors.[60] It should be remembered that Hazlitt's support for Kean was so great initially – effectively saving Drury Lane from closure – that rumours of Hazlitt being paid £1,500 to 'puff' the performer circulated around London.[61] This was not true of course, but it does suggest the extent to which this self-confessed voluntary 'reader' of the Shakespearean texts contributed actively to the creation of the greatest Shakespearean actor of the age.

The explanation for the apparent contradiction is that Hazlitt loved Kean as only an opponent can – with suspicion, fear and passion. Contrary to popular opinion, Hazlitt was not uncritical of Kean (particularly in the later years),[62] but when the actor performed some act of kindness towards the text or critic – a mutually agreed 'point' for instance, or the establishment of plausible meaning in a difficult passage of text – the victim felt nothing but love and identification, gasping enough to defer completely with claims like:

> it [the acting of Kean] was the finest commentary that was ever made on Shakespear.[63]

The crucial point in this extreme illustration of identification with the aggressor (attributing one's own function to the opponent) is that it was made *not in spite* of Hazlitt's preference for reading the plays, but *because* of it. Hazlitt's inherent suspicion of his status as an audience member in the theatre determined the preconditions for his love of Kean, because this critical suppression of affection could not last forever in a reordered world, which after all was what the theatre represented.

But this does not mean that the critic was passive, weak or misguided. Hazlitt was quite aware of this simultaneous destruction and creation of the opponent to which he dedicated himself:

> Nature seems (the more we look into it) made up of antipathies: without something to hate, we should lose the very spring of thought and action.[64]

He understood that hatred and love were alternative articulations of the same experience, each a precondition of the other, and that from a philosophical perspective, there was no contradiction between his preferred removal of Shakespeare to the closet, and his part in 'creating' the greatest Shakespearean actor of the age. And in this reconciliation of the discord lay the Schlegelian 'Romanticism' of Hazlitt's project.[65] It arose from the same Romantic belief of inherent goodness-in-evil and vice versa that in other incarnations led to the fascination with Satan-as-hero and *la belle dame sans merci*.

Hazlitt's theory of art – which in spirit could apply equally to the other 'bardolaters' – was constructed on a Platonic conception of pleasure and pain as the rulers of the aesthetic disposition, rather than law and the rational principles.[66] And the result of this was that in stage performances critics laughed at events which in real life did not amuse them,[67] and in practice they enjoyed those things which their theory had taught them to reject.

Far from being contradictory, however, these tensions between the good and the bad were an essential part of the theatrical experience – the agony which imagination turns into ecstasy, and the ecstasy to which piquancy is added by an unhealthy dash of agony. To adapt Coleridge's memorable example, the theatre was as pleasant and painful as making love to an ugly wife.[68] With the husband unable to control himself, the revulsion became integral to the attraction. Pain was compatible with co-existing pleasure, was amply repaid by thought and imagination, and as such was far superior to onions or shaving the upper lip.[69]

So while the contemporary theatre offered every reason for a sensitive Romantic to avoid it like the plague, for the very same reason it proved an enduring attraction that none of the supposedly anti-theatrical advocates could resist. There was an ecstasy in their theatrical affliction. Love and hate and sheer fascination drove them to Drury Lane and Covent Garden where they witnessed the adultery between Shakespeare and theatre. Their (collective) hundreds of thousands of words about Shakespeare and the theatre attest to just how exquisitely they felt the offence and the evil and the joy of an evening amid the egotistical actors, pusillanimous managements, rowdy audiences and superficial spectacle of the English Romantic theatre.

The Romantic critics showed how in the field of theatre, pleasure and pain began at the same points of moral, emotional and physical stimulation. Hazlitt's love and hate for Kean, his fury and his sentimentality toward other actors, his friendship and then rivalry with Coleridge, and his attraction and revulsion to the theatre were all manifestations of an aggressive impulse easily transformed into affection, and a capacity for identification ('disinterestedness') which without effort could be diverted into violent opposition.

In a turbulent world and as an individual with the backing of neither church nor state, Hazlitt suffered horrendously at the hands of a hostile opposition, vicious attacks which today would certainly result in libel suits and defamation convictions.[70] Hazlitt's survival – indeed his thriving – in the face of such vitriolic opposition is a tribute not just to his courage, but to his ability to absorb the extreme pleasures and pains of a life dedicated to aesthetic and political agitation.

In such a lifestyle where the object is both to kill and be killed, the rule of the passions in battle is such that it is rarely clear where horror ends and enjoyment begins. The murder of one's opponent is a source both of pride and humiliation, but even more intensely, of loss.

And with these great men and great antagonists lies the essence of the most dedicated modern theatrical audience, a public group of passionate individuals committed to creating in the theatre a mythical fabric of good and evil and love and hate according to the current modes of social interpretation. As Romantic inheritors of a fallen world it was their duty to produce and rage against imaginary forces of darkness, and as lovers, provocation and infuriation were integral to their method. So great were their abilities that scarcely any actor could satisfy their demands of rivalry. Kemble was failing and too easily resisted. Mrs Siddons too was now a less imposing figure than in her younger years.[71]

Amid such pathetic conflict between critics and actors, Kean's meteoric rise and fall – significantly almost identical to Hazlitt's period as a theatre critic[72] – was the satanic challenge demanded by the literary genius of the textual side in the war. In him was an opponent worthy of their hatred and their love, and it was on him that their passion was spent.

Such was the fury of the battle between Heaven and Hell that less than a decade after it had begun, the ardour of the combatants was spent and they retreated, never to be roused again. Hazlitt turned his attention to Napoleon, while Lamb lapsed into nostalgia. Coleridge for his part dabbled in church politics and opium addiction, while Hunt soldiered on until the middle of the century, his best work completed in his youth. Such was the brief and heady tenure of the Romantic passion.

6

THE DISINTERESTED
IMAGINATION

The status of actors
was the lowest of the low among the Romans
and an honourable one among the Greeks:
which is it with us?
We think of them like the Romans,
we live with them like the Greeks.
(La Bruyère, as quoted by Jean-Louis Barrault)

Historically, actors in the western world have been contemptible
lower-class figures, usually classified amid the ranks of slaves and
whores as lewd mercenaries devoted to the gratification of perverted
bourgeois impulses. In this capacity as butts for the fury of the
baser pleasures, a crucial element in their appeal has been their
offensiveness, with the lure of forbidden fruit sometimes proving
too great for the excitable Adams and Eves of the ruling classes to
resist.

When this occurs – when the desirability of the undesirable
overwhelms the Puritan – a curious catharsis of pent-up emotion
is released and a once-hostile society works itself into a sweat by
lavishing honours on its former libertines. Mistresses are kept in
regal splendour by fawning adulterers, slaves become confidantes
of their former captors, and actors are toasted by the very patrons
who condemned their ancestors to anonymity and poverty.

The rise of Tarlton, Armin and the better-known tragedians
Burbage and Alleyn (not to mention Shakespeare himself) from
a heritage of nomadic roguery to their often-revered membership
of various royal households is one example of this overwhelming
display of bureaucratic forgiveness in theatrical history. The
celebrated Quintus Roscius' elevation to equestrian status in

Republican Rome is another demonstration of the occasional bull-run of actors in the socio-aesthetic markets of authoritarian control, even though the impact of this particular promotion may be somewhat lessened by the subsequent appointment of a horse to the Senate.

In recent times, the actors have achieved blue-chip status in an overheated market, to the extent that imperial honours and political office are seen as a logical acknowledgement of society's debt to any actor who displays talent and endurance. In this extreme period of theatrical history, the kings-as-actors version of *theatrum mundi* is inverted, and the leading actors are hailed as majestic figures who are the envy and delight of their loyal subjects.[1]

It's another return of that bizarre, and inevitably temporary, period in the historical cycle when the oppressed are conscripted into the role of oppressors and bask in the uncustomary adulation of a placable and intimidated audience. It's a kind of Carnival inversion set on an indeterminate time-frame, with the fool being installed on the throne until such time as the former value of the stock returns with a vengeance, and the actor, like Antigonus, exits pursued by a bear.

But while he remains on the throne, the actor too, as a former victim, undergoes a catharsis, with the histrionic ego, suppressed over centuries by masks and traditional typecasting, suddenly bursting toward liberation and the administration of the very terror which it has endured. Texts, authors, audiences, social mores, all those theatrical prejudices which have previously inflicted their claims on anonymous and tormented actors, now become the victims as the thespian struts and frets his hour. He claims the stage for himself, associates with leaders and involves himself in causes, employs servants and minders, flaunts his wealth, and impersonates Midas with the fury of one who knows in his heart that his children or his children's children must inevitably return to the poverty from which he emerged. Hell hath no fury like the liberated ego of an impostor.

So profound has been this demonstration of released vanity during the twentieth century that the actors' personal, non-theatrical character has become mythologised. In possession of the fable, a society knows that professional actors tend to be fanatical narcissists, whether in fact individual actors possess these qualities or not, and their appeal resides in that very dubious characteristic.

The euphemisms through which the myth distances and displaces the unpleasant reality include such extra-theatrical terms as 'temperamental', 'highly-strung', 'emotional', 'eccentric' and 'colourful'. They mask a reality better-served by the terms 'rude', 'boorish', 'infantile', 'petulant' and 'egocentric', but to employ the implied terms rather than the rhetorical orthodoxy is to be heretical and, absurdly, to confirm the mystique of the actor. The wildness and egotism add to the appeal of the ravager, and publicity works overtime to ensure that every foible and imperfection repulses audiences into delight.

So an actor whose professional heritage has been one of anonymity and victimisation is unlikely to refuse the opportunity to thrust himself into the limelight once given a licence for fame. The result is that ever since the rise to prominence of named actors on the Shakespearean stage, the theatrical alienation from dramatic roles that Tarlton and Armin displayed has been a crucial tool in the histrionic trade and has become so welcome to adoring audiences that the greatest actors like Olivier and Gielgud often win a round of applause simply by walking on stage. Only after the applause has ended do they begin acting the character, with the audience's delight in the impending performance already a foregone conclusion, and the actor only needing to hint at the character as a gesture of goodwill toward these admirers and the play. This is why Sarah Bernhardt could keep acting despite her wooden leg. Audiences, who came to see her breathe as much as to see her act, were happy enough with her performance if she simply stayed alive on stage.[2]

By definition, famous actors are extreme cases, but with any actor basking in the reflected glory of their profession's newfound honour, the potential exists for a simultaneous dual identity to be presented on the inside and outside of plays. Successful careers begin as actors become larger than their characters, and unsuccessful careers fade as characters swamp actors, this latter reality being a particular problem for actors called on to double roles in naturalistic theatre.

In such a situation, talent is defined not by the versatility of the actor, but the power (or inability) of his own personality to dominate whatever role he is forced to assume. One of the saddest theatrical quotes from the past must surely be the minor Romantic actor who lamented, 'once establish a name for utility, and you throw down all hopes of eminence in the profession'.[3] The idea, rather, is to parade before an appreciative audience a colossal ego that through the illusion of conviction fills the theatre and simultaneously sketches something of the dramatic character within the play. In that way, the actor transcends his illegitimate roots while there is still an audience prepared to offer forgiveness and salvation.

Such alienation of actors from roles is ideally suited to comedy because, in the words of Charles Lamb, 'the same degree of credibility is not required of it as to serious scenes'.[4] Indeed for Lamb, the actor in comedy is *obliged* to take an audience into his confidence through Jack Bannister's 'thousand droll looks and gestures'[5] in their direction, thereby establishing dual points of delivery for the actor, between the audience and the other characters within the drama:

> There is something ungracious in a comic actor holding himself aloof from all participation or concern with those who are come to be diverted by him.[6]

The proffered Romantic reason for this is that comedy's appeal is primarily intellectual and, therefore, a degree of histrionic detachment is not inappropriate. Lamb could find any number of comedians of whom he approved and even befriended, among them Bannister, Munden, Farley, Suett, Knight and Liston.

Tragedy, however, being by the Romantic estimation fundamentally emotional in nature, required a very different degree of identification on the part of the actors, to the extent that by-play in tragic acting was seen as a heinous crime and the actor, to sustain the genuine tragic emotion, was expected to achieve 'acting degree zero'. Not surprisingly, the tragedians whom Lamb saw in the London theatres generally seemed incapable of, and unwilling to, suppress their own identities in a sympathetic, seamless interpretation of the Shakespearean tragic heroes.[7]

For Lamb, one of the best attempts at this voluntary submission of identity in the interests of dramatic credibility was Robert Bensley's Iago, in which artifice was suppressed to the extent that, with the exception of the soliloquies, the audience was offered no more evidence of dissembling than was Othello himself. Bensley represented Iago as a 'consummate villain', a satanic hero whose theatrical presence and evil motives were shared with the audience only as a last resort under the dictates of the text, and for the most part, Iago's attentions were devoted to his own scheming and to Othello, not to the spectators in the theatre.[8] Through this singularity of purpose, Bensley captured the idea of Iago without obvious recourse to practicalities and cheap theatrical stunts, and in transcending the self, won the approval of a critic whose strict criteria for artistic excellence were almost impossible to achieve.

Lamb's Romantic conception of the actor as anonymous animator of dramatic character in tragedy is naturally opposed to the style of comic acting developed by Tarlton and Armin and continued by Lamb's favourite contemporary comedians, as well as the egotistical and self-conscious performance of Shakespearean tragedy that Kemble had made his speciality.

In an age of newly-liberated and socially-acceptable actors, few aside from Bensley would voluntarily submerge themselves in tragic character to the extent demanded by Lamb, especially when the economic survival of the Patent theatres depended on the successful creation of a glamorous star system replacing the tradition of ensemble acting. Where an audience applauded an actor before he even began to act, the theatre had a future as a business enterprise, even if it didn't possess equally inspiring aesthetic prospects.

And so the battle lines were drawn between the egos of fêted tragic actors and the imaginations of the Romantic poets and essayists. And as suggested earlier, none fought harder nor better than William Hazlitt, for whom the celebrity which created the stage dualisms of famous actors was anathema to the true experience of tragic theatre, and the object of his finest critical ridicule. Hazlitt was a formidable opponent not just because of his courage, but because his passion was well-informed by intimate knowledge of, and affection for, the theatre of both past and present.

Like Lamb, Hazlitt argued that comedy takes a less sympathetic view of human nature and reduces the opportunities for histrionic identification with characterisation. But unlike Lamb, his rejection of the 'egotistical' acting of tragedy was grounded on a fully-articulated philosophical and theoretical base, originating in his first, and favourite, major work, *The Principles of Human Action*, published in 1805.[9]

In this attempt to refute the materialists' conception of self-love as the fundamental principle of human action, Hazlitt argued that sympathy leads the imagination to identify with whatever comes before it and that the truest philosopher is he who can forget himself. The theory of the disinterested imagination found favour with Keats, whose much more celebrated thesis of 'negative capability' is a paraphrase of it,[10] and other poets, but it did perilously little to further the cause of Classical acting in the style of Kemble. Hazlitt's highest conception of a tragic actor was that:

he shall assume the character once for all, and be it throughout, and trust to this conscious sympathy for the effect produced.[11]

And in playing the hero, the tragic actor, of whom Kean was usually Hazlitt's best example, ensured that the sense of personal identity is lost as the disinterested imagination allows the actor to place himself in the position of others and to speak and feel for and through them.

This facility for sympathy is a lot to ask of recently-rehabilitated lumpenproles, not only because the *nouveaux riches* are always reluctant to part with their fortune, but also because, by the critics' own admission, the demands for tragic acting were so opposed to the techniques of comedy. Throughout the recent history of acting, the intellect and empathy required by Hazlitt's disinterested imagination have been desirable rather than necessary qualities, and the application of them would appear to be more easily achieved when actors are slaves rather than kings.

But Hazlitt avoided the trap into which many of his subsequent admirers fell, by realising the difference between theoretical preference and practical reality. He knew that

> it would be ridiculous to suppose, that any one ever went to see Hamlet or Othello represented by Kean or Kemble; we go to see Kean or Kemble in Hamlet or Othello.[12]

And indeed there are times when one suspects that, incredibly, even this great critic loved Kean more than Shakespeare's characters. It's an emotional tendency which the usually-rational Hazlitt succumbed to more than once, this falling in love with hopelessly-unsuitable and ideologically-opposed partners.[13] Even he occasionally had to release the suppressed urges created by antagonism in outbursts of affection for rivals, and with his writing on Kean, the mixture of censure and adoration suggests that the actor had hypnotised the critic into a rapture in which Hazlitt, perhaps mistakenly, saw in Kean the disinterestedness which his theory advocated.

On the basis of surviving contemporary accounts alone, it is impossible to judge just how closely an actor like Kean ever approached a genuinely sympathetic interpretation of the Shakespearean heroes. The characteristics of that particular actor's theatrical style which have passed into mythology – his preference for a series of virtuoso 'points' over a consistently-developed 'through-line', his shortness and imperfect voice, his massive extra-theatrical ego and personal excesses, as well as his fame and financial value to Drury Lane[14] – tend to suggest that even he remained necessarily aloof from his characters for much of his performance.

Certainly there were some ways in which Hazlitt actually preferred the Classical style of Kemble to Kean's Romantic flashes of lightning,[15] and in his sadder moments such as his version of the familiar 'Lear cannot be acted' Romantic argument, Hazlitt acknowledged that perhaps his own theory of Shakespearean acting was a physical impossibility even for his favourite actor:

> no living actor can be expected to cope with Lear. . . . [Kean] chipped off a bit of the character here and there; but he did not pierce the solid substance, nor move the entire mass.[16]

It was a typical admission on Hazlitt's part, acknowledging that for all the passion of his rhetorical urging, the actor remained flesh and blood, ultimately incapable of achieving the wholeness of theatrical conception that the Romantic critics' imagination alone could sustain. The best that could be achieved was an occasional burst of 'gusto', that crucial moment when the sympathetic imagination defines the 'internal character' or 'living principle' of its subject.[17]

So theory aside, Hazlitt realised the undesirability of imaginative disinterestedness as a feature of populist Shakespearean acting. The history of twentieth-century British theatre has demonstrated that, while identification may be a seductive rhetorical ploy as well as a useful ambition for actors in creating a role, in terms of the aesthetic pleasure offered to audiences, acting anonymity and unmediated appeals to the imagination are by no means a guarantee of theatrical success.

Quite simply, in an age of reverence for the actor, Brechtian theory and passive audiences, it is not strictly necessary – and sometimes even damaging – for individual actors to submerge themselves into characters or to provide seamless interpretations of the familiar roles. Rather, the actor's the thing wherein audiences catch the conscience of the king.

The Carnival theory of tragedy and comedy discussed in the previous chapters, together with empirical examples from the history of modern Shakespearean acting, suggest that in contrast to the Romantic view, a degree of alienation is actually demanded from actors of Shakespeare's great tragic heroes. In terms of theory, the Romantic conception of the differing degrees of identification required for tragic and comic acting, which is implicitly predicated on a fundamental discrepancy between the two forms of Shakespearean drama, does not appear to be justified by a study of the origins of play and seriousness.

The simultaneous presentation of tragedy and comedy in Carnival and politics has been discussed already, but on a broader level, Huizinga's well-known theory that both tragedy and comedy derive from play can also be cited as a demonstration of the crucial similarity, and fluidity, between the two forms.[18] Drawing examples from Greek tragedy and Plato's *Symposium* and *Philebus* where according to Socrates the true poet must be tragic and comic at once,[19] Huizinga argues that the obvious genre of a play is not so important in determining its status as tragedy or comedy as the situation or thoughts expressed within it. Play of course can be serious and seriousness playful, and thus the apparent contrast between them is neither conclusive nor fixed.[20] And so any attempt to theorise on the basis of the distinction between comedy and tragedy appears to be misguided and doomed to failure, especially in the Shakespearean 'tragedies' where the comic structure is so pronounced and the grotesque content so frequent.

Alienation in the theatre is always fascinating, and usually amusing, which is why it could be welcomed by the Romantics in the strictly-defined comedies, and viewed suspiciously in the tragedies; but when the awareness of the tragicomedy of Carnival and play prevails, the techniques of comic-acting in so-called tragedy can be devastatingly effective. This tragic laughter generated by self-assured actors is one of theatre's most alarming powers, and while it may do little to reinforce Rousseau-inspired Romantic beliefs in the fundamental beneficence of human behaviour, it certainly offers every opportunity to forge a striking theatrical depiction of the moral and psychological struggles which are so crucial to Shakespearean tragedy.

These Elizabethan tragedies, which the Romantics loved so much, were written by Shakespeare for a theatre in which the newly-acquired fame of actors lured audiences to attend and enjoy the simultaneous dual appearances of actors and characters. As if in acknowledgement of the self-consciousness of his finest actors, Shakespeare's characters themselves tend to be constructed on the basis of their mortality-in-immortality, through images of majestic robes on dwarfish thieves, heroes bestriding oceans and then turning in battle like doting mallards, and motives spurred on by heaven and hell dissolving into the curses of a drab. Shakespeare apparently revelled in the realisation that Lear on stage was really only Burbage with a stick, and he tailored the imaginative world of his plays to embrace that physical reality. *Playing* rather than *being* the king is the issue at stake both within the drama and on the stage.

Thus, a faceless man, an actor solely devoted to complete transformation into his character, is curiously at odds with the dramatic and theatrical realities of Shakespearean tragedy. It's this uncomfortable truth about the necessity of histrionic ego in Shakespearean acting which accounts for the one consistent failure in the illustrious career of Sir Alec Guinness.[21]

Born in 1914 and beginning his career in the 1930s in successful portrayals of various minor Shakespearean characters, Guinness is indisputably one of the greats of twentieth-century British theatre and film, being known particularly for his ability as a mimic and so-called character actor. Yet in spite of his obvious talents and his popularity with British audiences, Guinness has never achieved success in his portrayal of Shakespearean heroes, while several of his contemporaries, possessing no obviously-greater natural abilities, have enjoyed one triumph after another – indeed created careers and legends – out of the same roles. Fifty years after his 1937 Richard II had been condemned, Guinness in his autobiography still felt ashamed of his performance.[22] So too, his attempts at Hamlet (1937–8, 1951) and Macbeth (1966) were also roundly criticised for their perverse and indecisive approach to characterisation.[23]

Guinness is notorious, not because of a characteristic appearance which is evident in every role, but for the opposite reason that he presents his characters with such facility that he as actor is often unrecognisable behind the dramatic role. One of his biographers has argued that:

> it was easy to pick out in advance a typical Gielgud or Richardson or Redgrave or Wolfit role, and though they were not necessarily confined to this sort of typecasting, one always knew just what face was behind the mask. Even Olivier, the most deliberately various of the greats, could be recognised by a certain directness which told one that even his Hamlet could not be a dreamer, but had to be a man of action, albeit contradictory action. But Guinness? What was his face really like? Though he was now playing the star roles, had he

that not precisely definable unity behind the diversity, that gift
for making all the faces his own instead of refashioning his own
face unrecognisably into whatever was required?[24]

Such awesome gifts, and such demonstrable sympathy toward his
characters, may win the plaudits of theorists and Hazlitt's successors,
and they may equip the actor admirably for many modern roles, but
the selflessness and 'negative capability' implied by the artistry has
been palpably unsuitable for a tragic Shakespearean stage demanding
the same degree of theatrical opacity as that brought to the comic
roles by Tarlton and Armin four centuries previously.

Guinness' tragic flaw, repeated over thirty years of Shakespearean
acting (before he gave away the tragedies altogether) was that, in his
own words, he eschewed the 'heroics, struttings and bellowings'[25] of
traditional, egocentric Shakespearean acting in favour of a sensitive,
selfless and transparent attempt to transform himself into the great
characters. And in presenting the characters of the play rather than
the characters of the actor, Guinness, an actor both before and after
his time, wrote his own epitaph as a Shakespearean tragic actor to
rival Olivier, Gielgud and Richardson. His generosity of spirit and
exquisite, humane talent for identification, could not compete with
self-possessed, consciously-heroic and intensely individual displays
of both dramatic and theatrical megalomania.

In refusing to depict the struggle between actor and character (a
struggle in which convention demands that the actor proves his
talent by winning) and concentrating instead on a less violent
demonstration of virtuosity, Guinness' Shakespeare could hold
little appeal for two theatrical generations raised during wars and
sustained by images of Henry V[26] subduing the foreign hoodlums
in manly battle. The rhetoric of militarism cannot be appeased
by the portrayal of theatrical unanimity, and existential despair
and isolation demand a fabulous demonstration of the triumph
of individuality.

From both chauvinist and philosophical perspectives, Shakespearean acting has proved its cultural potency in the making of
myths to sustain decadent colonialism, and the tradition of faceless
acting has succumbed to the irresistible swaggering and pride of
actors and audiences substituting the conquest of the stage for that
of the world.

A victim of Shakespeare's status as this cultural weapon, as well
as his own reluctance to flaunt the ego, Guinness had to resign his

interest in Shakespearean tragedy and to achieve fame in drama of less-overtly imperialistic application. It's the inevitable fate of a faceless and humble man in a society bent on the destructive assertion of the ancient and crumbling privileges of Empire.

But while the times may have been wrong for Guinness, they are undoubtedly right for Sir Ralph Richardson (b. 1902), whose style of acting is explicitly based on the portrayal of self, and whose Shakespearean roles have been lauded almost as fanatically as Olivier's and Gielgud's. A versatile actor whose career in London began at the Old Vic in the early 1930s, Richardson was particularly suited to tragicomic roles in both Shakespearean and modern drama.

The contrast between the unsuccessful sensitivity of Guinness and the successful narcissism of Richardson is demonstrated in Guinness' wry recollections of the ill-fated 1937 *Richard II*, in which Richardson played John of Gaunt. Refusing to wear the fourteeth-century collar designed for the production, and thus standing out from the other characters like 'a large, bearded Peter Pan', Richardson clearly stated his requirements from the leading actor Guinness: 'Never come within six feet of me on stage, old cock'. For Guinness,

> This meant that, as the King, I was often huddled with Bushy, Bagot and Green in a rather undignified way, while Ralph could free-wheel in plenty of space and air.[27]

Outside the confines of populist memoirs, one can only speculate as to the exasperation and confusion which Guinness must have suffered in response to Richardson's aggressive showmanship, the more so because, outside of this production, the scene-stealer achieved the Shakespearean success that had always eluded Guinness, as Othello, Timon, Prospero, as well as in many of the great comic roles including Falstaff and Shylock.[28]

More than thirty years after his stage-hog performance of John of Gaunt, Richardson was still being insulted and adored as an 'old poseur [demanding] everyone's undivided attention'.[29] In another age, his style would have seen him whipped unto the city gates rather than lauded with knighthoods and respect. The times, quite simply, are as right for the Richardson vanity as they are wrong for the Guinness diffidence, and the faceless man has had to content himself with brilliant portrayals of the minor characters, often doubling them in *As You Like It*, *Richard II*, and especially *Hamlet* and the comedies.[30] The slave mentality cannot sustain a performance when audiences expect to be diverted by kings.

The result of these pressures on actors is that acting, like politics, has its conservative ideology, sustained by knights like Richardson, Wolfit, Gielgud, and the greatest Shakespearean of them all, Lord Olivier, for whom displays of authority and conviction align with the Elizabethan comic tradition of histrionic alienation and virtuosity.[31]

During his first season at the Old Vic in 1937, Olivier established his Shakespearean career by playing Hamlet, Henry V, Macbeth and Sir Toby Belch in the extroverted (and where applicable) heroic manner which was to become his trademark, and then in the following season going on to Iago and Coriolanus. He remained at the Old Vic until 1949 and then embarked on a career as a manager in the 1950s, during which time he continued to perform the great Shakespearean roles on which his awesome contemporary reputation as a performer is based. In the 1960s he moved to the National Theatre Company and in roles such as Othello (1964) and Shylock (1970), he confirmed his reputation as the pre-eminent English Shakespearean actor of modern times. Knighted in 1947, he was made a life peer in 1970 and died in 1990.

The degree of authority which Olivier assigned to himself as actor in performances is indicative of an equal or even greater sense of histrionic imposition than that implicitly argued by the Elizabethan comedians, and explicitly argued by political aspirants. For Lord Olivier:

> Film is the director's medium, television the writer's, but the theatre is the actor's. When the actor is on stage, it is he and he alone who drives the moment. The audience have no choice but to remain in his faith or leave. That's the true excitement, the real magic of the profession. The actor on stage is all-powerful, for once the curtain rises he is in control. There is nothing the director or author can do once the house lights dim and the tabs go up. The actor can choose to do or say anything he likes, he is the governor, he cracks the whip.[32]

Conservatives celebrate this actor's theatre in which the terror of power-wielding is institutionalised and naturalised to the extent that the victim's admiration for aggression directed against him exceeds his feelings of helplessness.

Meanwhile, the all-powerful governor, once a slave himself, cracks his whip in excitement at the magic of his own authority. There is no text to be audited, no external reality to be emulated, no legitimacy or illegitimacy to be attributed, in this sublime moment when a charismatic and obsessive zealot claims his right to the dictatorship of the universe and with bravura and disdain asserts his control over the fate of his subjects. It's the alternative to the comedian's attainment of power through deceiving an audience into laughter; here, the hypnosis resides in the emphasis on capacity for and delight in authority, an implicit assertion of one's divine right to the throne. Olivier becomes the theatrical (and more successful) General Alexander Haig, enthusiastically proclaiming 'Right now, I'm in charge here'.

In a political and theatrical environment where truth is a casualty of credibility and rhetoric overcomes the limitations and contradictions of reality, the conservative is at an advantage because he brings to his display of conviction the authority and tradition of the oxymoronic myth of the benevolent dictator. Through familiarity with this myth, habit, and their belief in the inherent charity of human behaviour, spectators within a conservative dictatorship can be manipulated into the belief that their own position is privileged and that the victimisation falls on others. In this way, they are led into support for the conservative, whom they believe to be a statesman and servant of humanity. But the term 'statesman' is answerable only to the modes of credibility, not to the strictures of truth.

And so, provided that audiences are diverted and flattered by the power-play of the conservative actor, the concepts of morality, oppression and destruction are displaced by the urgency of the histrionic conviction, and virtuosity renders the player sovereign and inscrutable. The result of this deification founded on historical precedent and voluntary oppression is that the actor is given a licence for perversion and self-congratulation. For Lord Olivier, one manifestation of this elevation beyond the range of populist criticism, is that within the confines of the aesthetic charter, he could not only indulge in, but boast about, the maudlin preoccupations which are denied polite, uncommitted society.

In speaking of his fascination for the human body in general and his own in particular, Olivier recalled in his essay *On Acting* how he became a regular audience member at the operating 'theatre' of a London hospital. In an unfortunate choice of metaphor, Olivier remembered that at the first operation which he witnessed: 'From the moment the knife went in I was riveted.'[33] Olivier's enjoyment of the violence places him in the position of an audience member at a tragedy or execution, filled with a pleasure at the (improvement-oriented) suffering of others which can only be intensified if, still under the guise of beneficence, the violence is turned upon himself.

In Olivier's case, the fascination with the dissection of others was eventually turned to this desire to see *himself* as the unharmed victim when, faced with an operation to remove a kidney, he asked to remain conscious and to be provided with mirrors so that he could admire the workings, and examine the mutilation, of his internal organs:

> I feel that actors should know more about their bodies than perhaps they do. Maybe they should have a copy of Gray's *Anatomy* on their bookshelves along with Shakespeare. . . . You might think this morbid or macabre, but not at all. I simply wanted to know more about myself. I wanted to get under the make-up, really beneath the skin. I wanted to know every part of me. Every inch, duct and vessel. . . . When recently I had a kidney removed, I asked quite sincerely if it was possible to be operated on under local anaesthetic and watch the whole procedure in a mirror. They declined. A pity.[34]

Far from a display of elderly bravura, Olivier's disappointment at the refusal of this request is the typical reaction of an audience denied the privilege of witnessing a violent and uncompromising theatrical action directed against them. The personal improvement afforded by the brutality becomes all the more pleasurable if the horror of the means is consciously endured in the process. Olivier's loss of the kidney was not the true theatrical experience because he suffered the effect but did not savour the means of his own mutilation. The awesome trust bestowed by the victim in the aggressor was not put to the thrilling test of the stricken patient auditing the level of malevolence in the surgeon, and being mentally-aware but physically incapable of intervening if this exceeded the agreed limits.

Olivier's beloved kidney is a metaphor for a conservative post-feudal theatre, dominated by ageing imperialists committed equally to the celebration of their own bowels and their professional liberation from the bonds of slavery. It's a visceral theatre in which there is a Whitmanesque singing of the body electric aligned with a desire for the punishment of that same body.

If its leading practitioners are old poseurs strutting and preening and admiring themselves for the delight of an uncritical public, it is because theatre is doing penance for its sins and omissions of the past. There was a time, and there will be another time, when the conservative passion will fall on playwrights or directors or theatre-owners, and Olivier's kidney, so lovingly described by its infatuated owner, will provide an ample target for the savage boot of the cruel and bitter slavemaster, and the pleasure of the blow will be replaced by pain.

To forestall this moment of punishment, the Classical defence of theatre, arguing for *utile* deriving from *dulce*,[35] has been supplemented in modern times by the employment of the rhetoric of infantilisation and innocence. Actors and audiences are reduced to the emotional and psychological level of children by theatrical apologists avowedly wide-eyed in wonder at the nature of their game, and apparently eager to forestall the return of any anti-theatrical prejudice. Thus, Lord Olivier begins his essay *On Acting* by aligning his art with childish high-spirits and the discovery of forbidden fruits:

> Acting is like the first sip of beer, the one you probably steal as a child, the taste that you never forget, it makes such an impression on your palate.[36]

It's an appealing description, cloaked in the language of common experience and directed toward the development of trust between author and reader. With acting being depicted as childish simplicity and *joie de vivre*, the actor implicitly places himself in the position of the fool or half-wit, a sometimes-irritating but usually harmless 'natural' dedicated to the provision of delight and affection for his superiors. It introduces the audience to the actor a long way from the Machiavellian control and power-wielding which is glorified later in Olivier's essay.[37]

The rhetoric of infantilisation is so resonant of childhood innocence that in disputing it, the opponent is immediately labelled a philistine. The obverse is that the politician kissing the baby, or the actor identifying himself as a juvenile, generally attracts plaudits for his humanity and social concern. Realising this, second-rate authors are rarely reluctant to win sympathy for a character by writing scenes in which that character acts kindly toward children or animals. Theatrical apologists, it seems, are also more than eager to employ this cheapest form of sympathy-gathering through cynical alignment with innocents, transferring the incidental theatrical feature of 'play' into an essential one.

With childish games depicted as the foundation rather than a mere feature of theatre, actors are afforded the fools' licence to indulge in scurrilous behaviour. It's a popular position of safety. The result is that, as in *King Lear*, Mad Tom's hovel becomes ridiculously overcrowded as every man with a past, eager to escape censure through feigned madness, folly and childishness, races out into the heath seeking sanctuary and pity for his assumed infirmities.

This safety in infantilisation is entertaining not just for its Carnivalesque spectacle of geriatric legislators publicly proclaiming themselves as overgrown juveniles, but also because of its impassioned appeal to Huizinga's concept of *homo ludens*[38] in a nuclear society capable of destroying itself a hundred times over. Perhaps this oversimplification of the issue and crafty underestimation of one's own capacities is another manifestation of the same devoted spirit of art which led the band on the Titanic to serenade their sinking ship while others helped women and children scramble for lifeboats. Or perhaps the issue is more serious and sinister than this.

Acting may be a childish game, but as Huizinga has demonstrated, in any juvenile 'play', there is an element of exclusivity – a 'magic circle' from which outsiders are barred.[39] Those to whom access is permitted develop a kind of superiority, because they are in possession of unknown, and therefore unchallengeable, rules. As Paul Valéry once remarked, 'No scepticism is possible where the rules of a game are concerned, for the principle underlying them is an unshakeable truth.'[40] In other words, by applying the principle of gamesmanship, the actor removes his project beyond the level of moderate criticism, making himself a target only for those whose attack can be dismissed successfully as extremist. Moderates are precluded from anything but support for the theatre by the implied innocence of the theatrical rules and rhetoric.

As an audience member, Michael Goldman enjoys the same phenomenon of infantilisation as Olivier, but from the voyeuristic perspective:

> Part of the delight of the theater is that it recaptures the terror and pleasure of children spying on their elders. At the same time, though, the actor is like a child, performing as gracefully as he can to win the affection of the assembled grownups.[41]

It seems churlish to criticise such an affectionate description of naughty wide-eyed wonder, even though it so blatantly trivialises the theatrical experience in what purports to be an impassioned defence. But perhaps for the wrong reason, Goldman's claim for the audience's infantile lack of sophistication demonstrates a crucial feature of the audience's response to their theatrical encounter with actors, because the 'terror and pleasure' of infantilisation has been identified by psychologists as a precondition for identification with the aggressor.

According to Freud, the ego of children aged about five, just beginning to resolve the Oedipal complex, protects itself against anxiety-producing authority figures by identification out of fear rather than love,[42] in an effort to avoid the effects of anger and punishment. 'Introjection' – a form of imitative behavioural learning – can nevertheless still occur between aggressor and childish victim, particularly when this adoption of alien values seems likely to result in the victim's ultimate survival.[43]

If a theatrical audience is manipulated into this situation where it spies on its elders and betters with childish fear and excitement, the capacity for identification with the actor is correspondingly strong. An impressionable audience, reliant on the authoritarian figure on stage and susceptible to group reaction through the 'intimate alliance'[44] with its peers, can easily find itself approving the actions which it would rationally condemn in a world which was its own.

Thomas Strentz[45] has argued, however, that the hostage situation – to which the theatrical experience is likened – places the victim in a more regressive position than that of the Freudian 5-year-old. For Strentz, the 5-year-old is able to feed himself, speak for himself and has locomotion, whereas the hostage is more like the infant who, denied speech, must cry for food, may be bound and immobile, and in a state of extreme dependency and fright.[46]

Inevitably in this situation, the child begins to love the authoritarian protecting him from the outside world and on whom his information and very survival is dependent. It is the kind of love which Miranda feels for Prospero, oblivious toward her guardian's boorishness, authoritarianism and occasional cruelty because he offers the best chance for her survival and knowledge. Similarly, if an audience submits itself to the domination of the actor, then its chances of gaining from the theatrical spectacle increase accordingly. And its preferred method for achieving this is to regress into a position of dependence and passivity.

And so there is a twofold infantilisation in the theatrical experience, with the actor engendering trust by his proclamation of a fundamentally juvenile ambition and joy in playing, and the audience, rendered physically incapacitated by the architecture and techniques of theatrical production, also reverting to a position of hostage to the actor's authority. Bound by mutual need and desire to be nourished by mother-bird, both victim and aggressor wrestle for the status of wide-eyed innocent, claiming infantile deprivation as their defence, and eventually forming a secret society dedicated to survival in the face of attack from a hostile outer world, peopled by adults who are philistines[47] or spoil-sports ready to rob the play of its illusion.[48]

Both Olivier and Goldman appeal to the traditional conservative defence of logical and self-evident simplicity as a neutralising agent applied to symptoms suggesting violence and illegitimacy, and their employment of the infantile metaphor absolves the actor and audience of guilt even as the nature of the trope confirms their definitive irresponsibility.

Convinced of their right to rule and hailed by kings as 'wise justicers', conservative actors like Olivier can afford the luxury of disingenuous humility, but in doing so they make prominent targets for the barbs of Hazlitt's successors like Kenneth Tynan. For Hazlitt himself, the natural opposition toward conservative or 'Classical' acting resulted not just from aesthetic prejudice and a philosophy of sympathy, but from a radical political ideology which similarly rejected those poseurs cursed with an inability to see beyond their own ambitions. Acutely aware of political injustice and convinced of theatre's ability to influence the worldly actions of audiences,[49] Hazlitt developed a theatrical criticism which spurred his readers to action, but which nevertheless retained a sense of its own relative power.

Like his political rival Edmund Burke, Hazlitt understood that a theatrical audience's sensibilities were crude and cruel enough for them to leave a tragedy in order to watch a hanging.[50] Both engender the desirable power of *feeling* and an awareness of the consequences of evil,[51] and both offer a fascination deriving from emotional, moral and intellectual excitement. More in sadness than in anger, Hazlitt acknowledged the irresistible attraction in these displays of ego and power both on the scaffold and on the stage, even if he couldn't condone it. Provided the means be spectacular and the action unequivocal, the event gains an implied and even actual legitimacy. Not even Hazlitt could deny the urgency of compulsion. But this idealism tempered by realism which characterises so much of his writing, results in some extraordinary merging of perceptive political and literary comment in his criticism of Shakespeare's plays.

Hazlitt's political awareness has been underestimated by an

Anglo-American New Criticism which finds his radicalism repugnant to the middle-class values espoused in the language of Bible-belt literary evaluation. Supposedly, he lacks 'a disciplined sense of history, and of the complexity of the relation between literature and society,'[52] but Hazlitt's remarks on *Coriolanus* and *Henry V* alone are enough to refute such claims. In a mixture of passion and political provocation directed toward immediate social concerns, Hazlitt depicted *Coriolanus* as an example of political commonplaces and brutality which, combined with an audience's desire for identification with the aggressor, inevitably makes an attractive package out of distasteful materials. For Hazlitt:

> the cause of the people is indeed but little calculated as a subject for poetry. . . . The language of poetry naturally falls in with the language of power.[53]

And in such a world of power and its appreciation regardless of the motive, the actor who presents himself as hero will be lauded for his ability to subdue the tyrannical character, because the language of power must translate on stage into the acting of power.

Both the appeal of *Coriolanus*, according to Hazlitt, and the nature of Shakespearean acting itself, are founded on the seductiveness of strength. In explaining why the vile Coriolanus should survive and be hailed as a Shakespearean hero, Hazlitt writes that:

> we . . . take part with the lordly beast, because our vanity or some other feeling makes us disposed to place ourselves in the situation of the strongest party. . . . There is nothing heroical in a multitude of miserable rogues not wishing to be starved, or complaining that they are like to be so; but when a single man comes forward to brave their cries and to make them submit to the last indignities, from mere pride and self-will, our admiration of his prowess is immediately converted into contempt for their pusillanimity. The insolence of power is stronger than the plea of necessity.[54]

It's the Stockholm Syndrome depicted in the literary language of 1817. For Hazlitt, the inherent immorality of the character is of secondary interest, subordinated by the ruthless and compelling display of power, and proving that 'Wrong dressed out in pride, pomp, and circumstance, has more attraction than abstract right'.[55] It's a lesson which has not been lost on modern conservative political leaders who pledge to return their nations to strength, and who crush third world countries in an effort to prove it. And it is a political dictum which has ramifications not just pertaining to the characterisation of the plays (although in that alone it is exceptional), but within the *enactment* of that characterisation as well.

Within the *performance* of *Coriolanus* or for that matter any other Shakespearean play, the actor need not necessarily offer a sensitive, accurate or imaginative interpretation, provided that the acting embodies a display of conviction (pride, pomp and circumstance) and conveys the impression of domination. As Alec Guinness found to his cost, the only cardinal sin in the acting of Shakespearean roles is to be humble, because the poetic language of power, the heroism of the characterisation, together with the mythical status of the characters within British culture necessarily demands of its actors a decidedly 'interested' imagination. Preceded by centuries of Burbage's Hamlet, Garrick's Hamlet, Kean's Hamlet, and Gielgud's Hamlet, a contemporary actor will always be judged on prior possession of the character by egos which still reverberate years after their demise.

The conservative political notions of public institutions as private property, and massive inheritances passing down through privileged generations, ensure that a Shakespearean actor must necessarily assume the mantle of ego if he is truly to discharge his solemn duty. From this curious and naturalised perspective, only an apparent impostor like Guinness, unaware of the protocol pertaining to such revered traditions, would attempt to return the inheritance to its rightful owner. The nature of Shakespearean acting is, after all, this conservative appropriation and destruction of intellectual property. It is, in short, fundamentally aggressive in outward display, but prevented from being depicted as such by a rhetoric of innocence.

With no author to 'close' the interpretation of texts, and no flesh to imbue the printed roles with physical attributes, a Shakespearean performance becomes a battleground where jealous and ambitious men and women struggle and rage to fill the vacuum of the sublime with the activity of their own bowels and egos. The history of Shakespearean acting is a curiously poignant catalogue of these naïve and talented fanatics, convinced of their inherent right and destiny to achieve greatness by fulfilling the implied intentions of one greater.

Sadly, their project has been doomed to failure because mortality can never embrace the diversity and compulsion of myth, and the recurrent Sisyphean attempt to do so is at best an illustration of the triumph of the human spirit and at worst a demonstration of the vanity of individual ego. In either case, the performance of Shakespeare in the theatre is an example of vain Davids challenging mythical Goliaths, and attempting through stylised means to convey the illusion of victory. Plausibility achieved through rhetoric, posturing and, above all, conviction, necessarily must compensate for the absence of truth.

Ironically, and unintentionally, the Romantics in part established the conditions for their own dissatisfaction by hailing Shakespeare as the definitive example of negative capability *in absentia*. 'Shakespeare was the least of an egotist of anybody in the world', lauded Hazlitt.[56] 'Shakespeare could shift at pleasure, to inform and animate other existences', according to Lamb.[57] In stressing Shakespeare's ability to be nothing in himself, the Romantics drew attention to the resolutely 'open' texts, devoid of authoritarian ego and consequently incomplete from the perspective of early nineteenth-century materialism. As Jonathan Bate has demonstrated, they were ripe for appropriation.

For the Romantic critics, the appeal of 'open' texts was their potential for the weaving of political agitation and philosophical speculation in virtuosic prose around the contours of the Shakespearean plots,[58] while actors, blessed with fewer intellectual gifts but greater public exposure, could justify their masquerading as inheritors of the Shakespearean legacy by appealing to this necessity for Shakespearean 'completion' in stage representation.

This argument that characters needed actors was a form of imperialism very typical of nineteenth-century British attitudes. And by stressing its powers of supplementation, and its capacities for perfecting the imperfect, imperialism achieved the image of positivism and strength in its appeal to popular conservative sentiment. The problem though for the colonised is that paternalistic justification of imperialism renders itself irrelevant once the seductive myth of beneficent aggression becomes self-sustaining. In theatre, the analogous basis for histrionic exertion – namely, the argument that play texts imply an actor – similarly offers an opportunity in which a very limited legitimate function for actors nevertheless, through rhetorical agitation and tacit audience approval, often develops into a degree of unaccountability in areas outside of the immediate pretext for action.

In theory though, Kean was as eager as Hazlitt to avoid any suggestion that he was attempting to colonise Shakespearean texts as his own territory. Sensitivity to the integrity of the Shakespearean character was a hallmark of his remarks on his roles. For example, Kean was reported as saying that Shakespeare's

> scrutinizing research into human nature, and his sublime and pathetic muse, were to be comprehended only by a capacity alive to his mighty purposes.[59]

Kean of course could hope that in supporting Hazlitt's 'sympathetic' theory of great Shakespearean acting, he himself would be seen as the true inheritor of the Shakespearean legacy, but Hazlitt's testimony that moments of Kean's performances did actually achieve a union between actor, author and character, suggests that perhaps Kean's theorising on Shakespeare could escape claims of the usual cunning self-promotion and imperialism more than that of other actors. Yet with the explosive style adopted by Kean, these moments of sublimity undoubtedly were counteracted still by periods of alienation during which (in Hunt's words regarding his beloved Mrs Siddons) 'something of too much art was apparent'.[60]

Alternative contemporary acting styles seemed even less likely to satisfy the implied Shakespearean motives. Alan Downer[61] has identified the four styles which dominated nineteenth-century acting, ranging from the vulcanism of Kean's First Romantic School, to the opposed 'teapot' or Classical school of Kemble. Stylistically in between these extremes were the Second Romantic School of Macready, which was an amalgam of the previous two, and the Prince of Wales School in which the domesticity of Macready was merged with a more heroic style.[62] All in fact were responses to the openness of texts, offering theoretical and practical models on which the essentially arbitrary character of Shakespearean interpretation could be formalised, and all were capable of removing their characters to a position of subordination to their actors.

One celebrated example of this refusal by an actor to accommodate his character, immortalised by Hazlitt's brilliant criticism, was Kemble's performance in Massinger's *A New Way to Pay Old Debts*:

> Was this Sir Giles Overreach? . . . Mr Kemble wanted the part to come to him, for he would not go out of his way to the part. . . . He is chiefly afraid of being contaminated by too close an identity with the character he represents. This is the greatest vice in an actor, who ought never to *bilk* his part.[63]

Perhaps even more than a 'teapot' school, Kemble's was the 'kidney' school of acting, a style which celebrates the organs of the individual while incidentally portraying a fictional character. Fine interpretations of character may result from this method (and Hazlitt acknowledged these when they occurred), but they were only extreme instances of a style founded on the protocol of privilege.

Kathleen Coburn[64] has contrasted Hazlitt's criticism of Kemble's haughty refusal to compromise his own vanity in the interests of art with the praise offered by the same critic for Kean's Hamlet, wherein the actor:

> by an art like that of the ventriloquist . . . throws his imagination out of himself, and makes every word appear to proceed from the very mouth of the person whose name he bears.[65]

It's a form of praise which Hazlitt employed whenever he had been impressed by an actor, and often sounds more like a journalistic catchphrase rather than a philosophical theory. Eliza O'Neill, another of his favourites, drew a typical wave of enthusiasm:

> Her correctness did not seem the effect of art or study, but of instinctive sympathy. . . . There was no catching lights, no pointed hits, no theatrical tricks.[66]

There is no doubt that these comments are grounded on the theory of anti-Hobbesian disinterestedness, but in the heat of admiration and contempt, and under pressure of copy deadlines, they are popularised into a handy yardstick for 'I like/don't like' evaluation. This inevitable practical reduction of the theory in no way trivialises its impact, but it alters its focus from the intellectual to the emotional.

Thus, with the disinterested imagination being in application a metaphor, a subjective weapon with which Hazlitt attacked or defended actors who had offended or delighted his critical sense, it finds its most effective employment within a radical political context wherein selflessness in devotion to the cause is the greatest virtue. In a society in which a disaffected and violent proletariat was only just beginning to find its political voice, the theory served as a warning to those who would be king that their success depended on their displays of compassion, sensitivity and responsibility toward others.

That altruism founded on a revolutionary zeal – qualities demonstrated in genuine social revolution by Hazlitt's idol Napoleon – was the radical version of heroism, but it was to prove sadly unsuitable as a model for Shakespearean acting in a nineteenth-century Britain devoted equally to the Samuel Smiles concept of self-help and the Disraelian ambition toward global domination. Hazlitt and his metaphor of disinterestedness disappeared under the weight of conservative tub-thumping and a colonial mentality which was to depict Shakespeare as the definitive self-made man,[67] and employ his plays as the ultimate enforcers of British cultural imperialism.

The open text was closed by the imperial values of the actor. The rhetoric and display of military and cultural domination determined that the hero should divide and conquer as a prelude to occupation and administration, and Shakespeare's heroes, no less jewels in the crown of the Empire than India or the other colonies, were there to be subdued as they were celebrated and acquired by their actors.

7

DEATH OF THE ACTOR

There is a scene in Gustave Flaubert's *Temptation of Saint Antony* where the desert saint, exhausted by repeated resistance to temptation and bleeding from flagellation, finds his former pupil Hilarion returning from exile to offer him a means of transportation out of his wretched existence of misery, isolation and self-deprivation. Sorely tempted, but refusing to be swayed from his life of misery, Saint Antony endures and lives to suffer another day. He announces to Hilarion that he will not succumb because, after all, 'Suffering is blessed'.[1]

This fundamental tenet of monasticism has survived into modern times not just among the benedictine orders, but also in the theory of poetry and theatre, where literary and theatrical icons are deemed to be the result of holy and unholy psychological and even physical struggles between individuals and texts, each proclaiming their possession of and primary responsibility for the advocacy of the sublime. In a curious manifestation of the impulse toward beauty through mutilation and ritual sufferance, the monastic critic treats texts both sensually and forensically, appreciating the severity of the bruising which afflicts the verbal icon, while attempting to determine the nature of the instruments which caused the deformation.

A work's character is established by the degree of blessed suffering which it has endured, and its ability to triumph over ritualised aggression is a sign of moral and aesthetic strength. And so a text's value is ascertained not by its inner workings, but by its participation within the discursive space of a literary or theatrical culture as a whole, just as a physical object can be determined not by its mass, but by the displacement of air around it.

Harold Bloom[2] is one of the most prominent of these critics devoted to the creation of an heroic literary model in which battered texts struggle to the death with rivals and antecedents, and where authors hear the heavy stamp of parental feet gaining on their every advance. For Bloom, as for Saint Antony, the wretchedness of the aesthetically oppressed is a contemptible sign of weakness, and it is only the strong poet who will rage against tyranny and suffer a great physical defeat, even as he retains his greater dream of literary immortality through possession of the sublime.[3]

The Judaeo–Christian psychology of acquiescence has no place in such a paradoxical situation where corporeal exertion administers ascetic denial, and its place is taken by a world of Freudian self-assertion in which Oedipal and persecution complexes drive already-beaten men to mortal confrontation with their tormentors. The paradigm is the Romantic Satan-as-hero topos, and the related depiction of the poet as the heroic outsider, while the language derives from twentieth-century psychoanalysis:

> The anxiety of influence is so terrible because it is both a kind of separation anxiety and the beginning of a compulsion neurosis, or fear of a death that is a personified superego.[4]

With these words, Bloom creates a literary model wherein each poem achieves an identity of its own through a difficult relationship with a prior work, and where the poetic project represents not so much a poet's rage toward expression as his battle for survival during the assault of a previous poet.[5]

Bloom's *Anxiety of Influence* is a fine example of literary criticism as literature, and as in all great creative writing, the universal is treated through the individual. Thus, while Bloom increases the impact of his metaphor by concentrating on the simplified relationship between individual poems and poets, as a deference toward realism he is at pains to stress that in fact 'When we say that the meaning of a poem can only be another poem, we may mean a range of poems'.[6] And so, because of its 'literary' emphasis delivered through the medium of criticism, there is a fundamental tension in Bloom's work caused by the avowed diversity of influence being conveyed through a metaphor of finitude, with the result that what is essentially an argument for the intertextuality of discourse becomes little more than an alternative genetic theory in its dramatisation in Bloom's writing.[7] The intensity of the narrative necessarily simplifies the very premiss on which it is founded.

Displaying a Classical rather than Romantic predisposition, Roland Barthes offers the less flamboyant and less heroic version of Bloom's theory of literary discourse.[8] Where Bloom speaks biographically of the anxiety of influence, Barthes, following Julia Kristeva,[9] offers the term 'intertextuality' as the most appropriate description of the metaphorical relationship between an original literary work and its predecessors, and he broadens the field of influence well beyond the limits of mere literary icons. According to Barthes, intertextuality exists where prior texts (which need not be limited to literary works alone) function as contributions to a code which establishes the preconditions and determines the effects of signification.[10]

With the broadening of the semantic base implied by the term, intertextuality for Barthes is less a name for a work's Oedipal relationship with particular prior texts than it is a designation of its participation within the massive and variegated discursive space of a culture.[11] The specific prior discourses on which a work's meaning is predicated can never be catalogued with assurance, and Barthes goes so far as to say that 'the quotations of which a text is made are anonymous, untraceable, and nevertheless "already read"'.[12]

As a theoretical model, Barthes' intertextuality is an impressive exposé of the myth of originality in literary discourse, as well as an attractive alternative to the ubiquitous and insidious genetic theory of verbal creation, but because of its diversity, anonymity and downright vagueness, its applicability in practical criticism remains quite limited. Its value lies rather in its implicit acknowledgement of the impossibility of formalising an infinitude, and its revelation of the plenitude and anarchy which represent both the appeal of literature and its imperviousness to authoritative critical exegesis.

With the author dead and unable to 'close' his texts, the fundamental difficulty presented by intertextuality is that not only is a text a tissue of quotations, but so too is the newly-reborn reader a ragbag of prior texts, prejudices, interpretive imperfections and the dubious qualities generally resulting in Bloom's concept of 'misreading'.[13] Neither the printed word nor the interpreter is stable and meaning becomes arbitrary and anarchic, fixed only by social tradition and the masquerade of formal restraint.[14]

With both text and reader thus 'decentred', the intertextual experience of literature becomes a kind of high-class brothel where the nobleman which is the primary text gains and demonstrates its power and stamina through its deliciously immoral seduction and ravishing of every floozie or secondary text in sight. It's an extraordinarily democratic theory in that it advocates the capability of even the dirtiest whore to determine the demeanour and actions of the monarch, and its entry into modern critical debate has been roughly concurrent with the similar penetration of Genet's plays onto respectable stages.

Both Genet's plays and Barthes' theory are predicated on the eroticism and fascination of illegitimacy, and both enthusiastically reveal the furious perversions and vile absurdity which underlie formal ceremonial demonstrations of bourgeois power. As Genet creates his bestialising generals, so Barthes celebrates his works of literature which stand with one foot in the sewer even as they are hailed for their aristocratic bearing. The realism which underpins even the most excessive creations of French absurdism ensures that the rule of the guts is never lost amid the pomp of ceremonial splendour, and in Carnival spirit, the whip of the whore determines the wielding of the whip of the king.

Where Barthes accompanies Genet into a festive world of promiscuity and illicit semantic debauchery, Bloom's approach to literary conception is equally as diabolical in tone but based on a monogamistic system of dominance where the critic observes the jealous grappling of two splendidly-proportioned bully-boys modelled on the Satan of *Paradise Lost* Book 1. Revelling in the distorted, the perverse and the wilful,[15] Bloom argues that 'misprision' (mistaking, misreading, misinterpreting) necessarily occurs not only between one poet and another, but also between a critic and a text, because essentially, exact repetition and identity is slavery and a kind of death.[16] Bloom prefers the slave to strain against the manacles and actively dispute his right to freedom, all the while misinterpreting his master's cause and thus achieving liberty not through reason but through brute force and personal heroism. Judiciousness is for the weak poet only.

So with Barthes arguing for the poem's and the poet's construction by external poetic and extra-poetic forces, and Bloom urging the strong poets to rage against this alien pressure, from the theoretical perspective the poet is offered either anonymity and subservience to a pre-existing structural configuration, or fame and honour wherein the demonstration of personal power and individuality becomes the most important factor in the literary career.

Far from being antithetical, however, it is in fact characteristic of the madness of literary endeavour that in practice both conditions prevail simultaneously and the need for the individual artist to reconcile the impossibly-conflicting emotions of helplessness and power can account for the ultimate insanity of many authors. Schizophrenia and sado-masochistic perversions are admirably suited to a career where success depends on the ability to be a king and a slave simultaneously, and where the author is dead enough to lose responsibility for his own utterances, but alive enough to endure their consequences.

Acting too has its own version of intertextuality, and its own attendant psychopathy deriving from the necessity of the individual actor transcending the inherent bloodlust of the intertextual citations out of which she is constituted. Just as Bloom's and Barthes' authors are offered everything and nothing by this intertextual construction, so too actors are afforded the luxury of renting the intellectual and dramatic property of characterisation and through this limited licence conveying the illusion of the ownership and control which they will never truly possess.

In response to a reality which sees actors *made* rather than *born*, the star system of Shakespearean acting represented by the Oliviers, Gielguds and Richardsons favours the Bloom school of artistic heroism in the face of dispossession and oppression, while the more humble and character-serving Guinness style is more in keeping with Barthes' theory of democratic intertextuality. The former attempts to manipulate the pre-existing codes of acting into a vehicle for personal dominance and virtuosity, while the latter accepts the subjection as a contribution, through personal denial, to the greater aims of the art as a whole.

In transferring intertextuality from literature to theatre, the term itself can be retained because Barthes' 'text' can refer to anything, including the prior appearances of actors. However, the catchphrase of *déjà-lu* depicting the anonymous, vague and yet 'already-read' references which comprise a literary work needs to be altered to the catchier-still *déjà-vu*, *déjà-lu* which in the theatrical context refers to equally obscure prior visual *and* textual scenes which determine the conditions of signification within a staged spectacle. Each interplays with the other in a tussle for supremacy which essentially represents a conflict between the theatrical and literary approaches to drama, and each in itself is constructed from a diversity of prior events, ideas and suggestions which may be untraceable, but which are always-already in existence.

In the case of the Romantic critics, the dominance of the *déjà-lu* generally prevailed over the attractions of an equally-authoritative history of *déjà-vu*, and their response to Kean represented a temporary alignment of the two codes in a realisation of both the textual and theatrical potential of Shakespearean drama.

The recent thrust of dramatic debate, however, has tended to concentrate on the *déjà-vu* to the detriment of the *déjà-lu* in its references to actors and intertextuality. In referring to Olivier, Keir Elam for instance concludes that:

> A well-known actor will bring to his performance ... an 'intertextual' history which invites the spectator to compare it with past performances, thus drawing attention to the performer's idiolectal traits (common to all his performances).[17]

This is a modest and 'actor-centric' assessment of the intertextual function in acting, and its argument for the actor's positive function leading to emphasis on her identity does not suggest the profound impact which the *déjà-vu* and *déjà-lu* of intertextuality can have on a theatrical spectacle.

An actor's assumption of a part releases a vast range of intertextual agitation within both the text, the characterisation itself (the drama) and the body of the actor (the theatrical performance), as well as in the peripheral areas of the dramatic experience including the history, architecture, audience and physical orientation of the theatrical environment. In an adaptation of Veltrusky's celebrated phrase,[18] everything that is on-stage may be a sign, but it is no less true that everything immediately off-stage, as well as in the minds of the audience, also possesses the capacity to create meaning within the performance context.

Just as the verbal dimension of the play rubs itself up against a vast, even infinite, range of prior discursive practices, so the actor's participation in a world of intertextual citations is similarly constituted by not only her own prior appearances, but those of other actors in the same role, and a host of other theatrical and extra-theatrical historical, biographical and aesthetic details or prejudices which may influence an audience's misreading of her appearance. In theory, the actor is nothing but a space shaped, not internally, but by the interlocking of the various semantic masses which constitute its perimeters. In other words, the actor's body is delineated by a series of Saussurean differences with no positive terms, and the actor's sole active function is thus to displace the boundaries between herself and her outline with the most pleasing aesthetic impact possible.

In this demonstration of Sartrean being and nothingness, the existent is reduced to the series of appearances which manifest it,[19] and the actor only has to stand on stage for a tissue of factual and fictional quotations drawn from Barthes' 'innumerable centres of culture' to attend on her.[20] The result of such inactivity is that most curious of physical phenomena – a vacuum which achieves power through its sheer nothingness.

In assimilating and destroying her intertextual quotations and allusions, the actor is like a tornado, sucking in debris, whirling it around as a victim of the void, and then eventually succumbing to the overload of matter. For Hazlitt and Lamb, as well as Barthes with his wrestler, this detrimental filling of the tornado with too much substance occurred when actors (or wrestlers) were observed off-stage in all their factual mortality, emerging from the theatre 'with a spirit of lead [which] seems to seize on all their faculties'.[21]

A surfeit of reality and solidity is the actor's curse, and represents a misjudgement of the delicate balance between the assimilation of limited solid forms (an appropriately intriguing biography, a reputation for often-contradictory aesthetic and moral standards) which gives the actor power, and the overloading of the very same (imposing too much on an unwilling public and exposing mortality) which renders her powerless and the audience frustrated. In any case, the actor, powerful or powerless, is nevertheless in a state of total dependence, and the illusion of control and authority is sustained only by these occasional demonstrations of strength through a happy balance of matter and nothingness, and a capacity to disguise the negative as positive by focusing attention on the shape of the vacuum rather than on the movements of the external masses which determine it.

This positive depiction of the actor's own victimisation is much favoured by conservative theorists for whom the appeal of Carlyle's heroes and Smiles' self-made men has never waned, and who are enthusiastically predisposed toward the illusion of content independent of form in human endeavour. The conservative believes that the suggestion that communal forces greater than the individual determine the actions of humans is only for radicals and critics who are loathe to recognise divinity when they experience it.[22]

Acting, in this sense of intertextual constitution leading to the *discordia concors* of virtuoso display, indulges in an expression of the unrest, anxiety and bewilderment generated by a process of alienation, an anti-classicist statement which in Renaissance

scholarship has been labelled mannerist.[23] Art historians are fond
of identifying the 'decentralisation' of composition and the rise in
spatial and colouristic complexities in seventeenth-century Italian
art as having lead to increasing virtuosity of execution and highly-
decorative surface qualities, often associated with deliberate physical
and psychic ambiguities.[24] In responding to a chaotic world which,
in the words of John Donne,

> . . . is all in peeces, all cohaerence gone;
> All just supply, and all Relation:
> Prince, Subject, Father, Sonne, are things forgot . . .[25]

Mannerist art is always a demonstration of bravura and a conjuring
trick[26] built on paradox and expressing itself in extremes and pairs of
opposites.

This decentred mannerist mentality prepares an environment
where protagonists of Machiavellian political realism, finding
themselves in a world of post-Copernican and post-Montaignean
(and now post-Nietzschean) scepticism, can institute the unifying
myth of the superman for whom the demonstration of strength and
the heavy-handed wielding of power establishes an illusory order
which is severe enough to be mistaken for truth. At that moment
of *discordia concors*, when the void reveals itself as force, and as
apparent order takes the place of the chaos of reality, the cult of
the virtuoso begins and the uncertainty and anguish of the existential
nightmare dissipates with the institution of the philosophy of one
greater.

The phenomenon of the actor's simultaneous being and nothingness thus reveals a further elaboration of intertextual theory, in
that not just similitude, but indeed opposition as well determines
the conditions of signification within the theatrical experience. The
apparent virtuosity of the actor and her rage for power are referable
to a silence which proclaims the individual as insubstantial and
powerless except for the actions which the surrounding semantic
conditions and theatrical conventions invest in her. In making an
impression of skill on the intertextual space, the actor demonstrates
only the free-will which those same predetermined conditions have
permitted as part of their own broader project.

And so the actor 'brings' to her role not so much an intertextual
history as whatever semantic baggage (or debris) the theatrical-
experience-as-social-event demands of her. Deprived of real power
and yet observed for her demonstration of activity, the successful

actor is the void which can make its imposed mythological load appear to be manipulated voluntarily.

Intertextuality, then, employs myths which establish forms of communication recognised as sensible and significant by members of a society sharing a common background knowledge and range of experience. The range of these 'positive' myths is endless, but Hamlet's procrastination and his advertising of British cigars[27] are just two examples of prior discourses – accurate or inaccurate – which reverberate very substantially in the interpretive cogitations of an audience, and which can be instituted as a point of comparison and a touchstone of significance.

They should not be confused with the 'negative' myths which are the untruths, misinformation and misinterpretation which have raised the reputation of theatrical acting to an inappropriately authoritative position in Shakespearean scholarship. Examples of these negative myths include not just the claims for textual incompleteness outside of performance, but also outrageous and persistent overstatements such as Flecknoe's comment that Burbage was:

> a delightful Proteus, so wholly transforming himself into his Part, and putting off himself with his Cloathes as he never . . . assum'd himself again until the Play was done.[28]

When argued from the theoretical perspective alone, such implausible statements of histrionic divinity are passive and do not contribute to the intertextual function, but *can* be appropriated by the active and positive myths of artistic reality to act as practical 'decoding' devices when applied to specific instances of Shakespearean performance. In other words, the same ridiculous opinion is a negative myth in that it is untrue, but positive in that it may gain imaginative currency.

So in elaborating the way in which Shakespearean acting conveys meaning, the intertextual approach demands that discussion moves from the passive myths perpetrated by scholarly misrepresentation, to the active myths which can be extra-theatrical, imaginary or rhetorical, and which may achieve a degree of semantic authority unjustified by their internal constitution alone. Metaphorically, the validity of the premises on which the theory is based are not in question in the intertextual project, but they are now supplanted by the real (even if illusory) aura of their aesthetic perfection, which sustains the formula even as it undermines its rational foundation.

In the theatrical context, this translates into a destruction of the actor's voice and creative input at the very moment that she accepts her role as participant in the Shakespearean culture, because that is the point where the tyranny of history and the myths of beauty turn her into a reminder of what is already known.

It can be demonstrated in all types of dramatic performance, but in the case of Shakespearean acting, the actor's impotence is particularly abject, indeed deathly, because of the sheer weight of intertexts which constitute the cultural icon. From Shakespeare's name, which is both a standard of quality and an indication of stylistic uniformity,[29] through the mythological (because extra-theatricalised) status of the characters and plots themselves, to the vital participation of Shakespearean drama in the cultural and educational life of Britain and the western world as a whole, the extreme forces of Shakespearean signification determine that the actor possesses no internal creative power in theatrical productions of the plays.

In circumstances where the ambitions of the cultural icon may have been satisfied already, or when the prevailing discourses of bardolatry otherwise demand it, actors may be loaned some power for a moment or two in a production, but they are never the rightful possessors of it, and their authority must be sustained not by decree, but through the illusions of confidence and facility (and ultimately, destruction).

The greatest Shakespearean actors have to escape the awareness that in less congenial times in history, their position of aesthetic credibility has been successfully filled by juveniles and animals. In one of the favoured scholarly manifestations of this dilemma, wonder is expressed at the boy actors who impersonated Lady Macbeth and Cleopatra and theories of skill are espoused to explain why this seemingly impossible travesty did not appear to detract from the dramatic spectacle of Elizabethan times.[30]

The wonder, however, should be reserved for the fact that such speculation arises in inverse proportion to the creative function of the actor in the historical development of Shakespearean acting. Devoid of the distance which turns reality into myth, the acceptance of boy actors by Shakespeare's audience indicates the prevalence of theatrical conventions and related intertextual features which rendered the here-and-now of histrionic verisimilitude of only minor importance. In other words, not even when the plays were less well-known than their actors could the casting of individuals detract from the impact of the drama as a whole.

In the modern age, however, the plays and all their trappings tower over their actors to the extent that the very names of Shakespeare, Stratford, Hamlet, Lear, Goneril, Lady Macbeth, all bring with them such a range of intertextual citations that they are pleasing and resonant enough in themselves to be capable of life outside the theatrical context. The result of this should be the transformation of the actor into nothing more than the criminal lackey pretending to be dead on the street while her mistress picks the pockets of the assembled voyeurs and ghouls.

But in reality, the actors' theatre creates the extraordinary paradox of an omnipotently intertextual Shakespearean theory which nevertheless drastically overestimates the importance of flesh-and-blood in an imaginative, discursive world. The strictures of naturalism together with the unionised rhetoric of acting mythology, actively discourage the awareness of the comparative impotence of Shakespearean actors past and present. And so the lackey of the original Shakespearean performances astounds with his youth and unsuitability because he is mistaken as the sole attraction and the master of the game.

One of the more ironic myths of Shakespearean acting then is that actors are possessed of the negative capability which allows them to enter into the lives of their assumed characters. Indeed the very opposite applies in that, rather than actors' 'disinterestedness' creating characterisation, actors themselves are constituted on the basis of prior and foreign discourses. The would-be constructor is nothing more than a construct herself, rendered possible by the pre-existence of Shakespeare, his characters and their mystique. They lend her their lustre, their authority and their power because they exist independent of her brief tenure on them. Their immortality contrasts with her mortality and the best she can hope to achieve is to leave a little graffiti on the icon once she has disappeared.

Despite the anti-Romantic agitation to the contrary, contemptuous allegations of bardolatry cannot justifiably be levelled at such remarks, because the 'immortality' of Shakespearean characters is not a statement of relative moral or aesthetic values so much as it is an analysis of the modes of cultural signification. Prioritising characterisation at the expense of histrionic ego is the inevitable theoretical consequence of a Shakespearean mythology in which the discourses of power and alienable textuality dominate the naïve claims for an obsolete humanism. It is at this cruel point where the mortal individual must surrender her immanent identity to the irresistible claims of hegemonic discursive practices, that any veiled abuse of actors necessarily turns toward overt sympathy.

When Shakespearean theatre stops relating to things and turns instead to contemplation and representation of itself, its history, characters and social impact, then the actor dies and her rigor mortis is appropriated by a massive act of cultural signification which renders the natural only a curious and minor aspect of the expressive.[31] Mannerism knows this pathos of corporeality being humiliated by the urgency of ideas, allusions and texts which move ineluctably from the mimetic to the meta-mimetic, and the observer cannot but applaud the courageous efforts of the mortal individual continuing to assert her claim to power, like Bloom's strong poet beaten from the outset but attempting to summon up the non-existent fury of Satan to deny the brutal fact.

And so the *discordia concors* of Shakespearean acting is represented by the paradox of colonialism (which by definition should be active) being perpetrated by a fundamentally passive system of histrionic differences with no positive terms. The mannerist perspective would identify this paradox as an example of the irreducible tensions which characterise the truth of any post-sceptical phenomenon, but a reconciliation in fact can be effected because of the mediation of illusion and the impetus of ambition.

When the whim of established authority offers impotence a temporary licence for power, the ambition to colonise is realisable not through the inherent force of the overt protagonist, but through the displacement of the traditional source of paternalism. In other words, the actor is only invested with an interpretive capability which has been delegated by the intertextual space surrounding her, and at best this represents an illusory responsibility administered by default and proxy. And so while the immorality of virtuoso acting is that its ambition is always toward colonialism, the sorrow is that it can only indulge that hope on the volition of fickle and inscrutable external forces.

In that absurd, Beckettesque world of delusion, stasis and impoverishment, the actor must confront the painful difference between the illusion and reality of her existence. Hailed as the terrorist by those who lust to become her victim, there comes a time when the would-be heroine metaphorically has to stand naked in front of a mirror, ruefully observing the unaccommodated, poor, bare, forked animal whom king and fool alike hail for her pleasure, wisdom and power. Whether she responds with self-delusive pride, knowing cynicism, or schizophrenia, the actor cannot escape the consequences of the lie at the very foundation of her existence, and the awareness that her imperfect body necessarily satirises the myths of beauty and skill which the urgency of Shakespearean mythology and the absence of materiality has fostered in distant audiences.

The euphemism of acting displaces the reality of inaction and the reverence in which the name of an actor is held is the compensation for a life of suffering endured by an aspiring tyrant deprived of an executive decision-making capability. It's an untenable position of denial and flagellation where the individual is sustained only by the continual tormenting and temptation of ultimately unrealisable fantasies. But it possesses an enduring appeal both for the egocentric ascetics themselves and their spectators, because in a cruel world where suffering is blessed and humanity has given way to rhetoric, the beggar has achieved victory when an audience forgets itself long enough to feel pity.

It's unfortunate not just for Shakespeareans, but indeed for any actors, being ultimately at the whore-like service of a fickle and perverted public which is ready to admire the skilful performer able to disguise their humiliation and degradation of her as her pleasure. To maintain self-esteem, and to make the best of a bad situation, actors and whores alike generally employ assumed names and identities which both preserve an element of privacy for the meat of their corpse and which through their exoticism and mystique tend to titillate their abusers all the more.

Even as the victim of debauchery, there is a certain power in having one's identity either unknown or mistaken, and some of the great performers have done all they can to remove themselves from the martyrdom of biography, and to call to their aid the constitutive authority of intertextual myth alone. Yul Brynner[32] and Marlene Dietrich[33] were two such performers who did all they could to deny any factual background to their acting, revelling rather in the tinsel and glamour which intertextual citation, reputation and erotic speculation brought to their vacuous identities.[34]

In response to this dearth of reality furnishing identification with assumed character, Yul Brynner became known as the King of Siam, while Dietrich more sinisterly represented the mythical (Hollywood) caricature of European female sexuality. What they *were* was irrelevant because of what they *represented*, and in her last years, poignant pictures of the crippled and cadaverous Dietrich having to be carried because she was too weak to walk, and of the hollow-eyed Yul Brynner dying of lung cancer, did nothing to disrupt the memory and the legend of the performers, because they were only physical reminders of a phenomenon which was and is specifically imaginative.

Devoid of a physical body to attach to it, Dietrich's name still elicits hushed tones and sycophancy and Brynner is still a symbol of exoticism, regardless of the parody of human form that their ailing bodies came to be. Physically, even in their primes, they were nothing more than a bald head and a svelte body through which the products of and the consumables for imagination could be conveyed, and outside of the body they represented the images which sustained the curiosity of generations. They had transcended the category of acting and existed rather as pleasing myths, images of qualities which are cultural in general rather than theatrical in particular. As with James Dean, John F. Kennedy and Marilyn Monroe, their significance in death has already exceeded that in life.

And so with actors gaining in fame when they are no longer able to act, the supposed 'terror' of acting is revealed to be something of a misnomer, describing intentions rather than reality and demonstrating the fundamental impotence of the actor to determine her own fate in a theatrical environment controlled from outside the immediate actor-audience relationship. Quasi-mortal abrogations of the actor's responsibility, such as drunkenness or accidental business leading to increasing audience applause also confirm this dependence of the actor on that which she cannot control.

The amusing stage legends and ironic anecdotes about bold interpretive innovations arising independent of the will of their perpetrators indicate the extent to which many a true word about the function of intertextuality is delivered in jest.[35] The drunkenness and drug addiction which afflicted Romantic critics and actors alike was never likely to be a hindrance while interpretation of action or writing eschewed any dependence on the intention of its medium or its author.[36]

With actors literally and metaphorically approaching the same mortal fate as authors, intertextuality offers a new perspective on the phenomenon of an audience clapping a performer before she has even begun to act. Rather than merely acknowledging the primacy of the actor's theatre, the gesture in fact embraces the very opposite phenomenon – ultimately illustrating the actor's insignificance in a theatre constructed through the urgency of that which is pre-existing. The applause is not a celebration of life, but an artistic death-knell symbolising the sufficiency of all which has gone before, and a bizarre reversal from art to ritual as the future is deemed unimportant because of the triumph of the past.

The actor, whose early career is usually devoted to the heavy-handed demonstration of the illusion of ego, is helpless to stop this wave of *a priori* sentiment which renders her redundant even as it confirms her real or imaginary past successes. She is placed in the unenviable position of the premature museum exhibit, situated alongside the stuffed animals as a token of what was *once*, while her own heart mockingly beats as strongly as ever, refusing to acknowledge the death which is her reason for being there. The insult of unearned applause only confirms the vulnerability which has always characterised a career predicated on the imagination and lust of others, and their fury to purge emotions through their appreciation and employment of the physical exertion of others.

And so to summarise, the experience of theatre is not so much an act of observation as it is an invitation to remember, with that which is present being interpreted on the basis of that which has been seen and heard already. With the *déjà-lu* of literary intertextuality supplemented in theatre by the *déjà-vu* of previous experience both in theatre and in life – as well as the *déjà-écoute*, *déjà-imagine* and *déjà-toutes-choses* of personal subjectivity – the immediate physical experience of the theatre, which is most obviously that confrontation between actors and their audiences, is removed to a position of secondary semiotic importance and the status of those protagonists becomes not an identity but a function.[37] The actor is in fact deprived of the very action on which her title is based. This fundamental realignment of traditional conceptions of theatrical signification is rendered possible by an acknowledgement of the crucial operation of myth in intertextual communication and in the society of which Shakespearean theatre and its criticism is still an important part.

Shakespearean actors, then, are little more than the myths out of which they are created and then destroyed, and the tragedy comes when the mythical, disguised for so long as the natural, eventually comes to be regarded by its momentary object of attention as her essential human quality. Pleasing though it may be at first, it is entirely dependent on the indulgence of the socio-historical discourses of the mutable culture which surrounds it, and, by its essential constitution, can only be rendered meaningful by its dominance over the rival language of slavery and powerlessness. Thus, as with the opposition between life and death, the actor's primary function in Shakespearean theatre enjoys only one certainty, and that is that it will eventually come to an end.

The Shakespearean actor has never enjoyed the privilege of the primitive shaman or mask or trance-dancer who has been able not to disguise herself as her character, but in fact to *become* the thing itself. Instead, the westerner has been forced to content herself only with the illusion of doing so, studiously attempting to emulate the tremblings, screamings and frothings-at-the-mouth which occur spontaneously as a consequence of the complete divine or diabolical possession and identification of eastern performers. A surreptitious tear, a cracking voice, are the civilised theatre's versions of such fanatical transformations, delivered in accordance with a strict code of intellectual and emotional display sanctioned both by authority and the actor's own sense of dignity. It occurs this way in the west because unlike in primitive society, the characters exist primarily as textual creations independent of actors and the body necessarily can only enjoy limited tenure on the imaginative property, and must handle it with extreme care. The actor is always answerable to a character greater than herself and her triumph is brief.

Indeed the celebration of the actor in Shakespearean theatre is rendered possible only by this competition and temporary victory over the antagonistic voices of Shakespeare read. The appeal of the theatre is therefore ineluctably attached to the awareness of its limited tenure and the impending success of its opposition. The previous chapters have outlined the reasons for Shakespearean acting's eventual demise in confrontation with the rhetoric of its accusers. The present chapter necessarily heralds the lament for that very departure, as one rhetoric is supplanted by another and establishes a dominance that in turn will only be temporary. It is part of a cycle which, independent of human motives outside of mythmaking, is manifested in the rise and fall from grace not just of actors, but political leaders as well.

Because she seeks to fill the very same void with her own presence, the actor has followed the author on a journey toward death. Indeed, the well-known arguments for the latter's disappearance can be transposed with equal force onto the grid of the theatrical experience. Foucault has suggested that where the tales of Scheherazade were framed as a deliberate enactment of writing as a means to immortality, as it was in Greek narrative and epic, modern western culture has inverted the process so that

> Where a work had the duty of creating immortality, it now attains the right to kill, to become the murderer of its author . . . we find the link between writing and death manifested in the total effacement of the individual characteristics of the writer.[38]

It's a concept of mortality-through-writing which is much older in fact than Foucault implies (his examples of it come from Beckett, Flaubert, Proust and Kafka), and is closely related to the famous passage in 2 *Corinthians 3:6*, 'The letter kills but the spirit gives life'.[39] Simply by employing the medium of writing, the author cancels out the signs of her own individuality in the interests of a writing which is greater than she and which in turn, through the function of intertextuality, is constituted by other writings. It's a sacrifice that condemns the author always to a position of slavery to her own work and her eternal absence from the seat of semantic power attributed to her.

Foucault, along with Barthes before him,[40] stresses that the author, or in the present case the actor, does have an identity known to all who read fan magazines or newspapers. The important point about this, however, is that such information arises not out of the individual's biography itself, but from a psychological reconstruction of material deriving from the handling of the texts. Baudelaire is interesting as an individual only in so far as he informs the texts which go under his name. The sexual biography of a Baudelaire who hadn't written 'Don Juan in Hell' would never be as interesting as the same story of the author.

Similarly, actor-biographies provide angles on performances rather than on actors as individuals. Olivier's biography provides an elucidation of the heroic images of Hamlet and Henry V and Othello more than a contribution to the identity of an individual. Olivier the person presumably lurked somewhere behind Olivier the myth, but there was no guarantee that this was so, nor that he was especially interesting. Even Olivier's wife despairingly claimed that he was never himself, but always acting.[41] He was a great actor, because he sent his audience to every place but the scene of his death. He was a western Scheherazade, paradoxically surviving through self-obliteration.

The myth of Scheherazade is so pleasing to western audiences because it suggests that through extreme physical endurance and imaginative vigour, the inevitable onset of death can be forestalled as the aggressor's attention is distracted. Scheherazade in fact makes herself disappear for the duration of her tales, and in that sense she in fact is as typical of modern authorship (and acting) as any of Foucault's examples. It's a curious phenomenon which ensures that survival is guaranteed through disappearance and disappearance through textual survival.

But it is wrong to suggest that Scheherazade is exclusively focused on narrative as salvation. Indeed, there is a famous Arab legend, deriving from the fourteenth century, geared to the very same hostility toward print as Corinthians, that anyone who reads the *1,001 Nights* right through will die.[42] It's a story about narrative's power to destroy and the ways of forestalling or encouraging its horrible work. Scheherazade disappears at the moment that she assumes the role of narrator and acknowledges her indebtedness to both the myths which she relates and the myths out of which she herself is constructed in the mind of her audience, Shariar.

The same thing happens with Shakespearean actors who, from the moment of taking the stage, disappear behind the very actions which they assume. The case is particularly obvious in the teapot school of classicists such as Kemble, whose conventional gestures and method of delivery – so ridiculed by Hazlitt and Hunt – effectively created a range of intertextual (one could say 'intertheatrical') citations which adhere to schools of signification and interpretation which operate independent of the individual performing them.

The actor destroys herself at the very moment of performance because, her actions being predictable, she forms a library of gestures and a repertoire of competence rather than an individual expression alive to the present scene. The characteristics of Kemble as an actor are effaced by the operation of the stylistic model which he represents, and as he as an individual dies, his place is taken by the audience, who are the next in line for mortality, and the eager distributors of meaning into the semantic vacuum created by the departure of both author and now actor.

Unlike the author's, however, the actor's death is of a special kind, because regardless of the power of the intertextual citations attaching to her, and her dependence on them for significance, there is still always going to be a moving body present, waving its arms and shouting to the audience. This physical figure is not dead in the literal sense, but it is a body devoid of any cultural authority, ultimately isolated from the security of the very rhetorical covering which protects it temporarily from censure. Energy, that much-celebrated actor's quality, seeks to provide what nature has failed to bestow – a guarantee of safety and the illusion of power.

Every physical and mental resource must be brought to the confident portrayal of narrative and character in a story which takes its listener to another world deemed to be created by a master. But when Scheherazade momentarily forgets her tale, and Shariar's attention turns toward her, he will in fact see her shivering in the fear of exposure and death, just as the actor when suddenly confronted with a lapse in the mythical covering is revealed in her embarrassment as a fragile and guilty naked mortal desperately trying to improvise some story to deflect attention from her wholly inadequate and sanctionable body. Death is the next thing to be faced; but nakedness, as its living incarnation and a reminder of unavoidable destiny, is the immediate problem which must be (ad)dressed.

In order to achieve this distraction, the actor participates within a semiological system in which a vast range of textual, social and historical theatrical languages and media – the theatrical equivalent of Bakhtin's *heteroglossia* – strive for supremacy in a battle between the centrifugal forces of alien discourses and the centripetal intentions of the would-be unitary languages within the whole network.[43]

The actor aims to achieve her own version of this centripetal force, by turning the attention inward from the plethora of potential meanings within the theatrical *heteroglossia* (which can be defined as everything which is a sign in the theatre), to one prioritised human system which gives the illusion of internal consistency and power. Being nothing, she is able to suck in the debris of her semantic surroundings and thus form a temporary but effective solid mass.

And so, in successful acting, the centrifugal force, which in effect is created from this vast range and energy of the intertextual citations available to the theatrical performance as a whole, is reversed and drawn centripetally into the vacuum of the actor's absent 'identity', to offer the impression of one unitary mode of signification possessing specific content and embodying individual utterance. Unlike in *King Lear*, something comes of nothing.

In Shakespearean acting, the achievement of this reversal of semantic forces from outwards to inwards is extraordinarily difficult, so powerful is the referability of the great speeches to a host of wider cultural discourses. There are Shakespearean words which, independent of the tempering efforts of any actor, explode into a thousand pieces of semiological business and which defy any mortal attempt to make them appear the individual utterance of a unitary and original subject:

> To be, or not to be: that is the question:
> Whether 'tis nobler in the mind to suffer
> The slings and arrows of outrageous fortune,
> Or to take arms against a sea of troubles,
> And by opposing end them . . .[44]

At these points where the actor cannot speak in his own language, nor that of Shakespeare, nor of Hamlet, but only in that pertaining to a vast field of cultural endeavour, the best that can be hoped for is that the inevitable centrifugation will be interpreted as a convention and that, once the too sullied passages are completed, the attention will once more turn inward to the poor (but apparently rich) man attempting to present the language as his own original and spontaneous outburst.

The crisis which every Shakespearean actor must face occurs not just in these familiar passages, but in any speech where the deictic markings are heavily underlined. The 'I's and 'you's and the 'here's and 'now's are potentially the linguistic robes which can humiliate any dwarfish actor by their majestic hanging from her paltry thievish body. For all its emphasis on these deictic functions in Shakespearean drama, recent semiotic theory with its complex charts and arrowed diagrams[45] has not yet fully established the inherent absurdity of these simple words stretched in one direction toward dramatic magnificence and in the other toward theatrical pathos.

The function of the actor must be to naturalise the deictic expressions and to reduce them to a single meaning. The more successful actors generally pretend that the two extremes of monarchy and mortality are in fact the same point, a situation which was not so illusory for Lord Olivier as for lesser Shakespearean and political pretenders. In successfully subduing the deictic crisis, the actor is generally able to reverse this centrifugal trend.

One further way to achieve this centripetally-created illusion of histrionic responsibility is through mutilating the text, both by editorial emendation (shocking the audience into not knowing what comes next), and the wilful misinterpretation of conventions already inscribed in the language of the text ('TO be or [*pause*] not TO be'). Traditionally, such mutilations are described as 'interpretations' but such a euphemism renders innocent a procedure which can at times be spectacular in its irresponsibility.

But even in their most violent forms, these transgressions of textual inviolability are only partially successful, because even perverse acts of destruction necessarily focus attention on the known beauties which have been savaged to facilitate the ambitious centripetation of the performers' interpretation. Indeed Hamlet's 'To be or not to be' soliloquy would arguably gain maximum impact in a production if it were to be deleted altogether, because its very absence would raise a host of questions concerning its meaning and importance and the justifiability of its excision. Complete annihilation is, and on the evidence of the folk tales apparently always has been, the ultimate demonstration of interpretative ability, and for an actor to make an impact on the icon, this destruction and silencing is possibly the last alternative available in a community where Shakespearean texts speak regardless of the individual who presumes to be their mouthpiece.

The interpreter's words being exhausted in this way in all but the opinion of distant idealists, the only response is that of the unsuccessful political negotiator – a recourse into violence and terror. This of course is not the end of Shakespearean theatre, but its beginning, where actions finally take the place of words and the actor, liberated at last from the illusion of civility, sets out on a blatant attack on the Shakespearean models. And so at that point where borrowed words no longer provide an adequate clothing for the naked actor or political zealot, the distraction which prolongs life can only be sustained through the demonstration of an uncompromising and fearless power.

NOTES

1 BARDOLATRY

1. Ernest Hemingway in his edition of *Men at War: The Best War Stories of All Time* (New York, 1942), noted that 'As they get further and further away from a war they have taken part in all men have a tendency to make it more as they wish it had been rather than how it really was' (p. xvi). Refusing to be so deceived himself, Hemingway argued that 'The last war, during the years 1915, 1916, 1917 was the most colossal, murderous, mismanaged butchery that has ever taken place on earth. Any writer who said otherwise lied. . . . The writers who were established before the war had nearly all sold out to write propaganda during it and most of them never recovered their honesty afterwards' (xiv–xv).

2. All page references for Lamb's writings are to *The Works in Prose and Verse of Charles and Mary Lamb, vol. 1*, ed. Thomas Hutchinson (Oxford, 1924), hereafter referred to as *Works*. For general biographical information see David Cecil, *A Portrait of Charles Lamb* (London, 1983); George L. Barnet, *Charles Lamb* (Boston, 1976); E.V. Lucas, *The Life of Charles Lamb*, 6th edn (London, 1914). For Lamb and Romanticism see Thomas McFarland, *Romantic Cruxes: The English Essayists and the Spirit of the Age* (Oxford, 1987).

3. Among these titles are 'G.F. Cooke in Richard the Third' (1803), 45–8; 'Play-House Memoranda' (1813), 200–3; 'My First Play' (1821), 592–6; 'On Some of the Old Actors' (1822), 636–8; 'On the Acting of Munden' (1819), 656–8; 'Ellistoniana' (1831), 680–5, in the Lambs' *Works*, ibid.

4. Lamb, 'On Some of the Old Actors', *Works*, ibid., 645.

5. Lamb, 'G.F. Cooke in Richard the Third', *Works*, ibid., 48.

6. All page references for Hazlitt's writings are to *The Complete Works of William Hazlitt*, ed. P.P. Howe (London, 1930–4), hereafter referred to as *Works*. For general biographical information, see Herschel Baker, *William Hazlitt* (Cambridge, Mass., 1962); John Kinnaird, *William Hazlitt: Critic of Power* (New York, 1978); Ralph M. Wardle, *Hazlitt* (Lincoln, 1971); David Bromwich, *Hazlitt: The Mind of a Critic* (Oxford, 1983); Stanley Jones, *William Hazlitt: A Life, From Winterslow to Frith Street* (Oxford, 1989). See also Jonathan Bate's

Shakespearean Constitutions: Politics, Theatre, Criticism 1730–1830 (Oxford, 1989), esp. 129ff.

7. Hazlitt, *A View of the English Stage*, in *Works*, ibid., V.357.

8. Hazlitt, *Characters of Shakespear's Plays*, in *Works*, ibid., IV.189.

9. For a general introduction to depictions of Lamb, Hazlitt and their contemporaries as enemies of Shakespeare performed, see Joseph W. Donohue, *Dramatic Character in the English Romantic Age* (Princeton, 1970), 280–348, and Joan Coldwell, 'The Playgoer as Critic: Charles Lamb on Shakespeare's Characters', *Shakespeare Quarterly* 26 (1975), 184–95. Among many other available references, see also Stanley Wells' articles on 'Shakespeare in Leigh Hunt's Theatre Criticism', *Essays and Studies* 33 (1980), 118–38, and 'Shakespeare in Hazlitt's Theatre Criticism', *Shakespeare Survey* 35 (1982), 43–55. The topic has been an academic hot potato ever since Harley Granville-Barker began his analysis of *King Lear* in *Prefaces to Shakespeare* 2 (London, 1930), 7–8, with an overt answer to Lamb's contention that Lear is impossible to represent on the stage, and while Barker reserves his greatest contempt for A.C. Bradley, Lamb's reputation has never recovered from the assault.

10. Hazlitt, *Characters of Shakespear's Plays*, in *Works*, ibid., IV.357.

11. R.W. Babcock, *The Genesis of Shakespeare Idolatry, 1766–1799* (Chapel Hill, 1931), xxvii–xxviii.

12. ibid., 225.

13. See for instance Seymour Kleinberg's article on 'Eighteenth Century Criticism' in Oscar James Campbell (ed.), *A Shakespeare Encyclopedia* (London, 1966).

14. See the anonymous article on De Quincey, ibid., 181.

15. Howard Felperin, 'Bardolatry' (unpublished paper, 1988), *passim*.

16. Charles Marowitz, 'Reconstructing Shakespeare or Harlotry in Bardolatry', *Shakespeare Survey* 40 (1987), 1–10.

17. George Bernard Shaw, *The Complete Prefaces of Bernard Shaw* (London, 1965), 750.

18. Felperin, op. cit., 4–5.

19. G.B. Harrison, *Introducing Shakespeare*, 3rd edn (Harmondsworth, 1966), 21.

20. Jonas Barish, *The Antitheatrical Prejudice* (Berkeley, 1981), 328.

21. The most recent contributions to the debate include W.B. Worthen, 'Deeper Meanings and Theatrical Technique: The Rhetoric of Performance Criticism', *Shakespeare Quarterly* 40 (1989), 441–55; Marvin and Ruth Thompson (eds), *Shakespeare and the Sense of Performance: Essays in the Tradition of Performance Criticism in Honour of Bernard Beckermann* (Newark, 1989); Jean E. Howard and Marion F. O'Connor (eds), *Shakespeare Reproduced: The Text in History and Ideology* (New York/London, 1987); Richard Levin, 'Performance-Critics vs Close Readers in the Study of English Renaissance Drama', *M.L.R.* 81 (1986), 545–59.

22. The claim is made by Marvin and Ruth Thompson, 'Performance Criticism from Granville-Barker to Bernard Beckermann and Beyond', in their *Shakespeare and the Sense of Performance: Essays in the*

Tradition of Performance Criticism in Honour of Bernard Beckermann (Newark, 1989), 13–23. The article offers a full exposition of the history of performance criticism.

23. Worthen, op. cit., 441.

24. Richard David, *Shakespeare in the Theatre* (Cambridge, 1978), 16–17.

25. Presumably, Brown was thinking of L.C. Knights, about whom, as Kenneth Muir remarked, 'one sometimes gets the impression that Knights regards the stage as a vulgar place where we must expect to see only perversions of the plays'. See Kenneth Muir, '[Review of] The Shakespeare Play as Poem: A Critical Tradition in Perspective', *M.L.R.* 78 (1983), 140.

26. John Russell Brown, *Discovering Shakespeare: A New Guide to the Plays* (New York, 1981), 1.

27. Sidney Holman, *Shakespeare's 'More Than Words Can Witness': Essays on Visual and Non-Verbal Enactment in the Plays* (Lewisburg, Pennsylvania, 1980), 10. Richard Levin in his op. cit., 584, points out the logical and grammatical impossibility of Holman's claim.

28. See Worthen, op. cit., 447.

29. Howard and O'Connor, op. cit., 4.

30. As one example, see John Russell Brown's 'The Nature of Speech in Shakespeare's Plays', in Marvin and Ruth Thompson, op. cit., 48–59. According to Brown, 'Shakespearean critics and students . . . have suffered by being confined to university departments of English where plays are never seen in performance by skilled and practiced actors'.

31. Harold Goddard, *The Meaning of Shakespeare* (Chicago, 1951), I.82–3.

32. Harry Berger, Jr, 'Text against Performance in Shakespeare: The Example of Macbeth', *Genre* 15 (1982), 49–79; Harry Berger, Jr, 'Bodies and Texts', *Representations* 17 (1987), 144–66; René Girard, 'To Entrap the Wisest', in *Literature and Society*, ed. Edward Said (Baltimore, 1980), 100–19. In his 1982 article, Berger attempts to 'correct' Girard's approach. He notes, 'I shall argue not only that the text differs from the script but also that the Shakespeare play as a text to be interpreted by readers provides a critique of the play as a script – that is, as the basis of performance. I hasten to add that obviously if such a critique can be demonstrated we should not expect it to be so thoroughly antitheatrical as to advocate a ban on performance' (50). 'Girard's approach, thus corrected, may guide us toward an account of the tension between the ideologies of performance and text as Shakespeare presents it . . .' (53). See also Jackson G. Barry, 'Shakespeare with Words: The Script and the Medium of Drama', *Shakespeare Quarterly* 25 (1974), 161–71, for a partial attempt to reconcile the positions.

33. Richard Levin, op. cit., 558, notes that: 'The conclusion is quickly stated: so far as we can tell, most people in this period, and certainly most of the dramatists themselves, believed that plays existed, first and foremost, in the written texts, which contradicts the claims of the extreme performance-critics that the plays really exist only on the stage. But they also believed that these texts were written with a performance in mind, and therefore should be read as if they were

being performed, which contradicts the claims of the extreme close readers, whose thematic or ironic interpretations are unperformable.' Shakespeare's characters are by no means pro-theatrical in their own observations on the art which animates them. Some of the most famous quotes find them speaking of rotten players who strut and fret and speak more than is set down for them.

34. Worthen, op. cit., 452, 455.
35. Terry Eagleton, *Criticism and Ideology* (London, 1978), 66.
36. ibid.
37. In referring to Hazlitt's praise for him as a young man, Macready noted that his career was launched by an 'authority . . . almost supreme on subjects of theatrical taste'. See John Kinnaird, *William Hazlitt: Critic of Power* (New York, 1978), 166. Interestingly enough, Macready seems to have been something of a 'closet critic' himself. His notes in his copy of *King Lear* are apparently 'intensely personal, and concerned with the poetry, with his experience as a reader: creating a performance certainly, but primarily the performance in the mind, as described by Charles Lamb. They are so private, so removed from, even opposed to, any idea of usefulness to a stage manager, that they are chiefly in Latin, with excursions into Greek'. See J.S. Brattan, 'The Lear of Private Life: Interpretations of King Lear in the Nineteenth Century', in Richard Foulkes (ed.), *Shakespeare and the Victorian Stage* (Cambridge, 1986), 128.
38. Samuel Taylor Coleridge, *Table-Talk of Samuel Taylor Coleridge*, with an introduction by Henry Morley (London, 1884), 38.
39. See J.R. de Jackson, 'Coleridge on Dramatic Illusion and Spectacle in the Performance of Shakespeare's Plays', *Modern Philology* LXII/1 (1964), 13, and T.M. Raysor's introduction to Samuel Taylor Coleridge, *Shakespearean Criticism*, vol. I (London, 1960), xlvi. According to Raysor, 'Like Lamb and Hazlitt, he [Coleridge] did not hesitate to say that he preferred reading Shakespeare to seeing his plays performed on the stage. Whatever reason there may be in such a preference – and it is not without reason – it betrays an unfortunate tendency to handle Shakespeare's plays as closet-dramas, which is characteristic of Romantic criticism.' See also Raysor II.57, 68, 230.
40. Nicholas Brooke, *Shakespeare's Early Tragedies* (London, 1968), 2. Any number of similar statements could be extracted from other common Shakespearean texts. This particular example is employed as a definitive statement of the misconception, and as evidence that even the finest critics have fallen into the trap. Another typical remark from recent scholarship is J.S. Brattan's offering that '[*King Lear*] remained on the defensive throughout that time [after George III's death in 1820], and never shook off the dead hand of misplaced critical adulation of the Bard outside the theatre.' See Brattan, op. cit., 126.
41. Lamb, 'On the Tragedies of Shakespeare', *Works*, op. cit., 129.
42. Even Coleridge in his kinder moments could have claimed his part in establishing Kean's immortal Shakespearean reputation, noting in a letter to Godwin in 1823:

As to Kean, it would be superfluous to say a word – a man, whose genial originality, whose unique and multiform energy in the evolution of Thought, Passion, and Character, in one word whose intense Genius in re-creating the creations of the World's first Genius, are granted – I had almost said – *conclaimed* – even by those whose Preconceptions of Tragedy are at variance with his.

See *Collected Letters of Samuel Taylor Coleridge*, ed. Earl Leslie Griggs (Oxford, 1971), V.269. The fact that he said this about Kean as he was about to send him one of his own play-scripts possibly coloured Coleridge's judgement. For general biographical information on Kean, see Raymund Fitzsimons, *Edmund Kean: Fire from Heaven* (London, 1976); Joseph Donohue, *Theatre in the Age of Kean* (Oxford, 1975); Giles Playfair, *The Flash of Lightning: A Portrait of Edmund Kean* (London, 1983).

43. John Russell Brown, *Shakespeare's Plays in Performance* (London, 1966), 10.

44. Barish, op. cit., 331.

45. Nevertheless Styan appears to be particularly enamoured of the Granville-Barker phrase, repeating it in another book ten years later. See J.L. Styan, *Shakespeare's Stagecraft* (Cambridge, 1967), 3; *The Shakespeare Revolution: Criticism and Performance in the Twentieth Century* (Cambridge, 1977), 5. Aside from Granville-Barker, the ba[r]ker's dozen of scholars whom Styan singles out for individual praise in this latter work are William Poel, Muriel Bradbrook, E.E. Stoll, Levon Schucking, G.F. Reynolds, G.R. Kernodle, G.E. Bentley, Cranford Adams, Walter Hodges, Leslie Hotson, Glynne Wickham, Richard Southern, Bernard Beckermann and Richard Hosley, because 'each shares the idea of non-illusory Elizabethan performance, controlled by the medium of the playhouse' (5).

46. J.L. Styan, *Shakespeare's Stagecraft*, ibid.; in *The Shakespeare Revolution*, ibid., Styan argues that 'It is questionable whether the real advances in Shakespeare scholarship in this century have come through verbal and thematic studies' (4). 'The search is on, for the theatrical effect and experience of the original performance, in the belief that the meaning is in the experience' (9). Aside from Granville-Barker, Styan has also been influenced by Richard David, 'Actors and Scholars: A View of Shakespeare in the Modern Theatre', *Shakespeare Survey* 12 (1959), 77, who argues that 'outside the theatre Shakespeare can have only the thinnest and most unsubstantial of existences'. According to Styan in *The Shakespeare Revolution* 30, David 'sought, as we all do, the essential Shakespeare, and his theme was that the actor and the scholar needed each other'.

47. Barish, op. cit., 3.

48. ibid., 467–8. Given this kind of approach, it is extraordinary to read William B. Worthen's assessment of Barish's book in his *The Idea of the Actor: Drama and the Ethics of Performance* (Berkeley, 1984): 'Barish's examination of antitheatrical prejudice fittingly subordinates

the chorus of protheatrical writers to the voices of their critics' (7). Worthen too at this point in his career appears to have been a would-be 'objective' observer, but his sympathies, which ultimately are not so different from those of Barish, can be established through his statement that 'The site of drama is the site of acting. . . . Our assessment of the drama is enabled by our response to its histrionic means. To capture it in a formula, the ethics of drama are the ethics of acting' (3). There is cause for concern if the anti-theatrical voice truly rests in the custody of these theatrical apologists. Significantly, in his subsequent writing, op. cit., Worthen seems to have moderated his tone on this matter.

49. According to Roland Barthes, *Mythologies*, trans. Annette Lavers (London, 1973), 'the very principle of myth [is that] it transforms history into nature . . . what causes mythical speech to be uttered is perfectly explicit, but it is immediately frozen into something natural; it is not read as a motive, but as a reason' (129). 'In fact, what allows the reader to consume myth innocently is that he does not see it as a semiological system but as an inductive one' (131). Thus the purpose of Barthesian myth is to distort language so as to offer the illusion of commonsense, which in itself is nothing but another form of ideology sustained by the operation of semiological systems.

50. See Mario Praz, *The Romantic Agony*, trans. Angus Davidson (London, 1960), *passim*, for the Romantic answers to the discourses of innocence and authority. Praz traces the development, largely under the influence of the Marquis de Sade, of a literary tradition of perversion, cruelty, horror and hysteria which shapes both the lives and the writings of the great English and European Romantic authors.

51. Quoted in Percy Fitzgerald, *The Kembles* (London, 1871), I.32–3. For another version of Mrs Siddons' writings, see *The Reminiscences of Sarah Kemble Siddons 1773–1785*, ed. William Van Lennep (Cambridge, Mass., 1942).

52. She played Lady Macbeth in the provinces in 1774 and then in London at Drury Lane in February 1785, recreating the role at irregular intervals for another thirty years after that date. See Roger Manvell, *Sarah Siddons: Portrait of an Actress* (London, 1970), 356.

53. Among actors, there is a superstition about the play which precludes them from mentioning it by name. Generally it is known as 'that Scottish play' or 'the Scottish tragedy'. With the number of famous Shakespearean actors who have failed in the leading roles, together with the diabolical subject-matter of the play itself, the superstition seems to be founded on convincing historical and theatrical precedent. Gareth Lloyd Evans calls it 'the curse that gives the stage-history of *Macbeth* a Gothic piquancy'. See his 'Macbeth: 1946–80 at Stratford-upon-Avon' in John Russell Brown (ed.), *Focus On Macbeth* (London, 1982), 103.

54. For a description of modern-day suspicion of writing and textuality, Walter J. Ong, *Orality and Literacy* (London, 1982), 78–81. The relationship between voice and sign is a crucial issue in Jacques Derrida's critique of Saussure in 'Linguistics and Grammatology', *Of Grammatology*, trans. Gayatri Chakravorty Spivack (Baltimore, 1977).

Derrida identifies the implict privilege afforded to speech (*parole*) by Saussure in an argument which explicitly is founded on *langue*, and the apparent tension is aligned with the relative priority of spoken over written discourse in the western philosophical tradition. See Christopher Norris, *Deconstruction: Theory and Practice* (London, 1982), 26–32, for a discussion of Derrida's critique.

55. Walter Benjamin, 'Theses on the Philosophy of History', in *Illuminations*, ed. Hannah Arendt (New York, 1969), 256.

56. Walter Ong, op. cit., 81.

57. All page references for De Quincey's writings are to [*Selections from*] *Thomas De Quincey*, ed. Bonamy Dobrée (London, 1965). For general biographical information, see H.A. Eaton, *Thomas De Quincey* (New York, 1936); J.S. Lyon, *Thomas De Quincey* (New York, 1969); see also *De Quincey as Critic*, ed. John E. Jordan (London, 1973).

58. Quoted in Eaton, op. cit., 374. De Quincey's most familiar celebration of murder comes in his lengthy paper, 'Murder Considered as one of the Fine Arts', in De Quincey, op. cit., 84–103.

59. Thomas De Quincey, 'The Knocking at the Gate in Macbeth' in op. cit., 80–3. The final paragraph, which, after a closely-reasoned argument, represents a massive stylistic shift, is often hailed as a definitive example of the language of bardolatry: 'O mighty poet! Thy works are not as those of other men, simply and merely great works of art, but are also like the phenomena of nature, like the sun and the sea, the stars and the flowers, like frost and snow, rain and dew, hail-storm and thunder, which are to be studied with entire submission of our own faculties, and in the perfect faith that in them there can be no too much or too little, nothing useless or inert, but that, the farther we press in our discoveries, the more we shall see proofs of design and self-supporting arrangement where the careless eye had seen nothing but accident!' The anonymous author of the article on De Quincey in Oscar James Campbell (ed.), *A Shakespeare Encyclopedia* (London, 1966) refers to this paragraph as 'flamboyant bardolatry'.

60. De Quincey, op. cit., 80.

61. ibid., 82.

62. ibid., 83.

63. Shakespeare's employment of the plea includes Rosalind's invitation to 'bid me farewell' in *As You Like It*, Puck's 'Give me your hands if we be friends' in *Midsummer Night's Dream*, and Prospero's famous request for the audience to 'release me from my bands/With the help of your good hands' in *The Tempest*. Less explicit, but still typical pleas for applause come at the end of countless other plays, including in the Epilogue to Massinger's *A New Way to Pay Old Debts*.

2 TERRORISM

1. Charles Humana, *World Human Rights Guide* (New York, 1986), xv. (The initial quote from Sarah Bernhardt appears in Joanna Richardson, *Sarah Bernhardt and her World* (New York, 1977), 202.)

2. For an account of these methods, see for instance Beth Day Romulo,

Inside the Palace: The Rise and Fall of Ferdinand and Imelda Marcos
(New York, 1987); Raymond Bonner, *Waltzing with a Dictator: The
Marcoses and the Making of American Policy* (London, 1987); Iain
Grahame, *Amin and Uganda: A Personal Memoir* (London, 1980).

3. Michael Goldman, *The Actor's Freedom: Toward a Theory of Drama*
(New York, 1975), 3. Goldman's other works on the subject include
Shakespeare and the Energies of Drama (Princeton, 1972); *Acting and
Action in Shakespearean Tragedy* (Princeton, 1985).

4. Goldman (1975), ibid., 6.

5. In this project, Goldman aligns himself with the general thrust of
theatrical theorists such as Eric Bentley, whose major theatrical writings
were preceded by a work on *The Cult of the Superman* (London, 1947).
It is perhaps not entirely frivolous to suggest that this early work by
Bentley on Carlyle and Nietzsche on heroism shaped his subsequent
attitude to the function of the actor.

6. Quoted in Sheridan Morley, *Great Stage Stars* (London, 1986), 413.

7. ibid., 413.

8. ibid., 418.

9. ibid., 419.

10. ibid., 418.

11. ibid., 418.

12. Roland Barthes, *Mythologies*, trans. Annette Lavers (London, 1973),
16.

13. Gustave Flaubert, *Flaubert in Egypt: A Sensibility on Tour*, trans. and
ed. Francis Steegmuller (London, 1983), 220.

14. John Gielgud, *An Actor and his Time*, in collaboration with John Miller
and John Powell (London, 1979), 85. Similarly, the difficulty of 'being'
Richard III without 'being' Olivier preoccupies Anthony Sher in *Year
of the King* (London, 1985). Louis Potter describes how such anxieties
have often lead to actors 'drying' on their lines in 'Actors' Memories
and Plays of the 1590s', *Shakespeare Survey* 42 (1989), 85–6.

15. John Milton, *Paradise Lost* 1.121–4.

16. Billington, op. cit. refers to Williamson's 'attack' on Hamlet, and the
word is also used by Kenneth Tynan to describe Donald Wolfit in *The
Clandestine Marriage* of 1951.

17. Percy Bysshe Shelley, 'On the Medusa of Leonardo da Vinci in the
Florentine Gallery', *The Complete Poetical Works of Percy Bysshe
Shelley*, ed. Thomas Hutchinson (Oxford, 1923), 577–8 (l.35); See also
Mario Praz, *The Romantic Agony*, trans. Angus Davidson (London,
1960), 41–2.

18. Praz, ibid., 121.

19. Frederick J. Hacker, *Crusaders, Criminals, Crazies: Terror and
Terrorism in our Time* (New York, 1976), 297.

20. Praz, op. cit., 113–214.

21. ibid., 125, 186 n.41. Praz also provides the French text of the original
version of the death by lightning, treated in a more conventional
manner.

22. The full quote, which substantially alters the impression conveyed
by the usual extract from it, is: 'Kean is original, but he copies

from himself. His rapid descents from the hyper-tragic to the infra-colloquial, though sometimes productive of great effect, are often unreasonable. To see him act, is like reading Shakespeare by flashes of lightning. I do not think him thorough-bred gentleman enough to play Othello.' See *Table-Talk of Samuel Taylor Coleridge*, with an introduction by Henry Morley (London, 1884), 38.

23. 'Mr Young's Merits Considered', in *Leigh Hunt's Dramatic Criticism, 1808–1831*, ed. Lawrence Huston Houtchens and Carolyn Washburn Houtchens (London, 1950), 25. Quoted also in Joseph W. Donohue, *Dramatic Character in the English Romantic Age* (Princeton, 1970), 318.

24. Morley, op. cit., 38.

25. Hacker, op. cit., 90–1, gives the example of the mass-murderer Stephen Nash who, condemned to death, 'wanted to die, imagining that his execution would be a big public event attended by important persons. He was afraid of nothing except being deprived of his last spectacular opportunity . . .'.

26. *Henry V*, Prologue 19–25.

27. Morley, op. cit., 38.

28. See *European Romanticism: Self-Definition*, compiled by Lilian R. Furst (London, 1980), 98.

29. Paul Feyerabend, *Against Method: Outline of an Anarchist Theory of Knowledge* (London, 1975), 24.

3 THE STOCKHOLM SYNDROME

1. The aborted robbery and the siege which followed were described in intimate detail in various contemporary newspaper reports. See, for instance, *Newsweek*, 10 September 1973, *Die Presse*, 29, 30 August and 8 September 1973, *Chicago Tribune* 23, 27, 29 August 1973. Subsequently, the 'Stockholm Syndrome' has become the favoured topic in books and scholarly texts dealing with hostage crises from counter-terrorist, victimological and psychiatric perspectives. Among the more important of these articles are Thomas Strentz, 'The Stockholm Syndrome: Law Enforcement Policy and Hostage Behaviour', in Frank M. Ochberg and David A. Soskis (eds), *Victims of Terrorism* (Boulder, 1982), 149–63; Hans Joachim Schneider, 'Victims of Terror', in *The Victim in International Perspective* (Berlin, 1982), 298–304; Ronald D. Crelinsten (ed.), *Dimensions of Victimisation in the Context of Terrorist Acts* (Montreal, 1977); Frederick J. Hacker, 'Poor Devils', in *Crusaders, Criminals, Crazies: Terror and Terrorism in our Time* (New York, 1976), 105–18.

2. *Newsweek*, 10 September 1973, 28.

3. Hacker, op. cit., 109; *Newsweek*, ibid., 29.

4. Hacker, ibid., 109–10.

5. ibid., 108.

6. *Newsweek*, op. cit., 29.

7. There is considerable confusion over who said what and to whom at the end of the siege. Certainly one of the hostages, probably Enmark, said

'See you again' to one of the criminals, probably Olofsson. A report in *The Washington Post, Parade Magazine* supplement of 14 November 1976, suggested that in fact Enmark became engaged to Olofsson. See Strentz, op. cit., 161.

8. Strentz, ibid., 150; Hacker, op. cit., 111.
9. *Newsweek*, op. cit., 29; Hacker, ibid., 110.
10. See Anna Freud, *The Ego and the Mechanisms of Defence* (New York, 1974), 42. See also Strentz, op. cit., 150–2; Schneider, op. cit., 301.
11. Strentz, op. cit., 161. Another fascinating example comes in Richard Brockman's 'Notes While Being Hijacked', quoted in Abraham H. Miller, *Terrorism and Hostage Negotiations* (Boulder, 1980), 44. At the end of an American airline hijacking in which he had been a hostage, Brockman remembered the aircraft captain making an announcement over the intercom:

> 'This is the captain speaking.' His voice is clean, no cracks. 'We have all been through an incredible experience. But it is over for us. No one is hurt. However, it is not over for our hijackers. Their ordeal is just beginning. They have a cause. They are brave committed people. Idealistic dedicated people. Like the people who helped to shape our country. They are trying to do the same for theirs. I think we should all give them a hand.'
>
> I look around me. The hijackers are smiling. The audience is applauding. It has come full turn. We arrive at the theater. Stop clapping, you fools. The cadence continues. Tinker. Tailor. Actor. Fool. Let me out of here. Open the gate. Please let me out of here. No, the last curtain call.

12. Hacker, op. cit., 137–78.
13. ibid., 112.
14. Schneider, op. cit., 302.
15. ibid., 298–9.
16. The refusal to make any concessions to the ideology of his captors was one of the factors which British ambassador to Uruguay Geoffrey Jackson believed contributed to his survival at the hands of his Tupamaro captors during a 244-day ordeal in 1971. See Geoffrey Jackson, *Surviving the Long Night* (New York, 1973). Jackson maintained his dignity to such an extent that his guards were changed regularly because it seemed that he might convince them of the foolishness of their cause and the justice of his own (p. 49). Another captive of the Tupamaros, the American agronomist Dr Claude Fly, also maintained sanity and self-respect during his imprisonment, in his case by writing a 600-page autobiography and a 50-page analysis of the New Testament. See C.L. Fly, *No Hope but God* (New York, 1973), 151ff.
17. For a detailed analysis of the Beilen train siege, see Frank M. Ochberg, 'A Case Study: Gerard Vaders', in Ochberg and Soskis (eds), op. cit., 9–35.
18. Ochberg, op. cit., 9–10; see also George Brock *et al.*, *Siege: Six Days at the Iranian Embassy* (Melbourne, 1980), 69.
19. See for instance, William Hazlitt, 'Mr Kemble's Retirement', *The*

Complete Works of William Hazlitt, ed. P.P. Howe (London, 1930–4), V.374–9.

20. Schneider, op. cit., 299.
21. Jerzy Grotowski, *Towards a Poor Theatre* (Denmark, 1968), 57.
22. Richard Schechner, 'Ethology and Theatre', in *Essays on Performance Theory 1970–1976* (New York, 1977). According to Schechner, p. 164, 'Drama connects two basic actions: (1) misunderstanding, a break in communication, a confusion of messages, irony; (2) violence – especially political and sexual violence, often associated in drama – rebellion against authority and decency.'
23. Frederick J. Hacker, op. cit., p. 3, makes the point that 'All violence is aggressive, but not all aggression is violent; there are aggressive and nonaggressive alternatives to violence. Essential and inevitable aggression manifests itself in innumerable forms, such as verbal aggression, competition, and aggressive pursuits, that are nonviolent and may be individually and collectively productive and creative.' The aggressive impulse, in short, can be channelled into theatre as well as violence, or simultaneously into both, or even from one into the other.
24. Antonin Artaud, 'The Theatre of Cruelty First Manifesto', in *The Theatre and its Double*, trans. Victor Corti (London, 1970, 1977), 77.
25. Antonin Artaud, 'Letters of Cruelty' in ibid., 79.
26. Schechner, op. cit., 164.
27. ibid., 180.
28. ibid., 164. This language of cultural anthropology has been popular among recent theatrical scholars. David Bevington borrows from Victor Turner in addressing stage language in terms of 'liminality' and 'communitas' in his *Action is Eloquence: Shakespeare's Language of Gesture* (Cambridge, Mass., 1984), 137–8.
29. Schechner, ibid., 189.
30. ibid., 189.
31. ibid., 190.
32. ibid.
33. ibid., 193; see also Konrad Lorenz, 'The Role of Aggression in Group Formation', in B. Schaffner (ed.), *Transactions of the Conference on Group Processes of 1957* (New York, 1959), 182.
34. Schechner, op. cit., 194.
35. Anne Righter, for instance, has argued that 'A curious sense of violence surrounds many of the mysteries, a suggestion that the actors themselves in their zeal sometimes confused illusion with reality.' See her *Shakespeare and the Idea of the Play* (London, 1964), 17.
36. Richard Clutterbuck, *Kidnap and Ransom: The Response* (London, 1978), 105–6.
37. It's the theatrical version of the technique of *ostranenie* identified by Victor Shklovsky. See Terence Hawkes, *Structuralism and Semiotics* (London, 1977), 62–3.
38. This problem was often the cause for humour in the popular drama of the Tudor Age, with audience members and dramatic characters often taunting actors for their unsuccessful impersonations. See Robert

Weimann, *Shakespeare and the Popular Dramatic Tradition*, ed. Robert Schwartz (Baltimore, 1978), 44–6.

39. It is now generally agreed that it is not just the quantity of time which determines identification, but more especially the quality. See Ronald D. Crelinsten, 'Terrorist Victimisation: The Interface between Research and Policy', in Ronald D. Crelinsten and Denis Szabo (eds), *Hostage-Taking* (Lexington, 1979), 142; see also Miller, op. cit., 43–4.

40. This is why Donald Wolfit actually made a deliberate habit of appearing with inferior performers. See Sheridan Morley, *The Great Stage Stars* (Sydney, 1986), s.v. 'Wolfit'; see also Ronald Harwood, *Sir Donald Wolfit C.B.E.: His Life and Work in the Unfashionable Theatre* (London, 1971); Donald Wolfit, *First Interval: The Autobiography* (London, 1954).

41. Wolfgang Amadeus Mozart, *Il Dissoluto Punito, Ossia Don Giovanni*, K.527, libretto by Lorenzo da Ponte (1787).

42. See especially, Hans Joachim Schneider (ed.), *The Victim in International Perspective* (Berlin, 1982); Stephen Schafer, *Victimology: The Victim and his Criminal* (Reston, Virginia, 1977); Ezzat Abdel Fattah, 'Towards a Criminological Classification of Victims', *International Criminal Police Review* 209 (1967), 162–9; Marvin E. Wolfgang, 'Analytical Categories for Research on Victimisation', in A.M. Schafer (ed.), *Kriminologische Wegzeichen, Festschrift für Hans von Hentig* (Hamburg, 1967), 167–85; Thorsten Sellin and Marvin E. Wolfgang, *The Measurement of Delinquency* (New York, 1964).

43. Sigmund Freud, *The Essentials of Psychoanalysis*, selected by Anna Freud (Harmondsworth, 1986), 302.

44. Plato, *The Republic*, 2nd revised edn, trans. Desmond Lee (Harmondsworth, 1974), 435 (#604e).

45. ibid., 436–7 (#606a–d).

46. This is treated more comprehensively in subsequent chapters.

47. Plato, op. cit., 157 (#398a).

4 VIOLENT COMEDY

1. See Thomas Sebeok (ed.), *Carnival!* (Berlin, 1984); Umberto Eco, 'The Frames of Comic Freedom', 1–10, in this volume notes that 'there is something wrong with this theory of cosmic carnivalisation as global liberation. There is some diabolic trick in the appeal of the great cosmic/comic carnival. Bachtin [*sic*] was right in seeing the manipulation of a profound drive towards liberation and subversion in medieval Carnival. The hyper-Bachtinian ideology of carnival as *actual* liberation may, however, be wrong' (3).

2. Occasionally these murders are reported during the contemporary accounts of the festivities, but usually this is only done in the context of there being fewer than in previous years. The subsequent reports then generally disprove this initial comment.

3. The major works on Carnival as a specifically social (as opposed to theatrical) phenomenon are Emile Durkheim, *The Elementary Forms of*

Religious Life, trans. J. Swain (London, 1915); Victor Turner, *Dramas, Fields and Metaphors: Symbolic Action in Human Society* (Ithaca, 1974); Victor Turner, *From Ritual to Theatre: The Human Seriousness of Play* (New York, 1982); Victor Turner, *The Ritual Process: Structure and Anti-Structure* (Ithaca, 1977); Roger Caillois, *Man and the Sacred*, trans. Meyer Brasch (Glencoe, Ill., 1959); LeRoy Ladurie, *Carnival in Romans*, trans. Mary Feeney (New York, 1979); René Girard, *Violence and the Sacred*, trans. Patrick Gregory (Baltimore, 1977); Natalie Zemon Davis, *Society and Culture in Early Modern France* (Stanford, 1975); Peter Burke, *Popular Culture in Early Modern Europe* (London, 1978).

4. Burke, op. cit., 187. Caillois, op. cit. and Girard, op. cit. treat violence in both literal and symbolic manifestations as the crucial feature of Carnival.

5. Burke, ibid., 183–4.

6. ibid., 212.

7. ibid., 204.

8. Ladurie, op. cit., concentrates on the Romans disturbance.

9. Burke, op. cit., 204.

10. Davis, op. cit., 119.

11. Burke, op. cit., 204; Davis, op. cit., 118–19.

12. On *charivari*, see ibid., *passim*; Violet Alford, 'Rough Music or Charivari', *Folklore* 70 (1959), 505–18; Martin Buzacott, *Charivari: A Novel* (Sydney, 1987).

13. Davis, op. cit., 117.

14. ibid., 100.

15. Alford, op. cit., 510.

16. On execution as a dramatic performance, see Burke, op. cit., 197–8; Ralegh's execution as a work of street theatre is described in intimate detail in chapter 1 of Stephen Greenblatt, *Sir Walter Ralegh: The Renaissance Man and his Roles* (New Haven, 1973).

17. On the 'balladisation' of executions, see Hazlitt, 'On Poetry in General', *Lectures on the English Poets*, in *The Complete Works of William Hazlitt*, ed. P.P. Howe (London, 1930–4), V.7.

18. The major works on Carnival's influence on literature and theatre are Mikhail Bakhtin, *Rabelais and his World*, trans. Helene Iswolsky (Cambridge, Mass., 1968); C.L. Barber, *Shakespeare's Festive Comedy* (Princeton, 1959); Robert Weimann, *Shakespeare and the Popular Tradition in the Theatre*, ed. Robert Schwartz (Baltimore, 1978); Michael Bristol, *Carnival and Theatre: Plebeian Culture and the Structure of Authority in Renaissance England* (New York, 1985).

19. Bristol, op. cit., 4, potentially offers the most radical view of Carnival, by articulating 'the capacity of popular culture to resist penetration and control by the power structure', but he concludes that in fact 'Carnival is not anti-authoritarian. But it is a general refusal to understand any fixed and final allocation of authority' (212). This is ultimately a partial restatement of the Bakhtin thesis.

20. See Bakhtin, op. cit., esp. 10–12; Barber, op. cit., esp. 4.

21. See James Black, 'King Lear: Art Upside-Down', *Shakespeare Survey*

33 (1980), 35–42.

22. On the possible doubling of Cordelia and the Fool, see Thomas B. Stroup, 'Cordelia and the Fool', *Shakespeare Quarterly* XII (1961), 127–32; Richard Abrams, 'The Double Casting of Cordelia and Lear's Fool: A Theatrical View', *Texas Studies in Language and Literature* 27 (1985), 354–68; see also Martin Buzacott, *Shakespeare's Actors and their Doubles* (M.A. thesis, University of Wales, 1986), 67–8.

23. Davis, op. cit., 111.

24. ibid., 97.

25. For a very different interpretation of *Hamlet* as a form of Carnival humiliation, see Bristol, op. cit., 207–9. According to Bristol, Claudius is the Carnivalesque Lord of Misrule, being 'a sovereign figure of authority who is also pleased to indulge in drinking bouts and indiscreet public fondlings' (207). But surely Bristol is mistaken and Hamlet is a more likely contender for the title of Lord of Misrule, while Claudius is the *victim* of Hamlet's *charivari* re-enactment of the crime.

26. *Hamlet* III.ii.238–41. See Shakespeare's *Complete Works*, Stanley Wells and Gary Taylor (general eds) (Oxford, 1986).

27. It's a comedy which distances the emotions and which, under the guise of madness, is manipulated by the calculating, intellectual side of the fools for their own advantage. See Henri Bergson, *Laughter: An Essay on the Meaning of the Comic*, trans. Cloudesley Brereton and Fred Rothwell (London, 1911), 4–5.

28. The text which immortalised the 'wise fools' label is Robert H. Goldsmith, *Wise Fools in Shakespeare* (Liverpool, 1958); but see also Leslie Hotson, *Shakespeare's Motley* (New York, 1952, 1971) and the various works on Robert Armin, n.72 below.

29. See for instance Joseph Allen Bryant, 'Shakespeare's Falstaff and the Mantle of Dick Tarlton', *Studies in Philology* 51 (1954), 149–62; James Monaghan, 'Falstaff and his Forebears', *Studies in Philology* 18 (1921), 353–61; H.F. Lippincott, 'King Lear and the Fools of Robert Armin', *Shakespeare Quarterly* XXVI (1975), 243–53; Martin Buzacott, *Robert Armin at the Curtain and the Globe* (B.A. Hons thesis, Macquarie University, 1983), 35–64.

30. Weimann, op. cit., 44–6.

31. Quoted in Stephen Greenblatt, *Renaissance Self-Fashioning: From More to Shakespeare* (Chicago, 1980), 13.

32. Neither the actor nor the terrorist necessarily feels the passions which he enacts. The terrorist, for instance, rarely has anything personal against his victim, but will commit extreme acts of aggression against him nonetheless. He generally has to work hard to establish hatred and, as in the Stockholm Syndrome, often the opposite response is forthcoming. Similarly, the actor needn't necessarily feel the elderly rage of Lear to play Lear, provided that his actions are in accordance with the implied attitude. It is certainly often helpful to identify with the role, but by no means mandatory.

33. The term is adapted from Roland Barthes, *Writing Degree Zero*, trans. Annette Lavers and Colin Smith (London, 1967), to refer to a style of acting (the theatrical version of Barthes' *écriture*) which regards itself

as 'innocent' and not a style at all. The structuralist project of course is to reveal the ideology underlying this theory of 'natural' acting, and to expose the identification which it entails as nothing more than an alternative mode of presentation.

34. The Shakespearean company acquired the play from the Queen's Revels Company. An anonymous tire-man, Will Sly, John Sincklo, Richard Burbage, Henry Condell and John Lowin appear as themselves, discussing their acquisition of the play, their additions to it ('only as your sallet to your great feast' according to Burbage) and even their roles:

> BURBAGE: . . . I must leave you sir. *Exit*
> SINKLO: Doth he play the Malcontent?
> CONDELL: Yes, sir.
>
> (Induction 11.81–2.)

The Induction gives the players some opportunity for ribald jesting and closes with Sly's extemporised prologue to the play. See John Marston, *The Malcontent*, ed. Bernard Harris (London, 1967).

35. The extreme version of scholars arguing for actors playing themselves comes in T.W. Baldwin's *Organisation and Personnel of the Shakespearean Company* (Princeton, 1927), which is still the standard text for Shakespearean casting. On the basis of this supposition that actors play themselves consistently, Baldwin attempted to establish various 'lines' of specialisation within Shakespearean drama.

36. Bertolt Brecht, *Brecht on Theatre*, trans. John Willett (London, 1964), 136.

37. ibid., 137.

38. ibid., 138.

39. ibid., 139.

40. ibid., 136.

41. Jerzy Grotowski, *Towards a Poor Theatre* (Denmark, 1968), 117.

42. Petr Bogatyrev, 'Semiotics in the Folk Theatre', 33–49; 'Forms and Functions of Folk Theatre', 51–6 in Ladislaw Matejka and Irwin R. Titunik (eds), *Semiotics of Art: Prague School Contributions* (Cambridge, Mass., 1976).

43. Bogatyrev, ibid., 48.

44. ibid., 48.

45. Stanley Wells, *Literature and Drama* (London, 1970); S.L. Bethell, *Shakespeare and the Popular Dramatic Tradition* (London, 1948); Robert Weimann, op. cit.; Michael Goldman, *The Actor's Freedom: Toward a Theory of Drama* (New York, 1975); J.L. Styan, *Shakespeare's Stagecraft* (Cambridge, 1967).

46. Glynne Wickham, *Early English Stages*, 4 vols (London, 1963–7), 1300–1660 2, Preface vii–viii.

47. See for instance, Fabian's 'If this were played upon a stage, now, I could condemn it as an improbable fiction', in *Twelfth Night*, III.iv.125–6, quoted from Shakespeare's *Complete Works*, Stanley Wells and Gary Taylor (general eds) (Oxford, 1986).

48. The pictorial representations of Tarlton include the title page of

Tarlton's Jests (1613 edn) and the woodcut held in the British Library (Harleian MS 3885, f.19).

49. Bernard Spivack, *Shakespeare and the Allegory of Evil* (New York, 1958), 130–1. The only appearance made by the Devil in the approximately forty extant plays from the 1500–60 period is in *Lusty Juventus*. Prior to this, he appears in eight plays, usually as a helpless target for the Vice's scurrilous jests. After 1560 he appears in minor roles in five more plays.

50. For the most detailed of the many biographical outlines of Tarlton's life, see Halliwell's introduction to his edition of *Tarlton's Jests and Tarlton's News out of Purgatory* (London, 1844). All subsequent references to *Tarlton's Jests* are to this edition. Halliwell reprints most of the major contemporary references to Tarlton in this introduction. Other works on Tarlton include E.K. Chambers' *Elizabethan Stage* (Oxford, 1923), vol. II, 342–5; Muriel Bradbrook, *The Rise of the Common Player* (London, 1962), 162–77; J.A. Bryant, 'Shakespeare's Falstaff and the Mantle of Dick Tarlton', *Studies in Philology* 51 (1954), 149–62; W.J. Lawrence, 'On the Underrated Genius of Dick Tarlton', *Speeding up Shakespeare* (London, 1937), 17–38; David Wiles, *Shakespeare's Clown: Actor and Text in the Elizabethan Playhouse* (Cambridge, 1987), 11–23. In *Tarlton's Jests* there are several examples of Tarlton indulging in Vice-like boxing of people's ears. See for instance 'Tarlton's Jest of a Boxe on the Eare' in Halliwell's edition, 20.

51. An eighteenth-century engraving based on the woodcut on the cover of *Tarlton's Jests* (1613) and showing Tarlton with tabor and pipe is marked 'Richard Tarlton one of the first Actors in Shakespears Plays'.

52. Tarlton had made an inappropriate jest about Ralegh's influence on the Queen ('See, the Knave commands the Queen'), incurring the Queen's wrath, and then turning his attention to the overgreat power and riches of the Earl of Leicester in response. See E.K. Chambers, op. cit., II.342.

53. In this he seems to have been rather like Lear's Fool, certainly labouring continually under the threat of whipping, but never actually enduring the public humiliation.

54. Cusanus (Nicholas of Cusa), *De Docta Ignorantia* (1440); Thomas à Kempis, *Imitatio Christi* (1441), both quoted in Walter Kaiser, *Praisers of Folly: Erasmus, Rabelais, Shakespeare* (London, 1964), 9.

55. Ed. Harry Levin, *Selected Works of Ben Jonson* (New York, 1938), 12.

56. Quotations from the play are given in the style of the 1617 Quarto held in the British Library, which is preferable linguistically to the modern versions. However, owing to the inaccessibility of that volume, the line references are to Seymour Pitcher's modern edition in *The Case for Shakespeare's Authorship of the Famous Victories* (London, 1961). There are two extant texts, one printed in 1598 and this latter one in 1617, both of which refer to it as having been played 'by the Queen's Majesty's Players' and 'by the King's Majesty's Servants' respectively. See Pitcher, 166. It was entered in the Stationer's Register in 1594, but as Tarlton played in it – the proof is in one of *Tarlton's Jests*, op. cit.,

24–5 – it originally must have been written and performed before his death in 1588. The plot covers the same narrative span as Shakespeare's *Henry IV and V*, beginning with the pranks of young Hal, continuing through the war with France, and the eventual marriage to Katherine. A.R. Humphreys in his Arden edition of Shakespeare's *1 Henry IV* (London, 1960), notes that 'Reading that chaotic anonymous production *The Famous Victories* is like going through the *Henry IV–Henry V* sequence in a bad dream, so close to Shakespeare is it in fragments, so worlds removed in skill', xxxii.

57. *Famous Victories*, op. cit., Scene 2, ll.123–6.
58. ibid., Scene 2, ll.26–33.
59. Henry Peacham, *Thalia's Banquet* (London, 1620), Ep. 94.
60. Thomas Nashe, 'Pierce Penniless his Supplication to the Devil', *The Unfortunate Traveller and Other Works*, ed. J.B. Steane (Harmondsworth, 1972), 85.
61. Robert Greene, *News from Heaven and Hell* (1593).

62.   ROBIN: Hold him neighbour Cobler.
                Why I see thou art a plaine Clowne.
        DERICKE: Am I a Clowne, sownes masters,
                I am sure all we Gentlemen Clownes in
                Kent scant goe so
                Well: Sownes, you know Clownes very well.
                Heare you, are you Master Constable, and you be
                    speake:
                For I will not take it at his hands.

                                                    (2, ll.34–40.)

It appears that Tarlton is not in his usual russet outfit which distinguishes the rustic clown from the urban comedian.

63. The famous reference from Fuller's *Worthies*, quoted in Halliwell's edition of *Tarlton's Jests*, op. cit., xxvii.
64. *Famous Victories*, Scene 7, ll.1–14.
65. ibid., Scene 10, ll.56–9.
66. Robert Weimann, *Shakespeare and the Popular Tradition in the Theatre*, ed. Robert Schwartz (Baltimore, 1978), 12–13.
67. Weimann, ibid., 14, quotes Reich's struggle between a 'refined mythical idealism and a popular burlesque realism' in the Classical comedies. See Hermann Reich, *Der Mimus* (Berlin, 1903), 28.
68. T.W. Baldwin, *Organisation and Personnel of the Shakespearean Company* (Princeton, 1927), insert pp. 228–9, suggests that Armin played Touchstone, Feste, First Gravedigger, Evans, Clown (*Othello*), Pompey, Fool (*Timon*), Lear's Fool, Porter (*Macbeth*), Clown (*Antony and Cleopatra*), Lavache, Boult, First Citizen (*Coriolanus*), Cloten, Autolycus, Trinculo. It is assumed that Armin took over Will Kemp's role of Dogberry. A reference in the Dedication to Armin's translation of *The Italian Taylor and his Boy* (1609) makes the allusion: 'Pardon I pray you, the boldness of a Beggar, who hath been writ downe for an Asse in his time ... notwithstanding his Constableship and Office' (A3).

69. For an interpretation of the Gravediggers' scene from the Carnival perspective, see Michael Bristol, *Carnival and Theatre: Plebeian Culture and the Structure of Authority in Renaissance England* (New York, 1985), 188–96.

70. A modern edition of *Thersytes* appears in Marie Axton's *Three Tudor Classical Interludes* (Cambridge, 1982). Possibly written by Nicholas Udall (1504–56), *Thersytes* was printed in about 1562. In the plot, the cowardly anti-hero sets off for war with swaggering words and a Herculean club, browbeating Mulciber into forging him some armour. Loftily resisting his mother's entreaties to stay at home, Thersytes shows his valour in combat with a passing snail, but soon takes refuge when an honest English soldier, Miles, appears. A letter arrives from Ulysses, seeking a cure for his son Telemachus' worms, and Thersytes' mother effects the cure. Thersytes launches a Skeltonic tirade against the old 'witch' until he is finally chased away once and for all by the return of Miles, who points the moral 'That great barking dogges do not most byte'.

71. 'How Tarlton made Armin his adopted sonne, to succeed him', *Tarlton's Jests*, op. cit., 22–3: 'Tarlton keeping a tavern in Gracious street. . . . And this Armin, being then a wag, came often thither. . . . The boy . . . so loved Tarlton after, that regarding him with more respect, hee used to his playes, and fell in a league with his humour: and private practise brought him to present playing, and at this houre performes the same, where, at the Globe on the Banks side mean may see him.'

72. For biographical information on Robert Armin, see Charles S. Felver, *Robert Armin, Shakespeare's Fool* (Kent, Ohio, 1961); Austin K. Gray, 'Robert Armine, the Foole', *P.M.L.A.* XLII (1927); H.F. Lippincott, 'King Lear and the Fools of Robert Armin', *Shakespeare Quarterly* XXVI (1975), 243–53; Alexander S. Liddie, *An Old-Spelling, Critical Edition of the Two Maids of More-clacke* (New York, 1979); Martin Buzacott, *Robert Armin at the Curtain and the Globe* (B.A. Hons thesis, Macquarie University, 1983); David Wiles, op. cit., 136–63. A facsimile edition of Armin's *Collected Works* has been compiled by John Feather in two volumes (New York, 1972). For a full bibliography, see John Feather, 'A Check-List of the Works of Robert Armin', *The Library* 26 (1971), 165–72. An annotated bibliography is in Buzacott, ibid., 99–101.

73. On the original title page of *Foole upon Foole*, Armin referred to himself as 'Clonnico de Curtanio Snuffe', but in the second edition of 1605 he altered this to 'Clonnico del Mondo'. When the whole work was revised and republished as *Nest of Ninnies* in 1608, it was attributed simply to 'Robert Armin'. For the various texts, see John Feather's facsimile edition, ibid. Another edition is H.F. Lippincott's *A Shakespeare Jestbook: Robert Armin's* Foole upon Foole *(1600); A Critical, Old-Spelling Edition* (Salzburg, 1973).

74. The major alteration was an additional moral commentary in which an extravagant woman seeks out the divine philosopher Sotto, who shows her the parade of ninnies in his crystal ball, and who provides various

opportunities for cynical and world-weary depictions of the stupidity of humanity.

75. 'Who's the Foole now?', *Quips upon Questions* (1600), B3ᵛ–B4ᵛ, which includes the couplet, 'Many seeme wise as long as they had us'd schooles,/When in the end God knowes most seeme but fooles'(B3ᵛ).

5 THE ROMANTICS

1. Colin Brooks, 'England 1782–1832: The Historical Context', in Stephen Prickett (ed.), *The Romantics* (London, 1981), 15.

2. ibid., *passim*; for further information on the internal and external politics of the age, see also David Thomson, *England in the Nineteenth Century, 1815–1914* (Harmondsworth, 1950); Anthony Wood, *Nineteenth Century Britain, 1815–1914* (London, 1960); Elie Halevy, *A History of the English People in the Nineteenth Century*, 6 vols (London, 1924–48); J.H. Grainger, 'The View from Britain II; The Moralizing Island', in Eugene Kamenka and F.B. Smith (eds), *Intellectuals and Revolution: Socialism and the Experience of 1848* (London, 1979); J.L. Talmon, *Romanticism and Revolt, Europe 1815–1848* (London, 1967).

3. Raymund Fitzsimons, *Edmund Kean: Fire from Heaven* (London, 1976), 116–17.

4. The major works on the English Romantic Theatre include Allardyce Nicoll, *A History of English Drama 1660–1900* (Cambrige, 1952–9); George Rowell, *The Victorian Theatre 1792–1914*, 2nd edn (Cambridge, 1978); Joseph Donohue, *Theatre in the Age of Kean* (Oxford, 1975); Joseph Donohue, *Dramatic Character in the English Romantic Age* (Princeton, 1970). See also Jonathan Bate's, *Shakespearean Constitutions: Politics, Theatre, Criticism 1730–1830* (Oxford, 1989) for an analysis of the politics of Shakespearean drama in the period.

5. The Letters Patent, or Charters, were first awarded to Thomas Killigrew for Drury Lane and Sir William Davenant for Lincoln's Inn Fields, the latter eventually descending to Covent Garden. The monopoly on 'serious drama' enjoyed by these theatres lasted until 1843. See Phyllis Hartnoll (ed.), *The Oxford Companion to Theatre*, 4th edn (Oxford, 1983), 629.

6. Rowell, op. cit., 3–4; for Leigh Hunt on the O.P. riots, see 'Covent Garden Redecorated', *Leigh Hunt's Dramatic Criticism, 1808–1831*, ed. Lawrence Huston Houtchens and Carolyn Washburn Houtchens (London, 1950), 26–31.

7. ibid., 4.

8. Samuel Taylor Coleridge, 'Genius and Public Taste', in *Shakespearean Criticism, vol. 1*, ed. T.M. Raysor (London, 1960), 184.

9. Charles Lamb, 'On the Custom of Hissing at the Theatres, etc.', 113. All page references for Lamb's writings are to *The Works in Prose and Verse of Charles and Mary Lamb, vol. 1*, ed. Thomas Hutchinson (Oxford, 1924), hereafter referred to as *Works*.

10. Joseph Donohue, *Theatre in the Age of Kean* (Oxford, 1975), 82.

11. On whores at the theatre, see William Hazlitt, 'Old Cloaks', XX.206–8;

all page references for Hazlitt's writings are to *The Complete Works of William Hazlitt*, ed. P.P. Howe (London, 1930–4), hereafter referred to as *Works*. See also his 'Our National Theatres', XX.287–8, for the 'disrepute' that had fallen onto the boxes with the departure of the nobility.

12. Kathleen Coburn, 'Hazlitt on the Disinterested Imagination', in James V. Logan *et al.* (eds), *Some British Romantics* (Ohio, 1966) refers to the 'moralistic Puritan background of [Hazlitt's] idealism' (188).

13. Gas-jets were situated in rows on the floor of the stage, or ornamentally on brackets around the circle front. See Richard Southern, *The Victorian Theatre: A Pictorial Survey* (London, 1970), 71. See also the same author's *Changeable Scenery: Its Origin and Development in the British Theatre* (London, 1952), 256.

14. Hartnoll, op. cit., 188, 231.

15. Rowell, op. cit., 25–7.

16. Leigh Hunt actually advocated the removal of the Fool in *Lear*, because the character was 'out of date'. See Hunt, op. cit., 15. Coleridge on the other hand thought that 'the contrast of the Fool wonderfully heightens the colouring of some of the most painful situations'. See Coleridge, op. cit., II.47. On another occasion, Coleridge called the Fool 'one of the profoundest and most astonishing of [Shakespeare's] characters', op. cit., II.197.

17. Rowell, op. cit., 14–16, 22.

18. ibid., 23; Hartnoll, op. cit., 81–2. In regard to animals on the stage, Hunt noted: 'That actors should make beasts of themselves is no new thing; but the *gravis Esopus* of our Stage, Mr Kemble, must turn beasts into actors; and accordingly, after having had dog actors at Drury-Lane, and jack-ass actors (emblematic wags!) at Sadler's Wells, we are now presented with horse actors at "classical" Covent-Garden'. See Hunt, *Dramatic Criticism*, op. cit., 45.

19. But at the very same time that Revolution gripped France, the neoclassical approach to Shakespearean interpretation still predominated, stressing the aesthetic value of unity and decorum, features which Shakespearean drama was deemed to lack, despite the obvious genius of the author. It was this view which Coleridge, Schlegel, Hazlitt and the other Romantics attacked as the *raison d'être* of their critical project. In the words of Coleridge, the ambition was to prove that in fact Shakespeare's judgement was equal to his genius, a statement which must have contributed as much to nationalism as it did to Shakespearean criticism. See for instance John Payne Collier's notes on Coleridge's lectures of 1811–12 in *Coleridge on Shakespeare: The Text of the Lectures of 1811–1812*, ed. R.A. Foakes (London, 1971), 58; and *Shakespearean Criticism*, ed. Raysor, op. cit., I.194.

20. Michel Foucault, *The Order of Things: An Archaeology of the Human Sciences* (London, 1970), 304.

21. Hazlitt, *The Characters of Shakespeare's Plays*, in *Works*, ibid., IV.300.

22. ibid., 301.

23. According to Hunt, '. . . that a mere rhymer, whose dullness has become proverbial, should create whole scenes of his own [in *King*

Lear] and adorn them with a few extracts from Shakespeare, that he should turn the current of our poet's feeling into scanty sprinklings over his own barren fancy and then cry out, "How fertile I am!" – is really a violation of a man's literary property.' See 'King Lear Revived', 28 May 1808, in Hunt, op. cit., 15; see also Stanley Wells, 'Shakespeare in Leigh Hunt's Theatre Criticism', *Essays and Studies* 33 (1980), 129; Stanley Wells, 'Shakespeare in Hazlitt's Theatre Criticism', *Shakespeare Survey* 35 (1982), 47.

24. Lamb, *Works*, op. cit., 134.
25. According to Hunt, 'Puffing and plenty of tickets were, however, the system of the day. It was an interchange of amenities over the dinner-table; a flattery of power on the one side, and puns on the other; and what the public took for a criticism on a play was a draft upon the box-office, or reminiscences of last Thursday's salmon and lobster-sauce.' See *The Autobiography of Leigh Hunt* (London, 1891), 138.
26. Lamb, 'On the Tragedies of Shakespeare', *Works*, op. cit., 136.
27. Lamb, 'On the Custom of Hissing', *Works*, ibid., 112.
28. For an analysis of Coleridge's *Remorse*, see Joseph Donohue, *Dramatic Character in the English Romantic Age* (Princeton, 1970), 291–300.
29. Fitzsimons, op. cit., 128.
30. ibid., *passim*; Byron was among the many authors with whom Kean had a fiery relationship. See Jonas Barish, *The Antitheatrical Prejudice* (Berkeley, 1981), 332.
31. ibid., 129.
32. Included in Hunt's *Critical Essays on Performers of the London Theatres*, 21, and quoted in Alan S. Downer, 'Players and Painted Stage: Nineteenth Century Acting', *P.M.L.A.* 61 (1946), 530. Downer gives an authoritative account of the 'teapot' school of Kemble. Another celebrated insult by Hunt, quoted by Stanley Wells, 'Shakespeare in Leigh Hunt's Theatre Criticism', *Essays and Studies* 33 (1980), 125, is that 'it was not the man but his mask'. In 'King Lear Revived', *Dramatic Criticism*, op. cit., 20, Hunt says of Kemble that '. . . he is always stiff, always precise, and he will never, as long as he lives, be able to act anything mad unless it be a melancholy mad statue'. In 'The Tragic Actors', 104, Hunt also says of Kemble, 'He feels, as it were, in externals, and speaks in hyphens'.
33. Hazlitt, *A View of the English Stage*, in *Works*, op. cit., V.304.
34. Samuel Taylor Coleridge, *Shakespearean Criticism, vol. 1*, ed. T.M. Raysor, op. cit., 74.
35. On Hazlitt's 'disinterested imagination' and its influence on Keats, see Jonathan Bate's *Shakespeare and the English Romantic Imagination* (Oxford, 1986), 161–74. Bate, p. 164, notes that 'it is to Hazlitt that [Keats] owes the aspiration to "annihilate" the self, as he later put it, for the purpose of artistic creation. . . . Within months of reading the essay "On Gusto" Keats was using the term himself and writing of negative capability, the willingness to be in uncertainties and doubts that renders the mind open to acts of sympathetic identification.'
36. Lamb, 'On the Tragedies of Shakespeare', *Works*, op. cit., 127.

37. ibid., 133.
38. ibid., 142. Jonathan Bate notes that 'The argument has a certain force. . . . Lamb's essay marks a watershed in the history of one particular appropriation of Shakespeare: the tradition which singles out character, which psychologizes and internalizes, which Romanticizes and novelizes.' See his *Shakespearean Constitutions: Politics, Theatre, Criticism 1730–1830* (Oxford, 1989), 131–2.
39. J.S. Brattan, 'The Lear of Private Life: Interpretations of King Lear in the Nineteenth Century', in Richard Foulkes (ed.), *Shakespeare and the Victorian Stage* (Cambridge, 1986), 124–37.
40. Lamb, *Works*, op. cit., 126. This analysis of Lamb on Lear is much less aware of, or sympathetic towards, Lamb's pro-theatrical bias than is Harley Granville-Barker's *Prefaces to Shakespeare 2* (London, 1930), 7–9, the notorious work on which Brattan's attitude nevertheless would appear to be based.
41. Lamb, *Works*, op. cit., 129.
42. The major (but not sole) thrust of Lamb's criticism is directed toward the stage potential of the one play, *King Lear*, which he had only seen in Tate's mangled version. Harley Granville-Barker, ibid., 7, suggests that this fact contributed to his rejection of Shakespeare in the theatre: 'One cannot prove Shakespearean stage-worthiness by citing Tate, but how far is it not Tate rather than Shakespeare that Lamb condemns?'.
43. Lamb, *Works*, op. cit., 133.
44. See Terence Hawkes, 'Opening Closure', *Modern Drama* (1981), 353–6. See also Hawkes' *That Shakespeherian Rag: Essays on a Critical Process* (London, 1986), esp. 76–9, for alternative ways of 'recuperating' a play-text. Lamb and other critics are not alone in experiencing a let-down when physical reality replaces imaginative splendour. Actors feel it too. Sarah Bernhardt wrote that 'I regretted my visit to Elsinore. The reality did not come up to the expectation. The so-called tomb of Hamlet is represented by a small column, ugly and mournful-looking; there is little verdure, and the desolate sadness of deceit without beauty.' See Sarah Bernhardt, *My Double Life* (London, 1984), 344.
45. Hawkes, ibid. (1981).
46. Hazlitt, *Works*, op. cit., IV.237.
47. ibid., IV.247.
48. Stanley Wells, 'Shakespeare in Hazlitt's Theatre Criticism', *Shakespeare Survey* 35 (1982), 49.
49. Herschel Baker, *William Hazlitt* (Cambridge, Mass., 1962), 303, argues that 'Although Hazlitt knew the plays almost by heart . . ., his scholarship was shaky'. The response of these critics to Coleridge's chaotic literary-based Shakespearean ramblings in comparison with Hazlitt would be interesting to read. Perhaps they would be of Allardyce Nicoll's party of hatchet critics and agree that 'Coleridge had no idea as to what constituted a good play'. See J.R. de Jackson, 'Coleridge on Dramatic Illusion and Spectacle in the Performance of Shakespeare's Plays', *Modern Philology* LXII/1 (1964), 13.
50. Donohue, op. cit., 282.

51. Joan Coldwell, 'The Playgoer as Critic: Charles Lamb on Shakespeare's Characters', *Shakespeare Quarterly* 26 (1975), 184–5.

52. Lamb, 'On the Artificial Comedy of the Last Century', in *Works*, op. cit., 649.

53. Lamb, 'My First Play', *Works*, ibid., 596.

54. Lamb, 'Play-House Memoranda', *Works*, ibid., 202.

55. See Lamb, 'On Some of the Old Actors', *Works*, ibid., 636–48. According to Lamb, 'There is something strange as well as sad in seeing actors – your pleasant fellows particularly – subjected to and suffering the common lot – their fortunes, their casualties, their deaths, seem to belong to the scene, their actions to be amenable to poetic justice only. We can hardly connect them with more awful responsibility' (643). Hazlitt, 'Mr Kemble's Retirement', *Works*, op. cit., V.374 suggests that 'There is something in these partings with old public favourites exceedingly affecting. They teach us the shortness of human life, and the vanity of human pleasures.' Similarly, in 'Mrs Siddons', V.312, he notes that 'Players should be immortal, if their own wishes or ours could make them so; but they are not. They not only die like other people, but like other people they cease to be young, and are no longer themselves, even while living.'

56. Coleridge, ed. T.M. Raysor op. cit., 1.199.

57. J.R. de Jackson, op. cit., 20. Coleridge's ambivalence is well-illustrated in his letters concerning Kean, which range from references to '*the* sublime, tremendous, super-tragical Kean' (VI.1051) to the allegations that 'To destroy all sense of Metre is the avowed aim of Mr Kean, no less than his constant practice' (V.179). See *Collected Letters of Samuel Taylor Coleridge*, ed. Earl Leslie Griggs (Oxford, 1971).

58. See for instance Coleridge, 'Genius and Public Taste', op. cit., I.186; Lamb, *Works*, op. cit.; Hazlitt, *Works*, op. cit.

59. Hazlitt, *A View of the English Stage*, in *Works*, ibid., V.174.

60. Occasionally, Hunt could even find kind words for Kemble. See for instance 'The Tragic Actors', in *Dramatic Criticism*, op. cit., 103–6. Hunt felt that Kemble excelled in parts of 'loftiness and austerity', such as Coriolanus (104).

61. Fitzsimons, op. cit., 75.

62. Even from the earliest reviews, Hazlitt felt Kean tended toward an 'overdisplay of the resources of the art' (V.179), that he was sometimes 'deficient in dignity' (V.181), and that 'his voice and person were not altogether in consonance with the character' (V.189). In *Works*, op. cit.

63. Hazlitt, *Works*, op. cit., V.188.

64. Hazlitt, 'On the Pleasure of Hating', *The Plain Speaker*, in *Works*, op. cit., XII.128; see also Sylvan Barnet, 'More on Hazlitt's Preference for Tragedy', *P.M.L.A.* 73 (1958), 444.

65. According to A.W. Schlegel, '[the Romantics] strive in their poetry to reconcile and indissolubly fuse the two worlds between which we are torn, the spiritual and the sensual . . . a deeper interpenetration of the two is sought as a union of contraries.' See *European Romanticism; Self-Definition*, compiled by Lilian R. Furst (London, 1980), 35.

66. Plato, *The Republic*, trans. Desmond Lee (Harmondsworth, 1974), 437 (#607a).
67. See Sylvan Barnet, 'Charles Lamb's Contribution to the Theory of Dramatic Illusion', *P.M.L.A.* 69 (1954), 1150.
68. In his notes from a Coleridge lecture of 1818, John Payne Collier wrote 'but Coleridge took the opportunity of enlarging eloquently on the manner in which young poets have frequently connected themselves with women of very ordinary personal and mental attractions, the imagination supplying all deficiencies, clothing the object of affection with grace and beauty, and furnishing her with every accomplishment'. See *The Collected Works of Samuel Taylor Coleridge 5: Lectures on Literature 1808–1819*, ed. R.A. Foakes (Princeton, 1987), II.246.
69. ibid., 1.181.
70. On Hazlitt's 'unrelenting persecution by the Tory press', see John Kinnaird, *William Hazlitt: Critic of Power* (New York, 1978), 265–7, and Stanley Jones, *Hazlitt: A Life, from Winterslow to Frith Street* (Oxford, 1989), esp. 285–7, 300–3, 350.
71. Hazlitt lamented in the review of her comeback at Covent Garden in 1817 that 'we certainly thought her performance the other night inferior to what it used to be'. See *Works*, op. cit., V.373.
72. Both Kean and Hazlitt came and went – at least in terms of their greatest theatrical powers – within the decade beginning around 1812, and both achieved their greatest triumphs between the years 1813 and 1818.

6 THE DISINTERESTED IMAGINATION

1. The sceptical view is as old as kingship and acting themselves and was a favourite topic among the Classical authors. Seneca, for instance, in his 'Epistle LXXVI' in *Epistulae Morales*, trans. Richard Gummere (London, 1962), II. 165, writes that:

> None of those whom you behold clad in purple is happy, any more than one of these actors upon whom the play bestows a sceptre and a cloak while on the stage; they strut their hour before a crowded house, with swelling port and buskined foot; but when once they make their exit the foot-gear is removed and they return to their proper stature.

Similar views appear in one form or another throughout Shakespeare's writing, and indeed throughout the writing of the Renaissance in general. It's in the jest-books, it's in the plays such as Webster's *Duchess of Malfi*, and it's in the poems, this recurrent Senecan comparison of the monarch with the actor. For instance, Robert Armin in his *Foole upon Foole* (1600) reminds his audience that 'Wise men and fooles, all one end makes' (F4). In *Duchess of Malfi* see the Duchess' weary comment that 'I account this world a tedious theatre,/For I do play a part in't'gainst my will' (IV.i.84–5). References to theatricality abound in *Duchess of Malfi*, including Ferdinand's comment that 'a good actor many times is curs'd/For playing a villain's part' (IV.ii.289–90), and Bosola's dying reference in V.v to 'Such a mistake as I have often seen in a play'. See John Webster, *Duchess of Malfi*, ed. Jonathan Dollimore and Alan Sinfield (Cambridge, 1983). A similar reference occurs in the Epilogue to *All's Well That Ends Well*, where the French king announces that 'The King's a beggar now the play is done' (Epilogue l.1). Marvell's 'Horatian Ode' immortalised Charles I as the 'royal actor' (l.53). See Andrew Marvell, *Selected Poetry*, ed. Frank Kermode (New York, 1967), 152. Thomas Heywood in *An Apology for Actors* (1612) refers explicitly to Julius Caesar's histrionic activities: 'Iulius Caesar himselfe for his pleasure became an Actor, being in shape, state, voyce, iudgement, and all other occurrents, exterior and interior excellent' (E3ᵛ).

Linked with the more general *theatrum mundi* topos, the comparison of political leaders with actors is often a subtle means of disputing the truthfulness and honesty of one's betters, or challenging their achievements. (Authors throughout history have preferred a clever literary remark to a slit nose.) Such comparisons avail themselves of the pejorative connotations (of deceit, sleight of hand, illegitimacy) so often associated with the histrionic arts, and operate as a form of gentle and witty subversion. On *theatrum mundi*, see Ernst Robert Curtius, *European Literature and the Latin Middle Ages*, trans. Willard Trask (New York, 1953), 138–44; Frances Yates, *Theatre of the World* (London, 1969); Anne Righter, *Shakespeare and the Idea of the Play* (London, 1964); Elizabeth Burns, 'The Theatrical Metaphor: The World as a Stage, and the Theatre as Paradigm', *Theatricality: A Study of Convention in the Theatre and in Social Life* (London, 1972); Julia Briggs, *This Stage-Play World: English Literature and its Background, 1580–1625* (Oxford, 1983). The related phenomenon is known as *theatrum vitae humanae*, which was the subject of a well-known book by Jean Jacques Boissard printed at Metz in 1596.

2. William Emboden, *Sarah Bernhardt* (London, 1974), records that before the opening night in Paris of Louis Verneuil's *Daniel* in November 1920, the newspapers asked that no person attend without bringing at least one flower for Sarah whose ill-health and amputation had kept her absent from the stage for many years until this performance. She was to play a thirty-year-old man addicted to morphine. When the curtain rose for her initial entry (delayed until the third act) 'the audience at last saw their Sarah and for ten minutes called her name. She stood to bow, concealing her amputation. The audience applauded her delivery during the performance and then at the end a storm of flowers filled the stage' (161).

   Joanna Richardson, *Sarah Bernhardt and her World* (New York, 1977), has described how 'at the age of sixty-five, she played Joan of Arc again; and when, in the trial scene, she was asked her age, she turned slowly, very slowly, to face the audience. Gently but firmly she answered: "Nineteen". Every evening, at this point, she was given an ovation' (186).

3. Joseph Donohue, *Theatre in the Age of Kean* (Oxford, 1975), 74.

4. Charles Lamb, 'Stage Illusion', *The Complete Works in Prose of Charles and Mary Lamb*, ed. Thomas Hutchinson (Oxford, 1924), 676, hereafter

referred to as *Works*.

5. ibid., 674–5.
6. ibid., 676.
7. See Sylvan Barnet, 'Charles Lamb's Contribution to the Theory of Dramatic Illusion', *P.M.L.A.* 69 (1954), 1150–9.
8. Lamb, 'On Some of the Old Actors', *Works*, op. cit., 638–9; see also Joan Coldwell, 'The Playgoer as Critic: Charles Lamb on Shakespeare's Characters', *Shakespeare Quarterly* 26 (1975), 189.
9. William Hazlitt, *The Principles of Human Action*, in *The Complete Works of William Hazlitt*, ed. P.P. Howe (London, 1930–4), vol. 1, hereafter referred to as *Works*. All subsequent references to Hazlitt's works are to Howe's edition.
10. The influence of Hazlitt on Keats, particularly in the development of the theory of 'negative capability', is discussed at length in Jonathan Bate, *Shakespeare and the English Romantic Imagination* (Oxford, 1986), 161–74. See p. 163, note 35.
11. Hazlitt, *A View of the English Stage*, in *Works*, op. cit., V.184.
12. ibid., V.223.
13. In the early 1820s, Hazlitt fell hopelessly in love with Sarah Walker, the daughter of his landlord, expressing his adoration in *Liber Amoris* (1823), but predictably, she expressed little interest in the older man, and deceived him, even though he had terminated his own marriage for her.
14. See Raymund Fitzsimons, *Edmund Kean: Fire From Heaven* (London, 1976), *passim*.
15. One of the things which Hazlitt preferred in Kemble was his ability to present a consistent impression, in contrast to Kean's 'succession of striking pictures'. See Joseph Donohue, *Dramatic Character in the English Romantic Age* (Princeton, 1970), 331.
16. Hazlitt, 'Drama no. 6 from the London Magazine June 1820', *Works*, op. cit., XVIII.333.
17. Hazlitt, 'On Gusto', *Works*, op. cit., IV.77; see also W.P. Albrecht, 'Hazlitt's Preference for Tragedy', *P.M.L.A.* 71 (1956), 1045.
18. J. Huizinga, *Homo Ludens: A Study of the Play-Element in Culture* (London, 1949), 144.
19. ibid., 145; see also Plato's *Symposium* 223D and *Philebus* 50B.
20. Huizinga, ibid., 5.
21. For biographical information on Alec Guinness, see Alec Guinness, *Blessings in Disguise* (London, 1985); Sheridan Morley, *The Great Stage Stars* (Sydney, 1986); John Russell Taylor, *Alec Guinness: A Celebration* (London, 1984).
22. Guinness, ibid., 20.
23. Taylor, op. cit., 69–74.
24. ibid., 56.
25. ibid., 70.
26. See *Henry V*, by William Shakespeare, produced and directed by Laurence Olivier (London, 1945, text published 1984).
27. Guinness, op. cit., 20.
28. Although, like Guinness and several other 'name' actors, Richardson

suffered a disastrous Macbeth, in Richardson's case directed by Gielgud in 1952. See Gareth Lloyd Evans, 'Macbeth: 1946–1980 at Stratford-upon-Avon' in John Russell Brown (ed.), *Focus on Macbeth* (London, 1982), 91–2.

29. Mary Holland in *Plays and Players* (1971), quoted in Morley, op. cit., 330.
30. Guinness returned to Shakespeare with Shylock in 1984.
31. With the restriction of his stage appearances in his final years, Olivier turned toward authorship, completing the autobiographical *Confessions of an Actor* (London, 1982), and *On Acting* (London, 1986).
32. Olivier (1986), ibid., 246.
33. ibid., 242.
34. ibid., 242.
35. Horace, 'On the Art of Poetry', in *Classical Literary Criticism*, trans. T.S. Dorsch (Harmondsworth, 1965), 90.
36. Olivier, (1986), op. cit., 235.
37. See Olivier's description of the actor as the master, note 32 above.
38. J. Huizinga, *Homo Ludens: A Study of the Play-Element in Culture* (London, 1949).
39. ibid., 11.
40. Quoted in ibid., 11.
41. Michael Goldman, *Shakespeare and the Energies of Drama* (Princeton, 1972), 6.
42. See Thomas Strentz, 'The Stockholm Syndrome: Law Enforcement Policy and Hostage Behaviour', in Frank M. Ochberg and David A. Soskis (eds), *Victims of Terrorism* (Boulder, 1982), 151; see also Anna Freud, *The Ego and the Mechanisms of Defence* (New York, 1974), 120; C.S. Hall, *A Primer of Freudian Psychology* (New York, 1954), 78.
43. Strentz, op. cit., 151; see also J.C. Coleman, *Abnormal Psychology and Modern Life*, 5th edn (Glenview, Illinois, 1972), 122.
44. Goldman, op. cit., 5–6.
45. Strentz, op. cit., 151–2.
46. ibid., 152.
47. The term used by Olivier (1986), op. cit., 235.
48. Huizinga, op. cit., 11.
49. According to Hazlitt, 'The history of mankind is a romance, a mask, a tragedy, constructed upon the principles of *poetical justice*; it is a noble or royal hunt, in which what is sport to the few is death to the many, and in which the spectators halloo and encourage the strong to set upon the weak, and cry havoc in the chase though they do not share in the spoil. We may depend upon it that what men delight to read in books, they will put in practice in reality.' See Hazlitt *Works*, op. cit., IV.216.
50. See Hazlitt, 'On Poetry in General', *Lectures on the English Poets*, in *Works*, op. cit., V.7; Sylvan Barnet and W.P. Albrecht, 'More on Hazlitt's Preference for Tragedy', *P.M.L.A.* 73 (1958), 444.
51. Barnet and Albrecht, ibid., 445.

52. G.D. Klingopoulos, 'Hazlitt as Critic', *Essays in Criticism* VI (1956), 393.
53. Hazlitt, *Characters of Shakespear's Plays*, in *Works*, op. cit., IV.214.
54. ibid., 215.
55. ibid.
56. Hazlitt, 'Mr Wordsworth', *Spirit of the Age*, in *Works*, ibid., XI.92.
57. Lamb, 'Notes on Specimens of English Dramatic Poets', in *Lamb as Critic*, ed. Roy Park (London, 1980), 120.
58. Joan Coldwell, 'The Playgoer as Critic: Charles Lamb on Shakespeare's Characters', *Shakespeare Quarterly* 26 (1975), 188, suggests, for instance, that 'Lamb used a criticism of Cooke's performance in a mangled play [*Richard III*] as a peg on which to hang an interpretation he had developed through reading Shakespeare's own text'. Jonathan Bate's argument for Romantic 'appropriation' of Shakespeare is in his *Shakespearean Constitutions: Politics, Theatre, Criticism 1730–1830* (Oxford, 1989), esp. 1–9.
59. See Toby Cole and Helen Krich Chinoy (eds), *Actors on Acting*, 3rd edn (New York, 1957), 299.
60. See Stanley Wells, 'Shakespeare in Leigh Hunt's Theatre Criticism', *Essays and Studies* 33 (1980), 134.
61. Alan S. Downer, 'Players and Painted Stage: Nineteenth Century Acting', *P.M.L.A.* 61 (1946), 522–76.
62. ibid., 530–48.
63. Hazlitt, *A View of the English Stage*, in *Works*, op. cit., V.185. With acerbic remarks like this being typical of Hazlitt's style, it is bewildering to read Herschel Baker's comment in *William Hazlitt* (Cambridge, Mass., 1962), 309, that Hazlitt only writes well when his cue is admiration. This is a descriptive phrase of Baker's which Stanley Wells seems to have borrowed unconsciously in 'Shakespeare in William Hazlitt's Theatre Criticism', *Shakespeare Survey* 35 (1982), 54; cf. p. 164, note 49. Wells also shares with Baker a belief that Hazlitt's scholarship was 'shaky'; cf. p. 164, note 49.
64. Kathleen Coburn, 'Hazlitt on the Disinterested Imagination', in *Some British Romantics*, James V. Logan *et al.* (eds) (Ohio, 1966), 169–88.
65. Hazlitt, *A View of the English Stage*, in *Works*, op. cit., V.185. In fact, Hazlitt's quote refers to Shakespeare rather than Kean, but Coburn establishes the point none the less.
66. Hazlitt, 'Drama no. 2 from London Magazine February 1820', *Works*, ibid., XVIII.283.
67. Samuel Smiles, *Self-Help* (London, 1859); see also Thomas Carlyle, *Hero-Worship and the Heroic in History* (London, 1901) for another famous example of glorification for the self-made man. Both authors treat Shakespeare as one of the quintessential heroes, and Carlyle goes so far as to compare him favourably with the prophet Mohammed (343).

7 DEATH OF THE ACTOR

1. Gustave Flaubert, *The Temptation of Saint Antony*, trans. Kitty Mrosovsky (London, 1980), 94–5.

2. Harold Bloom's major texts in the present context are *The Anxiety of Influence* (New York, 1973) and *A Map of Misreading* (New York, 1975). For Bloom in the latter work (3), 'there are *no* texts, but only relationships between texts'.

3. The theory is developed most fully in *The Anxiety of Influence*, ibid., and the following discussion refers mainly to that work.

4. ibid., 58.

5. ibid., 5. Bloom remarks that 'My concern is only with strong poets, major figures with the persistence to wrestle with their strong precursors, even to the death.'

6. ibid., 95.

7. On Bloom's anxiety of influence tending toward a genetic theory, see Jonathan Culler, 'Presupposition and Intertextuality', *Pursuit of Signs* (London, 1981), 109.

8. For Barthes on intertextuality, see for instance his *S/Z*, trans. Richard Miller (New York, 1974); see also Barthes, 'The Death of the Author' and 'From Work to Text', *Image-Music-Text*, trans. Stephen Heath (London, 1984), 142–8, 155–64.

9. Julia Kristeva, *Semiotiké* (Paris, 1969) and *La Révolution du Langage Poétique* (Paris, 1974); see also Culler, op. cit., 104. According to Kristeva (1974), however, 'The term *intertextuality* denotes this transposition of one (or several) sign-system(s) into another; but since this term has often been understood in the banal sense of "study of sources", we prefer the term *transposition* because it specifies that the passage from one signifying system to another demands a new articulation of the thetic – of enunciative and denotative positionality.' See Julia Kristeva, *The Kristeva Reader*, ed. Toril Moi (New York, 1986), 111.

10. Barthes, (1974), op. cit., 21.

11. Culler, op. cit., 103.

12. Barthes, (1974), op. cit., 21.

13. See Bloom, (1975), op. cit., passim.

14. Michael Riffeterre notes that 'it is in and through intertextual mimesis that literature challenges representation most and most undermines its readers' views about the world . . . interpretation takes over at the very point where the text would seem closest to an objective recording'. See Riffeterre's 'Intertextual Representation: On Mimesis as Interpretive Discourse', *Critical Inquiry* 11.1 (September 1984), 159.

15. Bloom, (1973), op. cit., 30.

16. ibid, 94–5.

17. Keir Elam, *The Semiotics of Theatre and Drama* (London, 1980), 86.

18. Jiri Veltrusky, 'Man and Object in the Theatre', Paul L. Garvin (ed.), *A Prague School Reader on Esthetics, Literary Structure and Style* (Washington, 1964), 84.

19. Jean-Paul Sartre, *Being and Nothingness*, trans. Hazel E. Barnes (London, 1957), xlv.

20. Barthes, 'The Death of the Author', op. cit., 146.

21. Charles Lamb, 'Ellistoniana', *The Works in Prose and Verse of Charles and Mary Lamb*, vol. 1, ed. Thomas Hutchinson (Oxford, 1924), 682.

For very similar remarks, see William Hazlitt, 'Whether Actors Ought to Sit in the Boxes', *Complete Works of William Hazlitt*, ed. P.P. Howe (London, 1930–4), VIII. 272 and Roland Barthes, 'The World of Wrestling', *Mythologies*, trans. Annette Lavers (London, 1973), 25. For Barthes, 'When the hero or the villain of the [wrestling] drama, the man who was seen a few minutes earlier possessed by moral rage, magnified into a sort of metaphysical sign, leaves the wrestling hall, impassive, anonymous, carrying a small suitcase and arm-in-arm with his wife, no one can doubt that wrestling holds that power of transmutation which is common to the Spectacle and to Religious Worship.' Hazlitt writes, '[the actor] plays a number of parts disguised, transformed into them as much as he can "by his so potent art", and he should not disturb this borrowed impression by unmasking before company, more than he can help'.

22. Thomas Carlyle, *Hero-Worship and the Heroic in History* (London, 1901), 250.
23. Arnold Hauser, *Mannerism: The Crisis of the Renaissance and the Origin of Modern Art* (London, 1965), 111.
24. Rudolf Wittkower, *Art and Architecture in Italy, 1600 to 1750*, 3rd revised edn (Harmondsworth, 1973), 2.
25. John Donne, 'An Anatomie of the World: The First Anniversary', 11.213–15, *The Poems of John Donne*, ed. Herbert J.C. Grierson (Oxford, 1912, 1963), 237–8.
26. Hauser, op. cit., 13.
27. Terence Hawkes, 'Opening Closure', *Modern Drama* XXIV (1981), 353–6.
28. Richard Flecknoe, *A Short Discourse of the English Stage*, quoted in E.K. Chambers, *The Elizabethan Stage* (Oxford, 1923), IV. 370.
29. Michel Foucault, 'What is an Author?', trans. Donald F. Bouchard, *Screen* 20/1 (1979), 18–19.
30. See for instance John Russell Brown, *Shakespeare's Plays in Performance* (London, 1966), 37–8. According to Brown, 'In one respect the Elizabethan actors will continue to baffle our understanding: their use of boy actors for female roles. . . . The boys were helped, of course, by the dramatist, and in this Shakespeare was particularly careful . . . demanding roles, like Ophelia, are often given few appearances. . . . But Shakespeare used more than expert tact: he accepted the limitations of boy-actors without confining his imagination.' See also J.L. Styan, *Shakespeare's Stagecraft* (Cambridge, 1967), 40–2, who suggests that Shakespeare substitutes 'for the actuality a broad theatrical symbolism' (41–2); in similar vein, G.E. Bentley, *Shakespeare: A Biographical Handbook* (New Haven, 1961), 126, argues that the 'limitations of the boy actors' meant that Shakespeare 'could not create women's parts which show much development of character', and then is forced into an impossible argument to account for Rosalind, Imogen, Portia, Helena, Lady Macbeth, Cleopatra, Juliet and Viola. The whole issue of boys playing women is an embarrassing contradiction for the champions of Shakespeare-as-Shakespeare-wrote-it, and necessarily requires the employment of understated rhetoric such as Brown's

'of course' (above), or the oversimplification of Styan's analysis, to
disguise the perceived incompatibility of boy actors and powerful
histrionics. The Shakespearean theatrical bias and the predisposition
toward illusionist modes of performance (Brown argues for 'imitation
of life', 37) make decidedly uneasy partners in critical analysis.

31. See Foucault, op. cit., 15. To paraphrase Foucault, one could say that
'Acting is the interplay of signs freed from the necessity of expression'
(author's emphasis).

32. See Sheridan Morley, *The Great Stage Stars* (Melbourne, 1986), s.v.
'Brynner'.

33. ibid., s.v. 'Dietrich'.

34. ibid.

35. In *Confessions of an Actor* (London, 1982), 270, Laurence Olivier, for
instance, remarks on how concern for his feet inadvertently gave him
his famous swaying hips as Othello in 1964, 'so generously commented
upon, and regarded as the keystone of an elaborate characterisation that
even went to the lengths of studying the gait of the barefooted races!'.

36. See Alethea Hayter, *Opium and the Romantic Imagination* (London,
1967), for information on opium addiction. Coleridge and De Quincey
in particular, were notoriously addicted to opium, and more than one
of the former critic's lectures on Shakespeare were either cancelled
because of, or delivered under the influence of, the narcotic. Stage
actors, of whom Kean was just one of many, had their own drugs,
usually alcohol, which often accounted for either the excellence (G.F.
Cooke) or the disaster (Kean) of their performances. In both cases,
however, the origins of modern Shakespearean interpretation were
established by minds not always in a rational state. The rarer and more
extreme moments of Romantic sympathy for Shakespeare, such as the
final paragraph of De Quincey's 'Knocking at the Gate in Macbeth',
or Coleridge's fevered claim that 'Shakespeare . . . never introduces a
word, or a thought, in vain or out of place; if we do not understand
him, it is our fault or the fault of copyists and typographers', bear an
uncanny resemblance to medical reports on addicts' addiction to their
drugs. Addicts testify to the sense of elation, morality and love that
they can only feel when under the influence. The play of Shakespeare
on the mind of Coleridge, particularly in its relationship with his
improvisatory public lectures, seems to establish a direct connection
with the opium that enslaved his mind and body.

37. Foucault's replacement of the 'author' by the 'author-function' – a
'function' which is 'to characterise the existence, circulation, and
operation of certain discourses within a society' (Foucault, op. cit.,
19) – can be emulated in the present study by the replacement of the
'actor' with the 'actor-function'. And like Foucault's 'author-function',
the 'actor-function' 'is not formed spontaneously through the simple
attribution of a discourse to an individual, but results rather from a
complex operation whose purpose is to construct the rational entity we
call an actor. See Foucault, op. cit., 21. The suggestion in this present
study is that the myths of Shakespearean acting facilitate this illusory
construction of an actor through an 'actor-function'.

38. Foucault, ibid., 15.
39. See Walter J. Ong, *Orality and Literacy* (London, 1982), 81, for related quotes concerning the letter killing and the spirit giving life.
40. Roland Barthes, 'The Death of the Author', op. cit. 143.
41. This comment from Joan Plowright often appears in articles and reviews of Olivier's biographies. A friend of the actor confirms that Olivier wants to be remembered by his children 'not as some old fellow who was once an actor, but as a vital old boy who, when he went down, went down acting, and acting gloriously'. Quoted in Thomas Kiernan, *Sir Larry: The Life of Laurence Olivier* (alternative edition entitled *Olivier*) (London, 1981), 274.
42. See *Best Selections from the Arabian Nights Entertainments*, trans. Edward William Lane, ed. Edward Stanley Poole (New York, 1976), ix.
43. On centripetal and centrifugal forces within *heteroglossia*, see Mikhail Bakhtin, *The Dialogic Imagination*, trans. C. Emerson and M.M. Holquist (Austin, 1981), esp. xvii, 301–31.
44. *Hamlet*, III.i.56–60. Michael Goldman in *Acting and Action in Shakespearean Tragedy* (Princeton, 1985), 31–40, analyses this soliloquy by concentrating only on its 'histrionic articulation', from which perspective he concludes that the opening phrase 'is so abstract that it is in danger of being histrionically dead'. But he himself acknowledges that 'One could write volumes – volumes continue to be written – on the way these words resonate with the ideas and motifs of the play'(32). In other words, he (implicitly) argues that in fact the text *does* have a life of its own independent of the actor's function, although that is contrary to his (explicit) thesis of the actor's priority.
45. See for instance Keir Elam, *The Semiotics of Theatre and Drama* (London, 1980) and Alessandro Serpieri *et al.*, 'Toward a Segmentation of the Dramatic Text', *Poetics Today* 2:3 (1981), 163–200.

INDEX

175